MERCEDES-BENZ
ML Petrol Models
Series 163 & 164
WORKSHOP MANUAL
1998 - 2006

OWNERS EDITION

PETROL ENGINES COVERED
M111, M112, M113, M272. 4-Cyl., V6 & V8

BROOKLANDS BOOKS LTD.
P.O. BOX 146, COBHAM,
SURREY, KT11 1LG. UK
sales@brooklands-books.com

ABOUT THIS MANUAL

This 'Owners Edition' workshop manual covers the Mercedes-Benz petrol powered vehicles known as the 'ML Class', but built in two Series. Originally, they were introduced as Series 163 and were manufactured up to the end of 2004. There followed in 2005 the updated Series 164. Details of these models can be found on the following pages.

This manual has been compiled for the practical owner who wants to maintain their vehicle in first-class condition and contains comprehensive step-by-step instructions to enable them to carry out the bulk of their own servicing and repairs. With easy-to-follow instructions and hundreds of illustrations to amplify the text, many aspects of service, overhaul and repair are within the scope of an owner with a reasonable degree of mechanical aptitude.

Some operations, however, demand more skill whilst other jobs require the use of special tools and, in some cases, testing facilities and techniques that are not generally available. Only you can judge whether a job is within your capabilities. Whilst we do try to assist the reader to ensure that the information is correct it is obviously not possible to guarantee complete freedom from errors or omissions.

Information found in the driver's handbook is not necessarily duplicated here. It is not possible within this volume to cover every aspect to be found in the manufacturer's own workshop manual which is of greater size and complexity. However, it should be consulted if more detailed information is needed.

Always remember that you are responsible for your own safety, and that of others, when working on a vehicle. Particular care should be taken with safety related systems like the brakes and steering. If in any doubt professional advice should be sought. Never work under a vehicle unless it is properly supported (a single jack is not enough). Care should be taken with power tools and potentially harmful fuel, lubricants, solvents and sealers. These should always be stored in labelled, sealed containers. Always obtain your spare parts from an officially appointed Mercedes-Benz dealer.

With care and common sense the practical owner can make an excellent job of maintenance and overhaul. You will be adding to your knowledge too, knowing more about what needs to be done even if it does, in some instances, have to go to a professional repair shop.

The Mercedes-Benz ML Series of vehicles are built with care and precision. Given regular servicing and maintenance they will provide long and reliable service.

ISBN 9781783180523   MBLPWH

Brooklands Books Ltd. PO Box 146, Cobham, Surrey, KT11 1LG, England
Tel. 01932 865051   email: sales@brooklands-books.com

www.brooklands-books.com

Mercedes-Benz ML

Series 163 Model Years 1998-2004
Series 164 Model Years 2005-2006
2.3. 3.2, 3.5, 3.7, 4.3, 5.0 Litre Petrol
4-cyl., 6-cyl. and 8-cyl.

CONTENTS

---

0.   INTRODUCTION

Our 'Owners Manuals' are based on easy-to-follow step-by-step instructions and advice enabling you to carry out many jobs yourself. This manual will give you the means to avoid delays and inconveniences which may result from not knowing the correct procedures for carrying out repairs, which are often of a comparatively simple nature.

Whilst special tools are required to carry out certain operations, this manual shows you – whenever possible – how to improvise or use alternative tools. Experience shows that it is preferable to use only genuine parts since these give the assurance of a first class job. You will find that many parts are identical in the various makes covered, so our advice is to find out before purchasing new parts and suggests that you always buy your replacement parts from an authorised dealer.

0.0.   General Information

Four-cylinder, six-cylinder and eight-cylinder petrol engines and five, six-cylinder and eight-cylinder diesel engines are fitted to ML vehicles.
Only petrol models are covered in this manual:

Models 1998 to 1999

ML 230, four-cylinder: Four-cylinder engine, 2295 c.c., with 16 valves with a performance of 150 B.H.P. (110 kW) at 3800 rpm. Engine type "111.977" is fitted. Model identification 163.136. The vehicle is available with manual transmission (717.461) or automatic transmission (722.660).

ML 320, 3.2 litre six-cylinder: V6 engine with 18 valves, 3199 c.c., with a performance of 219 B.H.P. (160 kW) at 5600 rpm. Engine type "112.942". Model identification 163.154. The vehicle is fitted with an automatic transmission (722.662).

ML 430, 4.3 litre eight-cylinder: V8 engine with 24 valves, 4266 c.c., with a performance of 271 B.H.P. (199 kW) at 5500 rpm. Engine type "113.942". Model identification 163.172. The vehicle is fitted with an automatic transmission (722.663).

Models 2000 to 2001

Models ML230, ML320 and ML 430 were sold with the engines listed above to the end of 2001. The ML230 was discontinued for 2001.

Models 2002 to 2003

ML 320, 3.2 litre six-cylinder: V6 engine with 18 valves, 3199 c.c., with a performance of 219 B.H.P. (160 kW) at 5600 rpm. Engine type "112.942". Model identification 163.154. The vehicle is fitted with an automatic transmission (722.662).

ML 500, 5.0 litre eight-cylinder: V8 engine with 24 valves, with a performance of 292 B.H.P. (215 kW) at 5600 rpm. Engine type "113.965". Model identification 163.175. The vehicle is fitted with an automatic transmission (722.660).

Models 2002 to 2004

ML 350, 3.7 litre six-cylinder: V6 engine with 18 valves, with a performance of 234 B.H.P. (172 kW) at 3000 rpm. Engine type "112.970". Model identification 163.157. The vehicle is fitted with an automatic transmission (722.674).

ML 500, 5.0 litre eight-cylinder: V8 engine with 24 valves, with a performance of 292 B.H.P. (215 kW) at 5600 rpm. Engine type "113.965". Model identification 163.175. The vehicle is fitted with an automatic transmission (722.660).

Models 2005 to 2006

This sees the introduction of the new model series "164".

ML 350, 3.5 litre six-cylinder: V6 engine with 24 valves, with a performance of 272 B.H.P. (200 kW) at 6000 rpm. Engine type "272.967". Model identification 164.186. The vehicle is fitted with an automatic transmission (722.906 or 722.944).

ML 500, 5.0 litre eight-cylinder: V8 engine with 24 valves, with a performance of 306 B.H.P. (225 kW) at 5600 rpm. Engine type "113.964". Model identification 164.175. The vehicle is fitted with an automatic transmission (722.901).

The advantages of a multi-valve technology

One of the basic problems of a four stroke engine is the filling of the cylinders during the induction stroke with the necessary amount of the fuel/air mixture. The problem is increased with increasing engine speed, as the opening period of the valves is shortened. Technicians refer to filling loss. To compensate the valve diameters are selected as large as possible so that more fuel/air mixture can enter, but the disadvantage is, of course, the larger diameter of the compression chamber.

This is the main reason for the introduction of the multi-valve technology. Three or four valve heads make up a larger opening area than two large valve heads and the size of the compression chamber can remain the same.

The advantages of the four valves can therefore be given as follows:

- Four valves enable larger opening diameters for inlet and exhaust gases. This helps the engine performance and the fuel consumption. This is one of the reasons that an engine with four valves per cylinder has a better consumption than a valve with two valves.
- Engines with three/four valves per cylinder have smaller valves and thereby have less weight to be moved. A quicker response of the valve gear is therefore possible.
- Smaller valves are able to cool down quicker during the closing period.
- Engines with three/four valves per cylinder also enable to obtain a higher compression ratio.
- The spark plugs can be centred in the compression chamber to provide the best possible igniting of the fuel/air mixture.

The vehicles covered in this manual are fitted with a five or six-speed manual transmission or 5 or 7-speed automatic transmission.

The vehicles have a double wishbone front suspension with torsion bars and telescopic shock absorbers and a stabiliser bar in the case of model series "163" to the end of 2004. The torsion bars were replaced by coil springs on model series "164" with the introduction of model year 2005.

The independent rear suspension comprises double wishbones, coil springs and a stabiliser bar in the case of model series "163". With the introduction of model series "164" the rear suspension has been changed and now consists of a four-suspension arm suspension with coil springs. The stabiliser bar has been retained.

Disc brakes on all four wheels, with dual-line brake system and brake servo is fitted. The handbrake acts on the rear wheels.

A rack and pinion steering with servo-assistance is fitted.

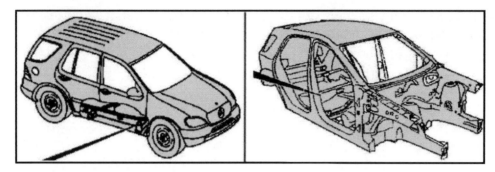

Fig. 0.1 – Location of the vehicle identification number. On the L.H. side for model series 163, on the R.H. side for model series 164 (from 2005).

0.1. Vehicle Identification

The type identification plate is located at the R.H. side at the position shown in Fig. 0.1, in the case of models 163 on the L.H. side and models 164 on the R.H. side. All vehicle identification numbers start and end with the Mercedes star and has 19 numbers Fig. 0.2 shows an example of an identification number. The number refers to the world manufacturing code (2 to 4), model designation (5 to 10), steering (11), manufacturing plant (12) and the production number (13 to 18).

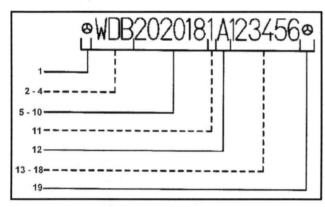

Fig. 0.2 – Vehicle identification number (shown on a different model). Numbers (1) and (19) show the Mercedes star. The remaining numbers are explained in the text.

Any other type identification plates will be given in the Owners Manual, for example chassis number, permissible maximum weight and the permissible axle load on front and rear axle, paint code, etc.

The engine number is stamped into the cylinder block on the side of the starter motor, immediately below the intake tube.

The code numbers and letters must always be quoted when parts are ordered. Copy the numbers on a piece of paper and take it to your parts supplier. You will save yourself and your parts department delays and prevents you from ordering the wrong parts.

0.2. General Servicing Notes

The servicing and overhaul instructions in this Workshop Manual are laid out in an easy-to-follow step-by-step fashion and no difficulty should be encountered, if the text and diagrams are followed carefully and methodically. The "Technical Data" sections form an important part of the repair procedures and should always be referred to during work on the vehicle.

In order that we can include as much data as possible, you will find that we do not generally repeat in the text the values already given under the technical data headings. Again, to make the best use of the space available, we do not repeat at each operation the more obvious steps necessary - we feel it to be far more helpful to concentrate on the difficult or awkward procedures in greater detail. However, we summarise below a few of the more important procedures and draw your attention to various points of general interest that apply to all operations.

Always use the torque settings given in the various main sections of the manual. These are grouped together in separate sub-sections for convenient reference.

Bolts and nuts should be assembled in a clean and very lightly oiled condition and faces and threads should always be inspected to make sure that they are free from damage burrs or scoring. DO NOT degrease bolts or nuts.

All joint washers, gaskets, tabs and lock washers, split pins and "O" rings must be replaced on assembly. Seals will, in the majority of cases, also need to be replaced, if the shaft and seal have been separated. Always lubricate the lip of the seal before assembly and take care that the seal lip is facing the correct direction.

References to the left-hand and right-hand sides are always to be taken as if the observer is at the rear of the vehicle, facing forwards, unless otherwise stated.

Always make sure that the vehicle is adequately supported, and on firm ground, before commencing any work on the underside of the car. A small jack or a make shift prop can be highly dangerous and proper axle stands are an essential requirement for your own safety.

Dirt, grease and mineral oil will rapidly destroy the seals of the hydraulic system and even the smallest amounts must be prevented from entering the system or coming into contact with the components. Use clean brake fluid or one of the proprietary cleaners to wash the hydraulic system parts. An acceptable alternative cleaner is methylated spirit, but if this is used, it should not be allowed to remain in contact with the rubber parts for longer than necessary. It is also important that all traces of the fluid should be removed from the system before final assembly.

Always use genuine manufacturer's spares and replacements for the best results.

Since the manufacturer uses metric units when building the cars it is recommended that these are used for all precise units. Inch conversions are given in most cases but these are not necessarily precise conversions, being rounded off for the unimportant values.

Removal and installation instructions, in this Workshop Manual, cover the steps to take away or put back the unit or part in question. Other instructions, usually headed "Servicing", will cover the dismantling and repair of the unit once it has been stripped from the vehicle it is pointed out that the major instructions cover a complete overhaul of all parts but, obviously, this will not always be either necessary and should not be carried out needlessly.

There are a number of variations in unit parts on the range of vehicles covered in this Workshop Manual. We strongly recommend that you take care to identify the precise model and the year of manufacture, before obtaining any spares or replacement parts.

Std.:	To indicate sizes and limits of components as supplied by the manufacturer. Also to indicate the production tolerances of new unused parts.
O/S	Parts supplied as Oversize or Undersize or recommended limits for such parts, to enable them to be used with worn or re-machined mating parts.
U/S	O/S indicates a part that is larger than Std. size U/S may indicate a bore of a bushing or female part that is smaller than Std.
Max.:	Where given against a clearance or dimension indicates the maximum allowable. If in excess of the value given it is recommended that the appropriate part is fitted.
TIR:	Indicates the Total Indicator Reading as shown by a dial indicator (dial gauge).
TDC:	Top Dead Centre (No. 1 piston on firing stroke).
MP:	Multi-Purpose grease.

0.3. Dimensions and Weights (typical)

Overall length – ML 230, ML 320, ML 430 – 1998/2001: ....4590 mm
Overall length – ML 320, ML 500 – 2002 : ....4535 mm
Overall length – ML 350, ML 500 – 2003/2004 : ....4640 mm
Overall length – ML 350, ML 500 – 2005/2006 : ....4578 mm
Overall width – ML 230, ML 320, ML 430 – 1998/2001: ....1830 mm
Overall width – ML 320, ML 500 – 2002 : ....1850 mm
Overall width – ML 350, ML 500 – 2003/2004 : ....1840 mm
Overall width – ML 350, ML 500 – 2005/2006 : ....1910 mm
Overall height – ML 230, ML 320, ML 430 – 1998/2001: ....1780 mm
Overall height – ML 320, ML 500, ML– 2002 : ....1840 mm
Overall height – ML 350, ML 500 – 2003/2004 : ....1840 mm
Overall height – ML 350, ML 500 – 2005/2006 : ....1815 mm
Wheelbase – ML 230, ML 320, ML 430 – 1998/2002: ....2820 mm
Wheelbase – ML 350, ML 500 – 2003/2004: ....2820 mm
Wheelbase – ML 350, ML 500 – 2005/2006 : ....2915 mm
Front track – ML 230, ML 320, ML 430 – 1998/2001: ....1560 mm
Front track – ML 320, ML 500 – 2002 : ....1555 mm
Front track – ML 350, ML 500 – 2003/2004 : ....1555 mm
Front track – ML 350, ML 500 – 2005/2006 : ....1630 mm
Rear track – ML 230, ML 320, ML 430 – 1998/2001:.................................1560 mm
Rear track – ML 320, ML 500 – 2002 : ....1555 mm
Rear track – ML 350, ML 500 – 2003/2004 : ....1555 mm
Rear track – ML 350, ML 500 – 2005/2006 : ....1630 mm
Kerb weight .... Refer to Owners manual

0.4. Capacities

Engines:
- Oil and filter change – 2.3 litre four-cylinder (111 engine): ....5.9 litres
- Oil and filter change – V6 (112 engine):...7.5 litres
- Oil and filter change – 4.3 litre V8 (113 engine):......................................9.5 litres
- Oil and filter change – 5.0 litre V8 (113 engine):......................................8.0 litres
- Oil and filter change – 3.5 litre V6 (272 engine):......................................7.5 litres
- Difference between Max/Min:..2.0 litres
Cooling system:.. Refer to Section "Cooling System"
Transmissions: .... See Section 3.0

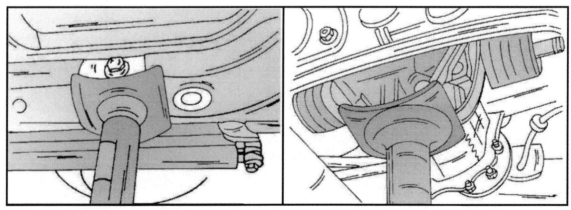

Fig. 0.3 – Jacking up the front end of the vehicle. The L.H. view shows where the jack is placed underneath the front crossmember. The R.H. view shows the jacking up of the rear of the vehicle. The jack is placed underneath the centre piece of the rear axle.

0.5.   Jacking up the Vehicle

To prevent damage to the underside of the vehicle, apply a jack or chassis stands only to the points specified below:

Fig. 0.4 – Jacking up one side of the vehicle. Place the jack (2) underneath the side of the body as shown. Chassis stands (1) are placed at the position shown. The R.H. side shows a 164 model.

The front end of the vehicle should be lifted up by placing a jack underneath the transverse crossmember (cross bridge) for the front axle carrier as shown in Fig. 0.3, taking care not to damage the undercover for the engine compartment. To lift the rear end of the vehicle, place the jack underneath the rear cross bridge for the rear axle carrier, similar as shown as shown in Fig. 0.3 on the R.H. side. Make sure the jack is sufficient to take the weight of the vehicle. The vehicle can also be jacked up on one side. In this case place the jack underneath the hard rubber inserts near the wheels, as shown in Fig. 0.4 on one side of the vehicle, as shown in the L.H. view. The R.H. view shows where a vehicle of series 164 is jacked up. Never place a jack underneath the oil sump or the gearbox to lift the vehicle.

Fig. 0.5 – Three-legged chassis stands are the safest method to support the vehicle when work has to be carried out on the underside of the vehicle.

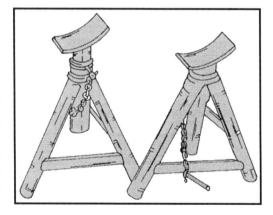

Chassis stands should only be placed on the L.H. and R.H. sides under the side of the body without damage to the paint work. A chassis stands of the construction shown in Fig. 0.5, should be used, but again make sure that they are strong enough to carry the weight of the vehicle. Make sure the vehicle cannot slip off the stands.

Before lifting the front of the vehicle engage first or reverse gear when a manual transmission is fitted or place the gear selector lever into the "P" (park) position when an automatic transmission is fitted. Use suitable chocks and secure the front wheels when the rear end of the vehicle is jacked up.

Always make sure that the ground on which the vehicle is to be jacked up is solid enough to carry the weight of the vehicle.

Note: *It is always difficult to raise a vehicle first on one side and then on the other. Take care that the vehicle cannot tip-over when the first side is lifted. Ask a helper to*

General Information

support the vehicle from the other side. Never work underneath the vehicle without adequate support.

0.6.   Recommended Tools

To carry out some of the operations described in the manual we will need some of the tools listed below:

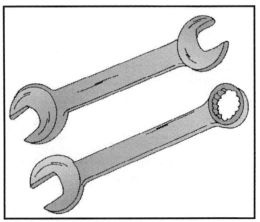

Fig. 0.6 – A double open-ended spanner in the upper view and an open-ended/ring spanner in the lower view. Always make sure that the spanner size is suitable for the nut or bolt to be removed and tightened.

As basic equipment in your tool box you will need a set of open-ended spanners (wrenches) to reach most of the nuts and bolts. A set of ring spanners is also of advantage. To keep the costs as low as possible we recommend a set of combined spanners, open-ended on one side and a ring spanner on the other side. Fig. 0.6 shows a view of the spanners in question. Sockets are also a useful addition to your tool set.

Fig. 0.7 – A graduated disc is used to "angle-tighten" nuts and bolts. "Torx" head bolts are shown on the R.H. side.

A set of cross-head screwdrivers, pliers and hammers or mallets may also be essential. You will find that many bolts now have a "Torx" head. In case you have never seen a "Torx" head bolt, refer to Fig. 0.7. A socket set with special "Torx" head inserts is used to slacken and tighten

these screws. The size of the bolts are specified by the letter "T" before the across-flat size.

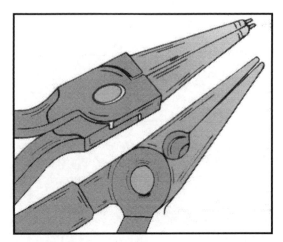

Fig. 0.8 – Circlip pliers are shown in the upper view. The type shown in suitable for outside circlips. The lower view shows a pair of pointed pliers.

Circlip pliers may also be needed for certain operations. Two types of circlip pliers are available, one type for external circlips, one type for internal circlips. The ends of the pliers can either be straight or angled. Fig. 0.8 shows a view of the circlip pliers. Apart from the circlip pliers you may also need the pliers shown in Fig. 0.9, i.e. side cutters, combination pliers and water pump pliers.

Every part of the vehicle is tightened to a certain torque value and you will therefore need a torque wrench which can be adjusted to a certain torque setting. In this connection we will also mention a graduated disc, shown in Fig. 0.7, as many parts of the vehicle must be angle-tightened after having been tightened to a specific torque. As some of the angles are not straight-forward (for example 30 or 60 degrees), you will either have to estimate the angle or use the disc.

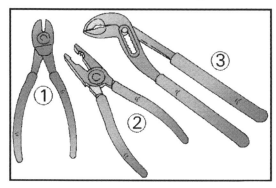

Fig. 0.9 – Assortment of pliers suitable for many operations.
1 Side cutter
2 Combination pliers
3 Water pump pliers

Finally you may consider the tool equipment shown in Fig. 0.10 which will be necessary from time to time, mainly if you intend to carry out most maintenance and repair jobs yourself.

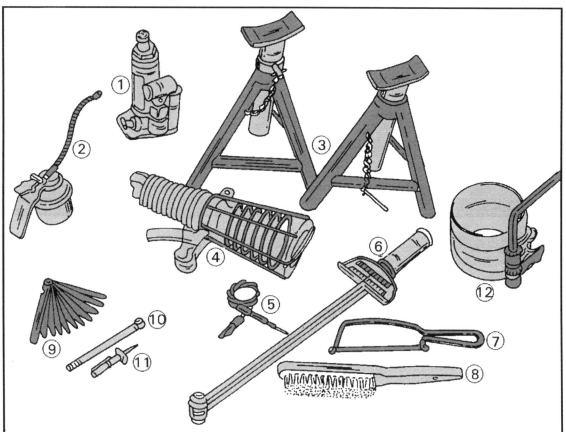

Fig. 0.10 – Recommended tools to service and repair your vehicle.

1 Hydraulic jack	7 Small hand saw
2 Oil can	8 Wire brush
3 Chassis stands	9 Feeler gauges
4 Electric hand lamp	10 Tyre pressure gauge
5 Test lamp (12 volts)	11 Tyre profile depth checker
6 Torque wrench	12 Piston ring clamp band

0.7.   Before you start

Before you carry out any operations on your vehicle it may be of advantage to read the following notes to prevent injuries and damage to the vehicle:
* Never carry out operations underneath the vehicle when the front or rear is only supported on the jack. Always place chassis stands in position (refer to next section). If no chassis stands are available and if the wheels are removed place

one wheel on top of the other one and place them under the side of the vehicle where you work. If the jack fails the vehicle will drop onto the two wheels, preventing injury.

- Never slacken or tighten the axle shaft nuts or wheel bolts when the vehicle in resting on chassis stands.
- Never open the cooling system when the engine is hot. Sometimes it may, however, be necessary. In this case place a thick rag around the cap and open it very slowly until all steam has been released.
- Never allow brake fluid or anti-freeze to come in contact with painted areas.
- Never inhale brake shoe or brake pad dust. If compressed air is available, blow off the dust whilst turning the head away. A mask should be worn for reasons of safety.
- Remove oil or grease patches from the floor before you or other people slip on it.
- Do not work on the vehicle wearing a shirt with long sleeves. Rings and watches should be removed before carrying out any work.
- If possible, never work by yourself. If unavoidable ask a friend or a member of the family to have a quick look to check thats everything is OK.
- Never hurry up your work. Many wheel bolts have been left untightened to get the vehicle quickly back on the road.
- Never smoke near the vehicle or allow persons with a cigarette near you. A fire extinguisher should be handy, just in case.
- Never place a hand lamp directly onto the engine to obtain a better view. Even though that the metal cage will avoid direct heat it is far better if you attach such a lamp to the open engine bonnet.
- Never drain the engine oil when the engine is hot. Drained engine oil must be disposed of in accordance with local regulation.
- Never place a jack underneath the oil sump or the gearbox to lift the vehicle.

1   ENGINES

1.0. Technical Data

Type: 4-stroke engine, with electronically controlled fuel injection and injection system

Fitted Engines:
- ML 230 (163 series):   111.977
- ML 320 (163 series):   112.942
- ML 350 (163 series):   112.970
- ML 430 (163 series):   113.942
- ML 500 (163 series):   113.965
- ML 350 (164 series):   272.967
- ML 500 (164 series):   113.964

Number of Cylinders:
- 111 engine: Four
- 112 engine: Six (V)
- 113 engine: Eight (V)
- 272 engine: Six (V)

Arrangement of cylinders:
- 111 engine: In-line
- 112 engine: 90° V

- 113 engine:	90° V
- 272 engine:	90° V

Camshafts:
- 111 engine:	Two overhead camshafts (chain)
- 112 engine:	2 x 1 overhead camshaft (chain)
- 113 engine:	2 x 1 overhead camshaft (chain)
- 272 engine:	2 x 2 overhead camshafts (chain)

Arrangement of valves:	Overhead

Cylinder bore:
– M111 engine (ML 230):	90.90 mm
– M112 engine (ML 320/ML 350):	89.90 mm
– M113 engine (ML 430):	89.90 mm
– M113 engine (ML 500):	97.00 mm
– M272 engine (ML 350):	92.90 mm

Piston stroke:
– M111 engine (ML 230):	88.40 mm
– M112 engine (ML 320/ML 350):	84.00 mm
– M113 engine (ML 430):	84.00 mm
– M113 engine (ML 500):	84.00 mm
– M272 engine (ML 350):	86.00 mm

Capacity:
– M111 engine (ML 230):	2295 c.c.
– M112 engine (ML 320:	3199 c.c.
– M112 engine (ML 350:	3724 c.c.
– M113 engine (ML 430):	4266 c.c.
– M113 engine (ML 500):	4966 c.c.
– M272 engine (ML 350):	3498 c.c.

Compression Ratio:
– M111 engine (ML 230):	10.4 : 1
– M112 engine (ML 320):	10.1 : 1
– M112 engine (ML 350):	10.1 : 1
– M113 engine (ML 430):	10.1 : 1
– M113 engine (ML 500):	10.1 : 1
– M272 engine (ML 350):	10.7 : 1

Max. kW/B.H.P. (DIN):	See Section 0.0.

Max. Torque:
– M111 engine (ML 230):	224 Nm (162 ft.lb.) at 3800 rpm
– M112 engine (ML 320):	316 Nm (227 ft.lb.) at 3000 rpm
– M112 engine (ML 350):	346 Nm (249 ft.lb.) at 3000 rpm
– M113 engine (ML 430):	408 Nm (293 ft.lb.) at 3000 rpm
– M113 engine (ML 500):	448 Nm (293 ft.lb.) at 2700 rpm
– M272 engine (ML 350):	350 Nm (252 ft.lb.) at 2700 rpm

Crankshaft bearings:	5 (4-cyl.), 4 (V6), 5 (V8) friction bearings
Cooling system:	Thermo system with water pump, thermostat, cooling fan with fluid clutch, tube-type radiator

Engines

Lubrication:	Pressure-feed lubrication with gear-type oil pump, driven with chain from crankshaft. With full-flow and by-pass oil filter
Air cleaner:	Dry paper element air cleaner
Injection system:	Fuel injection system

General Information

The engines fitted to the ML vehicles in the series 163 and 164 are different in many ways. The following information will tell you something about the new engines.

- The 2.3 litre engine (type 111.977) is fitted from the beginning of series 163 to the **ML 230.** Discontinued at the end of 2001.
- The 3.2 litre V6 engine with 18 valves is fitted to the end of series 163 to the **ML 320** (engine type 112.942) or **ML 350** (engine type 112.970).
- The 4.3 litre V8 engine with 24 valves is fitted to the end of series 163 to the ML 430 (engine type 113.942).
- The 5.0 litre V8 engine with 24 valves is fitted to the end of series 163 and from the beginning of series 164 to the **ML 500** (engine type 113.965 or 113.964).
- The 3.7 litre V6 engine with 24 valves is fitted from the beginning of model year 2005 to the **ML 350** (engine type 242.967).
- The cylinder head, as already mentioned, has three or four valves per cylinder either 16 valves in the case of a four-cylinder 111 engine or 24 valves in the case of a six-cylinder V6 or the V8. The cylinder head is made of light alloy metal. The valve seats, made of hardened steel, are pressed into the cylinder head. The valves are "gliding" in brass valve guides and are arranged as "overhead" valves, i.e. they are inserted vertically, valve head down, into the combustion chambers.
- A different number of camshafts are fitted, depending on the engine. The bearings for the camshafts are not machined directly into the cylinder head.
- The valve tappets are inserted between camshafts and valve ends. The cams push against the ends of the tappets to operate the valves. The tappets are known as bucket tappets.

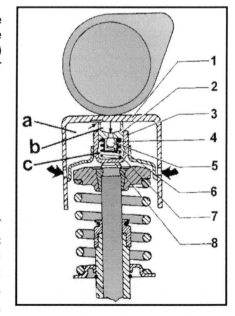

Fig. 1.1 – The operation of the hydraulic tappets. The oil enters via the bore (1) in the tappet into the valve tappet chamber (a), then into the smaller chamber (b) and then via the ball valve into the working chamber (c). The remaining parts are given below:

1 Valve tappet
2 Thrust pin
3 Retaining ring
4 Pressure spring
5 Ball guide
6 Ball
7 Ball guide
8 Guide sleeve

- The adjustment of the valves is no longer necessary on these engines. Hydraulic compensating elements are fitted which will ensure the correct valve clearance at all times. The function of the hydraulic valve clearance compensating elements is to eliminate valve clearance, i.e. the dimensional changes in the valve train (valve lash) due to heat expansion and wear are compensated by the elements. The rocker arm is in constant contact with the cam. The compensating elements cannot be repaired, but can be checked for correct functioning as described below. Fig. 1.1 shows sectional views of a valve with clearance compensation. We will give a short description of the operation. All references refer to Fig. 1.1.

The hydraulic valve compensating element are fitted into the rocker levers and operate the valves directly via a ball socket:

- The thrust pin with oil supply chamber and the return bores and the ball valve (check valve). The ball valve separates the supply chamber from the work chamber.

- The guide sleeve with the work chamber (c), the thrust spring (4) and the closing cap.

When the engine is stopped and the tappet is held under load from the cam, the element can completely retract. The oil displaced from the work chamber (c) flows through an annular gap, i.e. the clearance between the guide sleeve and the thrust pin to the oil supply chamber (b).

When the cam lobe has moved past the valve tappet, the thrust pin will be without load. The thrust spring (4) forces the thrust pin upwards until the valve tappet rests against the cam.

The vacuum resulting from the upward movement of the thrust pin in the work chamber (c) opens the ball valve and the oil can flow from the supply chamber into the work chamber. The ball valve closes when the valve tappet presses against the cam and puts the thrust pin under load. The oil in the work chamber acts as a "hydraulic rigid connection" and opens the valve in question.

When the engine is running and depending on the engine speed and the cam position, the thrust pin is only pushed down slightly.

The oil contained in the oil supply chamber is sufficient to fill the work chamber under all operating conditions of the engine. Oil or leak oil which is not required, as well as air are able to escape via the annular gap between the washer and the rocker lever. The oil ejected from the work chamber flows via the annular gap between the guide sleeve and the thrust pin and the two return bores into the oil supply chamber.

Important Notes when working on the Engine

Before any work is carried out in the engine compartment note the following points, mainly when the engine is running:

- The engine is fitted with electronic components with a very high voltage. For this reason never touch any electrical/electronic elements when the engine is running or when the engine is being started.

- Never touch any of the electronic elements with the ignition key in position "2" and the engine is cranked over by hand.

- Persons with pace maker should not carry out any operations on the electronic ignition system.

1.1.   Engine – Removal and Installation

The removal of the engine requires a suitable lifting device or a hand crane to lift the power unit out of the engine compartment. For this reason we recommend to read the instructions in full before you decide to remove the engine. The engine is a heavy unit and the hoist or crane must be strong enough to take the weight of the assembly, remembering that the weight is more than 200 lbs. The following description is a general guide line, as we cannot refer to every possible variation and/or equipment that may be fitted to your vehicle The removal and installation of the engine is described for the individual type.

Engines

2.3 Litre Engine (M111, ML230)

The following removal instructions will also give you information to refit a certain part or unit or the applicable tightening torque of bolts and/or nuts. All self-locking nuts and bolts must be replaced during installation. The removal and installation of many parts are described in separate sections and must be referred to where necessary. First disconnect the battery and drain the cooling system.

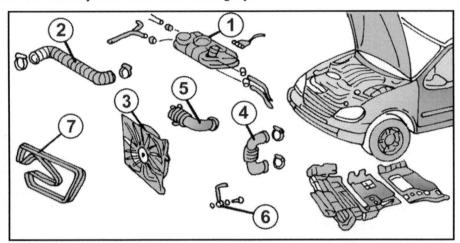

Fig. 1.2 – Details for the removal and installation of the M111 engine.(ML 230). The numbers are referred to in the text.

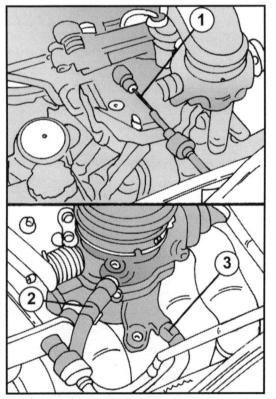

Fig. 1.3 – The throttle valve operating linkage (1) and the two vacuum hoses (2) and (3) must be connected on an M111 engine.

- Open the bonnet and secure it in upright position.
- Place the vehicle on secure chassis stands when operations are carried out from below.
- Remove the parts shown in Fig. 1.2. These are the visco fan (3), the fan shroud (2) and the air cleaner (1). If an air conditioning system is fitted you will have to insert a protective plate in front of the radiator and the condenser to prevent damage during removal of the engine. This can be made up of 1 mm thick plastic or metal sheet, but must have a dimension of 400 x 680 mm.
- Remove the Poly V-belt.
- Follow the throttle operating linkage and disconnect it at position (1) in Fig. 1.3. Also disconnect the two vacuum hoses (2) and (3) shown in the same illustration. One of them leads to the brake servo unit.
- Follow the fuel lines and disconnect them at the hexagon connection. The fuel is under pressure and the necessary care must be taken. For this reason unscrew the tank filler cap.
- Remove the coolant expansion tank, secured at two placed at the level of the filler cap.
- Disconnect all cable connections from the engine, i.e. the cables from the alternator, remove the cover from the fuse and relay module, disconnect an earth

cable from the engine, in the open fuse and relay module withdraw the cable connector plugs, withdraw a cable connector plug from the fuel injection control unit (Attention – secured by a locking arm), disconnect an earth cable between engine and body, unscrew a cable at the outside of the relay module and disconnect the starter motor cables (1) shown in Fig. 1.4. These are the cables connected to terminals "30" and "50".

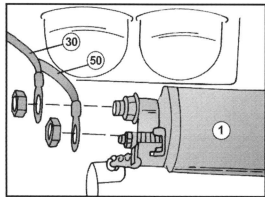

Fig. 1.4 – Cables must be disconnected from terminals "30" and "50" on the starter motor.

- The next operations are carried out with the help of Fig. 1.5. Remove the steering pump (7) without disconnecting the hoses. Push the pump to one side and tie it up with a piece of wire. The bolts are tightened to 2.0 kgm (14.5 ft.lb.) during installation.
- Remove the transmission mounting bolts (11) at the upper end. Note the instructions further on during installation.
- Remove the starter motor.

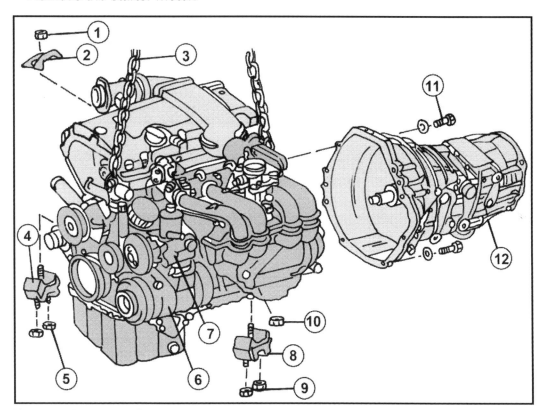

Fig. 1.5 – Removal of the M111 engine (ML 230). The numbers are referred to in the text.

- Disconnect the exhaust pipe from the exhaust manifold, unscrew a bracket from the exhaust pipe and remove. Also remove a pipe bracket from the bottom of the transmission.
- If air conditioning is fitted remove the compressor and push it to one side of the engine compartment with all pipes/lines connected and tie it up with wire.
- On the L.H. and R.H. side of the engine remove the front engine mountings (4). Tighten the bolts mounting/vehicle frame to 3.5 kgm (25 ft.lb.) and the bolts mounting/mounting bracket to 6.5 kgm (47 ft.lb.).

Engines

- The engine must now be lifted with a suitable hand crane or hoist and ropes or chains (3) attached to the engine lifting eyes. Carefully lift the engine without damaging the injection pipes. The workshop inserts, as already mentioned, a guard plate between the engine and the radiator/condenser to protect the items. This will prevent any damage.
- Place a mobile jack with a suitable protective plate underneath the transmission (12) until just under tension. Fully unscrew the engine mounting on the R.H. side. Note that the mountings are not the same on both sides. Mark them after removed.
- Remove the remaining bolts (11) from the transmission.
- The engine is now carefully removed. Make sure that none of the cables, pipes, etc. are damaged during the removal.

The installation is a reversal of the removal procedure noting the points and tightening torques already given above. When fitting the transmission note the following: M10 bolts with a length of 40 mm are tightened to 5.5 kgm (40 ft.lb.) if they have a yellow colour, otherwise to 4.0 kgm (29 ft.lb.). M10 bolts with a length of 90 mm are tightened to 4.5 kgm (32.5 ft.lb.) if they have a yellow colour, otherwise to 4.0 kgm (29 ft.lb.).
After filling the cooling system check all connections for leaks. The following points must also be observed:

- Engine mountings, oil and fuel pipes must be checked for damage before they are re-used.
- Check the oil level in engine and transmission and correct if necessary. If the engine oil has been drained fill it with the correct quantity of engine oil.
- Before filling the cooling system check that all drain points have been closed.
- Make sure that all bolts and nuts have been tightened to the correct tightening torque.
- After starting the engine and allowing it to warm up, check the cooling system for leaks. Drive the vehicle a few miles to check for exhaust pipe rattle.

Note: There is no need to remove the engine and the transmission when the engine mountings or the rear crossmember must be removed or replaced.

M112 und M113 Engine, ML320, ML350, ML430, ML 500, Series 163

In general the removal and installation of the V5 und V8 engine is carried out in a similar manner. We try to refer to any differences if applicable. Figs. 1.6 and 1.7 will help during the removal.

- Disconnect the battery earth cable.
- In the case of the ML 430 remove the air guide panel (7).
- Drain the cooling system. The coolant hose (13) between water pump and radiator must be disconnected.
- Drain the engine oil. The drain plug is tightened to 3.0 kgm (22 ft.lb.).
- Remove the visco fan. In the case of the ML 500 (engine 113.965) the fan bolt has right/hand thread (see under removal of fan).
- Remove the fan shroud (2). The bolts must be removed at the bottom. In the case of the ML 500 remove the electric fan.
- If an air conditioning system is fitted you will have to insert a protective plate in front of the radiator and the condenser to prevent damage during removal of the engine. This can be made up of 1 mm thick plastic or metal sheet, but must have a dimension of 400 x 680 mm.

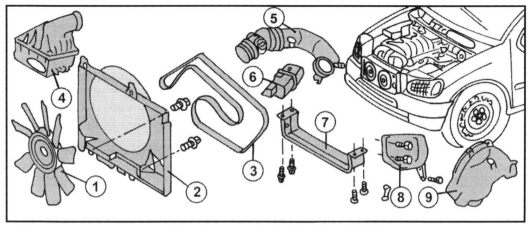

Fig. 1.6 – Parts to be removed in the case of the M112 and M113 engine as fitted to the ML 320, ML 350, ML 430 and ML 500 of series 163. The numbers are referred to in the text.

- Remove the coolant expansion tank.
- Remove the air cleaner housing (4) and the intake tube (5) from the resonance unit (6). To do this withdraw the connector plug from the hot film air mass meter and unscrew the tube from the cylinder head. The tube is attached to the rear of the inlet manifold with a plastic plate (engines M112 and M113.942/965).

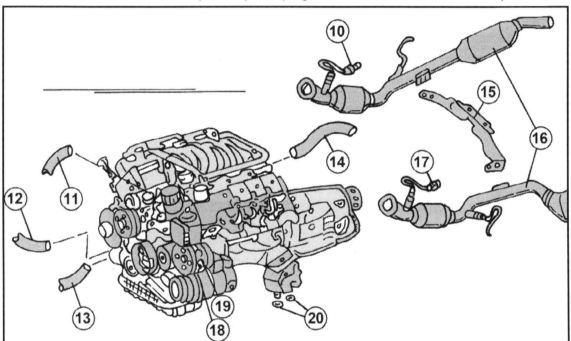

Fig. 1.7 – Parts to be removed in the case of the M112 and M113 engine as fitted to the ML 320, ML 350, ML 430 and ML 500 of series 163. The numbers are referred to in the text.

- Disconnect the coolant pipe (12) from the water pump and the pipe (11) from the thermostat housing.
- In the case of an M113 engine remove the radiator (section "Cooling System").
- Disconnect the vacuum pipe leading to the brake servo unit at the rear of the air intake pipe. Towards the right, slightly above, disconnect a further vacuum pipe.
- Empty the steering fluid reservoir with a hand pump and disconnect the return pipe and the pressure pipe from the pump.
- Disconnect the fuel pipe. The system must be free of pressure. The pipe connection can be located by referring to Fig. 1.8 (marked with 1). Tighten the union nut to 3.8 kgm (27.5 ft.lb.).
- Disconnect the coolant pipe (14).

Engines

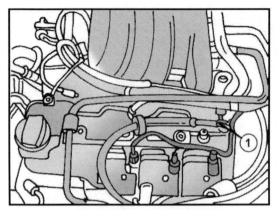

Fig. 1.8 – The fuel line is disconnected at location (1).

- Disconnect the electrical cable harness from the engine. If necessary mark their connection to facilitate the installation.
- Remove the Poly V-belt as described for this engine.
- Remove the connector plug from the A/C compressor (18) and unbolt the compressor from the timing housing cover. Attach the compressor with all pipes connected at the bottom of the engine compartment with wire. The securing bolts are tightened with 2.0 kgm (14.5 ft.lb.) during installation.
- If an M113 engine is fitted remove the panelling from inside the L.H. front wing (fender). Also on this engine the cover (8) must be removed.
- Disconnect the exhaust pipes (11) from the exhaust manifold. The connection is tightened to 2.0 kgm (14.5 ft.lb.) during installation. Hold the exhaust from below and unscrew the bracket (15).
- Remove the torque converter from the drive plate (3 bolts). The bolt are tightened to 4.2 kgm (30 ft.lb.) during installation.
- Withdraw the plug of the L.H. Lambda probe (17) upstream of the catalytic converter and from the R.H. probe (10). Remove the cable trap.
- Remove the starter motor without disconnecting the cables. Tighten the bolts to 4.2 kgm (30 ft.lb.).
- Remove the transmission securing bolts from the cylinder block. In the case of a 112.942 or 112.970 engine (ML 320 and ML350) do not remove the two upper bolts fully at this stage. In the case of a 113.942 or 113.965 do not remove the two lower bolts fully at this stage. Bolts are tightened to 4.0 kgm (29 ft.lb.) during installation.
- Remove the nuts (20) from the engine mountings. Tighten them to 3.5 kgm (25 ft.lb.) to the front axle carrier during installation.
- Remove the fluid filler pipe on the R.H. side of the cylinder head cover.
- The engine must now be lifted with a suitable hand crane or hoist and ropes or chains attached to the engine lifting eyes. Carefully lift the engine without damaging the injection pipes. The workshop inserts, as already mentioned, a guard plate between the engine and the radiator/condenser to protect the items. This will prevent any damage.
- Place a mobile jack with a suitable protective plate underneath the transmission until just under tension.
- Remove the two remaining two upper bolts or the remaining two lower bolts, depending on the engine.
- The engine is now carefully removed. Make sure that none of the cables, pipes, etc. are damaged during the removal.

The installation is a reversal of the removal procedure noting the points and tightening torques already given above.

After filling the cooling system check all connections for leaks. The following points must also be observed:

- Engine mountings, oil and fuel pipes must be checked for damage before they are re-used.
- Check the oil level in the engine and transmission and correct if necessary. If the engine oil has been drained fill it with the correct quantity of engine oil.
- Before filling the cooling system check that all drain points have been closed.

- Make sure that all bolts and nuts have been tightened to the correct tightening torque.
- After starting the engine and allowing it to warm up, check the cooling system for leaks. Drive the vehicle a few miles to check for exhaust pipe rattle.

M113 engine, ML500, series 164 (model 164.175)
M272 engine, ML350, series 164 (model 164.186)

Again you will have to refer to the chapter in question for details not described in the following description. The removal and installation is rather complicated, but is, however, described. Read the instructions in full and then decide.

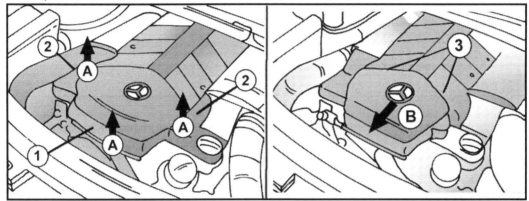

Fig. 1.9 – Removal of the engine cover in the case of an M113 engine. Refer to text.

Removal and installation of the two engine types is carried out in a similar manner, but there is no need to remove the two propeller shafts in the case of the ML 350.

- Open the bonnet and secure it in vertical position.
- Place the vehicle on secure chassis stands when operations are carried out from underneath.
- Disconnect the battery earth cable.
- Remove the engine trim panel by referring to Fig. 1.9 in the case of the M113 engine. Unlock the two mounting clamps (1) and (2) by lifting the panel slightly upwards in the direction of arrows (A), but only in the area of the mounting clamps (otherwise the trim panel can be damaged). The removal in the case of the M272 engine can be followed in the description of the removal of the L.H. cylinder head.
- Unlock the mounting clamps (1) and (2) by moving the trim panel in the direction of arrows (B). The trim panel can now be lifted off.
- Disconnect the fuel pipe from the fuel distributor pipe. Careful – the fuel is under pressure. The union nut is tightened to 3.8 kgm (27 ft.lb.).
- Using a hand pump draw the fluid out of the steering fluid reservoir.
- Drain the cooling system.
- Disconnect the coolant hose from the pipe on the thermostat housing and two further hoses at the top and bottom of the water pump. Check the condition of hoses and hose clamps before re-using them.
- Remove the fan shroud together with the fan.
- Remove the Poly V-belt.
- Remove a banjo bolt from the high pressure hose on the steering pump. Protect the open ends from entry of foreign matter. The bolt is tightened to 4.0 kgm (29 ft.lb.) during installation.
- The next operations are carried out by referring to Fig. 1.10. First disconnect the vacuum pipe leading to the brake servo unit (1). Disconnect the coolant hose (2) from the heat exchanger from the connection (3). In the R.H. view withdraw the connector plug (4) and disconnect the pipe (5) from the control valve (6). The

valve is now removed from its rubber mounting and placed over the engine with the pipe connected.

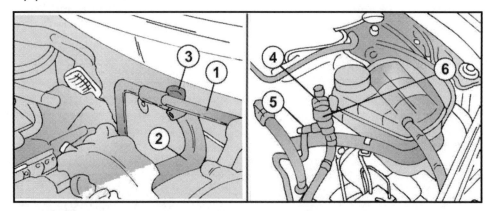

Fig. 1.10 – Removal and installation of the M113 engine (series 164). The numbers are referred to in the text.

•   Disconnect all electrical leads from the engine.

•   Remove the undercover from underneath the engine compartment.

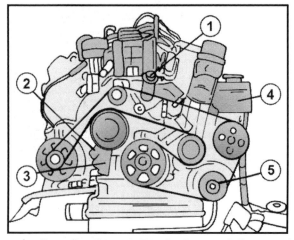

Fig. 1.11 – View of the engine front with the location of some of the items to be removed.

1   Fuel hose
2   Connecting pipe to thermostat
3   Lower connecting pipe on water pump
4   Steering fluid reservoir
5   Compressor, A/C system

•   Remove the A/C compressor. The compressor of this engine is attached at the position shown in Fig. 1.11. Attach the removed compressor with the connected lines/hoses at the bottom of the engine compartment. Tighten the compressor bolts to 2.0 kgm (14.5 ft.lb.) during installation.

•   Remove the complete exhaust system.

•   Disconnect the rear propeller shaft from the transfer box after marking the flange connection. Withdraw two cable connectors from the transfer box. The bolts are tightened to 5.5 kgm (40 ft.lb.) during installation. Make sure that the markings are opposite each other.

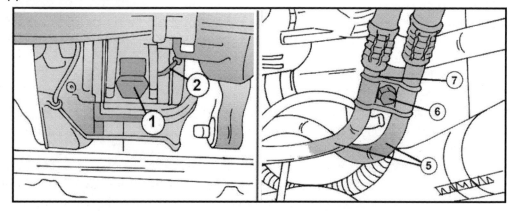

Fig. 1.12 – Remove the items at the positions shown.

- On the R.H. side of the transmission remove two bolts and take off the exhaust pipe bracket. Bolts are tightened to 2.0 kgm (14.5 ft.lb.).
- On the side of the transmission remove a cover (heat protection shield) and then withdraw the visible cable connector from the transmission control unit. The cover bolts are tightened to 0.8 kgm (6 ft.lb.).
- Remove the cover at position (1) in the L.H. view of Fig. 1.12 and through the opening unscrew the torque converter from the drive plate. The crankshaft must be rotated to reach all bolts. Bolts are tightened to 4.2 kgm (30 ft.lb.) during installation.
- Remove the bolt (4) from the double clamp on the alternator mounting bracket (5). The bolt is tightened to 0.8 kgm (6 ft.lb.).
- Remove a bolt securing the oil cooler pipe to the oil sump. Tighten the bolt to 0.8 kgm (6 ft.lb.).
- Disconnect the oil cooler pipes (3) in Fig. 1.12 from the transmission, remove it from the oil sump and push it to one side without bending it. Close the ends in suitable manner. Tighten the bolt to 0.9 kgm (7 ft.lb.).
- Place a mobile jack with a suitable protective plate underneath the transmission until just under tension. The workshop, of course, uses a special lifting plate.

Fig. 1.13 – Removal of the engine mounting crossmember.

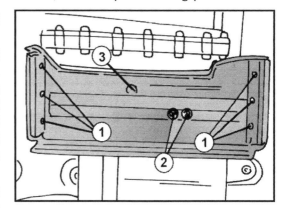

- Remove the engine mounting crossmember by referring to Fig. 1.13. Remove the bolts (1) and (2) and take off the crossmember (3). The bolts must be replaced and are tightened to 3.0 kgm (14.5 ft.lb.) to the transmission and 5.5 kgm (40 ft.lb.), when the crossmember is bolted to the body.
- Disconnect the front propeller shaft from the transfer box after marking the flange connection. The bolts are tightened to 5.5 kgm (40 ft.lb.) during installation. Make sure that the markings are opposite each other.
- Remove the bolts securing the engine to the transmission. Also remove a bolt from the venting pipe and remove the pipe. Note that the starter motor can drop after removal of the mounting bolts.
- Remove the transmission from below. Take care that the converter cannot drop out.
- Remove the bolts of the front engine mountings from the mounting brackets. Tighten the bolts to 5.3 kgm (38 ft.lb.) during installation.
- The engine must now be lifted with a suitable hand crane or hoist and ropes or chains attached to the engine lifting eyes. Carefully lift the engine without damaging any of the engine parts. As in the case of the other engines, the workshop inserts, as already mentioned, a guard plate between the engine and the radiator/condenser to protect the items. This will prevent any damage.

The installation is carried out in reverse order. The point already listed also apply to these engines.

1.2 Engine - Dismantling

Before commencing dismantling of the engine, all exterior surfaces should be cleaned, as far as possible, to remove dirt or grease. Plug the engine openings with clean cloth first to prevent any foreign matter entering the cavities and openings. Detailed information on engine dismantling and assembly is given in the sections dealing with

Engines

servicing and overhaul (sections commencing at 1.4.) and these should be followed for each of the sub-assemblies or units to be dealt with.

Follow the general dismantling instructions given below.

- Dismantling must be carried out in an orderly fashion to ensure that parts, such as valves, pistons, bearing caps, shells, tappets and so on, are replaced in the same positions as they occupied originally. Mark them clearly, but take care not to scratch or stamp on any rotating or bearing surfaces. A good way to keep the valves in order is by piercing them through an upside-down cardboard box and writing the number against each valve. Segregate together the tappets, the springs and retainers with collets for each valve, if possible in small plastic bags for each individual valve.

- If a proper engine dismantling stand is not available, it will be useful to make up wooden support blocks to allow access to both the top and bottom faces of the engine. The cylinder head, once removed from the block, should be supported by a metal strap, screwed to the manifold face and secured by two nuts onto the manifold studs.

1.3   Engine - Assembling

The assembly of the engine is described in the following section for the component parts in question.

1.4.   Engine - Overhaul
1.4.0.   Cylinder Head and Valves – Technical Data

Values for the various engines are similar but not identical and are either not available or too comprehensive to list. We therefore recommend to contact your dealer for any important value you may need. We strongly recommend to follow the recommendation in section "Cylinder Head Overhaul".

Cylinder Head:

Max. Distortion of Cylinder Head Faces:
- Longitudinal direction: 0.08 mm
- Across the face: 0.00 mm
Max. deviation of faces between upper and
  lower sealing faces (parallel to each other):   0.10 mm

Depth of valve head faces and cylinder head sealing face:
- Inlet valves: +0.17 to 0.23 mm
- Exhaust valves: +0.12 to 0.28 mm
- With re-cut valve seats: 1.0 mm – all valves

Valves

Valve Head Diameter:
- Inlet valves – Four-cylinder: 40.00 mm
- Inlet valves – 642 diesel engine: 25.30 – 25.50 mm
- Inlet valves – V6 – M112 engine: 36.00/38.00 mm
- Inlet valves – V6 – M272 engine: 28.50 mm
- Inlet valves – V8 – M113 engine: 38.00 mm
- Exhaust valves – Four-cylinder: 35.00 mm
- Exhaust valves – 642 engine: 28.40 – 28.60 mm

- Exhaust valves – V6 – M112 engine: 41.00/43.00 mm
- Exhaust – V6 – M272 engine: 25.40 mm
- Exhaust valves – V8 – M113 engine: 43.00 mm

Valve seat angle: 45° + 15'

Valve Stem Diameter:
- Inlet valves – M111:   6.955 – 6.970 mm
- Inlet valves – 642 engine: 5.945 – 5.975 mm
- Inlet valves – M112/M113:   6.975 mm
- Inlet valves – M272:   5.960 – 5.975 mm
- Exhaust – M111:   6.938 – 6.960 mm
- Exhaust valves – 642 engine: 5.945 – 5.975 mm
- Exhaust valves – M112/M113:   6.970 mm
- Exhaust valves – M272:   5.955 – 5.970 mm

Valve Seat Width:
- Inlet valves: 1.8 – 3.0 mm
- Exhaust valves: 1.5 – 2.5 mm
- Inlet and exhaust valves – V6 and V8:   0.8 – 1.2 mm

Valve Identification: Check with parts list

Valve Seats

Valve seat width – Inlet/exhaust valves: See above
Valve seat angles: 45° - 15'
Upper correction angle: 15°
Lower correction angle: 60°

Valve Guides

Inlet Valve Guides:
Length:
- Four-cylinder: 35.50 mm
- V6/V8 petrol: 50.00 mm
- Inner diameter, V6/V8 depending on engine: 7.000 or 8.000 mm
- Inner diameter – 642 engine: 6.000 – 6.015 mm

Exhaust Valve Guides:
Length:
- Four-cylinder: 35.50 mm
- V6/V8 petrol: 50.00 mm
- Inner diameter, V6/V8 depending on engine: 7.000 or 8.000 mm
- Inner diameter – 642 engine: 6.000 – 6.015 mm

Interference fit of valve guides – All guides:
- Std.   0.009 – 0.021 mm
- Repair size   0.011 – 0.024 mm

Valve Timing
M111 Engine   Depending on camshaft code

Cylinder Head on R.H. side: **642 Engine**
Inlet valves open: 19.6° after TDC
Inlet valves close: 5.6° after BTDC

Engines

Exhaust valves open:	17.9° before BTDC
Exhaust valves close:	27.9° before TDC

Cylinder Head on R.H. side:

Inlet valves open:	21.5° after TDC
Inlet valves close:	3.7° after BTDC
Exhaust valves open:	16.0° before BTDC
Exhaust valves close:	26.0° before TDC

Cylinder Head on L.H. side: **642 Engine**

Inlet valves open:	20.7° after TDC
Inlet valves close:	4.5° after BTDC
Exhaust valves open:	16.8° before BTDC
Exhaust valves close:	26.8° before TDC

Cylinder Head on L.H. side:

Inlet valves open:	21.5° after TDC
Inlet valves close:	3.7° after BTDC
Exhaust valves open:	16.0° before BTDC
Exhaust valves close:	26.0° before TDC

Camshaft

Camshaft Bearings:
Camshaft Bearing Diameter – M111 engine:

- Standard diameter:	28.00 – 28.021 mm
- Repair diameter:	28.50 – 28.521 mm

Camshaft Journal diameter – M111 engine:

- Standard diameter:	27.947 – 27.963 mm
- Repair diameter:	28.447 – 28.463 mm
Camshaft end float – M111 engine:	0.05 – 0.15 mm
Camshaft end float – V6/V8 engine:	0.08 – 0.12 mm

1.4.0.1. Cylinder Head – Working on the Cylinder Head

The following information should be noted when work is carried out on a cylinder head:

- The cylinder head is made of light-alloy. Engine coolant, engine oil, the air required to ignite the fuel and the exhaust gases are directed through the cylinder head. Glow plugs, injectors and valve tappets are fitted to the cylinder head. Also in the cylinder heads you will find the camshafts.
- The exhaust manifold and the inlet manifold are bolted to the outside of the head. The fuel enters the head on one side and exits on the other side.
- The cylinder head is fitted with various sender units, sensors and switching valves, responsible for certain functions of the temperature control.
- As the cylinder head is made of light alloy, it is prone to distortion if, for example, the order of slackening or tightening of the cylinder head bolts is not observed. For the same reason never remove the cylinder head from a hot engine.
- A cylinder head cannot be checked in fitted position. Sometimes the cylinder head gasket will "blow", allowing air into the cooling system. A quick check is possible after opening the coolant reservoir cap (engine fairly cold). Allow the engine to warm-up and observe the coolant. Visible air bubbles point in most cases to a "blown" gasket. Further evidence is white exhaust smoke, oil in the coolant or coolant in the engine oil. The latter can be checked at the oil dipstick. A white,

grey emulsion on the dipstick is more or less a confirmation of a damaged cylinder gasket.

The cylinder head must only be removed when the engine is cold. New cylinder head gaskets are wrapped in plastic und must only be unwrapped just before the gasket is fitted. The cylinder head can be removed with the engine fitted and these operations are described below, but note that operations may vary, depending on the equipment fitted. Many secondary operations are necessary before the actual cylinder head can be removed. The following description refers therefore in detail to the various jobs on different engines.

1.4.0.2. Removal and Installation of Cylinder Head

M111 Engine

Some preliminary operations must be carried out before the cylinder head can be removed.

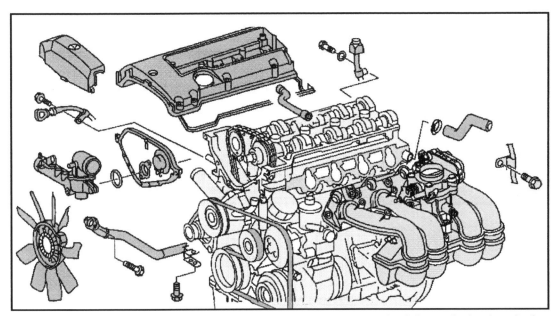

Fig. 1.14 – Some of the parts to be removed during the removal of the cylinder head of an M111 engine.

Removal and Installation of Cylinder head Cover

First remove the cylinder head cover. Fig. 1.14 shows the parts fitted to the cylinder head and the engine which must be removed.

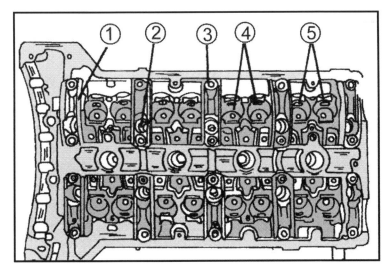

Fig. 1.15 – View of the cylinder head from above.
1 Camshaft bearing cap
2 Bearing cap bolts
3 Cylinder head bolts
4 Valve tappets
5 Lubrication bores for valve tappets

Before removal of the cylinder head read the following instructions. Fig. 1.15 shows the cylinder head with the location of some of the parts.

• The camshaft bearings

are marked with numbers 1 to 10 in the bearing caps (1). The numbers are also cast into the side of the cylinder head.

- The securing bolts for the camshaft (2) have a "Torx" head. To remove the bolts a "Torx" head socket is therefore required (size T40). The tightening torque of the bolts is 2.1 kgm (15 ft.lb.).

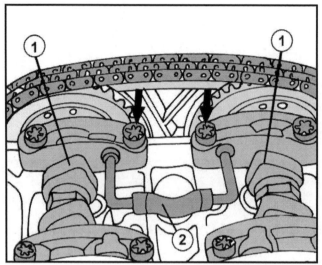

Fig. 1.16 – The two locking pins (2) of the special tool are inserted from the rear of the camshaft timing gears (1).

- The cylinder head bolts are located at positions (3) below the camshaft bearing caps and have an internal hexagonal head, i.e. an Allen key will be required to remove and tighten them. Each time the bolts are tightened, the bolts are stretched. It is therefore necessary to measure their length, between the underside of the bolt head and the end of the thread. Any bolt longer than 105 mm must be replaced. The tightening of the bolts is carried out in three stages, as described during the installation of the head.

Fig. 1.17 – The four bolts (A) secure the cylinder head. The locking pins are inserted from the rear into the camshaft timing gears.

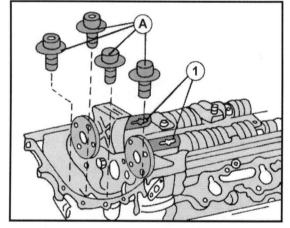

- The 16 valve tappets are fitted at position (4). To lubricate the tappets, two oil drilling are machined at positions (5), i.e. there are in total 16 such drillings in the cylinder head.
- The camshafts are arrested against rotation in the workshop by two locking pins (No. 111 589 01 15 00). These pins have a thread diameter of 5 mm and maybe substituted by pins of the same diameter. If the pins are not used, make sure that the camshafts cannot rotate after the timing chain has been removed. Fig. 1.16 shows where the locking pins are inserted. Fig. 1.17 shows where the pins are inserted from the rear of the camshaft timing gears.
- The guide rail for the timing chain must be removed. The bearing bolt for the guide rail has a tight fit in the cylinder head. The bolt can be removed by screwing in a threaded insert and attach an impact hammer to the end of the insert.
- The slackened cylinder head is removed by means of a suitable lifting device (hand crane for example). Ropes or chains can be attached to the front and rear lifting eye at the front and rear of the cylinder head to lift off the head. The cylinder head is lifted upwards.
- The inlet manifold must be removed and is taken off together with the connected cables and pushed away from the cylinder head until it is free of the threaded studs.
- New cylinder head gasket is shrink-wrapped in plastic which must be removed just before the gasket is fitted.

Removal and Installation of Cylinder Head

The removal and installation of the cylinder head is described below, but again note that some of the operations are only referred to briefly and the relevant sections must be consulted for details.

- Set the engine bonnet in the vertical position as mentioned during the removal of the engine. Disconnect the battery cables.
- Drain the cooling system. The drain plug is the cylinder block should also be removed. Remove the coolant expansion tank.
- Remove the cylinder head cover as described.
- Remove the exhaust pipe from the exhaust manifold and push the pipe away from the engine. If a bracket is attached to the exhaust system remove it.
- Remove the thermostat housing cover.
- Disconnect all electrical cable connectors from the cylinder head.
- Remove the inlet manifold (intake manifold) from the cylinder head and push it away from the head until it is free of the threaded studs. Remove the gasket. The component parts of the cylinder head cover are shown in Fig. 1.14.
- Below the flange connection of the inlet manifold and cylinder head disconnect a venting hose.
- If fitted, remove the bracket shown in Fig. 1.14. Also disconnect the coolant hose shown in the same illustration at the rear of the cylinder head after slackening of the hose clamp.
- At the rear of the cylinder head remove the position sensor for the camshaft (1 bolt).

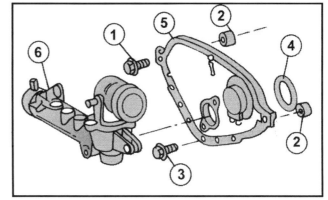

Fig. 1.18 – Removal and installation of the front cover of the cylinder head.

1 M8 x 35 mm bolt
2 Dowel sleeve
3 M6 x 22 mm bolt
4 "O" sealing ring
5 Cover
6 Thermostat housing

- Locate the Lambda probe and withdraw the cable connector.

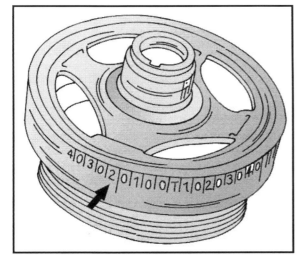

Fig. 1.19 – The crankshaft must be rotated until the vibration damper (crankshaft pulley) is aligned as shown.

- Remove the front cover. This is the cover which encloses the chain housing at the front of the cylinder head. The parts to be removed are shown in Fig. 1.18. Remove the thermostat housing (6) on the side of the cylinder head, remove a solenoid valve, remove the cover (5) at the upper end and remove. During installation tighten the M6 bolts (22 mm long) to 1.0 kgm (7.2 ft.lb.), the M8 bolts (35 mm long) to 2.5 kgm (18 ft.lb.). The cover sealing face must be coated with sealing compound during installation. "Omnifit FD 10 sealing compound is used in the workshop.

Engines

- Remove the bolt securing the oil dipstick guide tube from the cylinder head. If an automatic transmission is fitted you will have to remove the fluid dipstick tube at the R.H. rear end of the cylinder head (one bolt, refer to Fig. 1.14 for location).

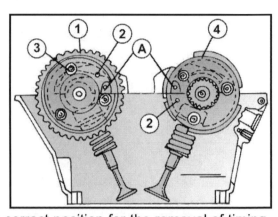

Fig. 1.20 – Basic position of the camshafts of a four-cylinder engine. The locking pins are inserted into the bores (A).
1   Exhaust camshaft
2   Pins
3   Securing bolts
4   Inlet camshaft

- Rotate the crankshaft until the angle scale on the crankshaft pulley (vibration damper) is in the position shown in Fig. 1.19. The 20° mark has a longer line. In this position the piston of No. 1 cylinder is at the top dead centre position, i.e. the correct position for the removal of timing mechanism parts.

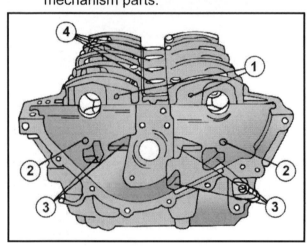

Fig. 1.21 – View of the cylinder head. The bores (1) are used to lock the camshafts in their basic position.
1   Bores
2   Oil bores
3   Oil return bores
4   Spark plug tubes

- The camshafts must now be locked in their installed position. As already mentioned, locking pins are used in the workshop. These are inserted in accordance with Figs. 1.16 and 1.17 into the cylinder head. Fig. 1.20 shows a further view. The basic position of the camshafts is guaranteed by means of the 6.5 mm bores in Fig. 1.21. If the locking pins are not available, you will have to make sure to lock the camshafts by other means. Mark the sprockets and the chain at opposite points with a spot of paint.

- Remove the chain tensioner and the camshaft timing gears of the inlet and exhaust camshafts or, if fitted, the camshaft adjuster. Bolts are tightened to 2.0 kgm (14.5 ft.lb.) and a quarter of a turn.

Fig. 1.22 – Removal of the bearing bolt (1) for the timing chain guide rail. Screw in the threaded bolt (2) and remove with the impact hammer (3).

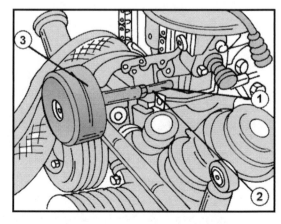

- The bearing bolt for the chain guide rail must now be removed from the cylinder head. To do this, you will need a suitable bolt, screwed into the bearing bolts and an impact hammer. By hitting the weight of the impact hammer against its outer stop, the bearing bolt will be released. Fig.1.22 shows details. Otherwise screw in a screw of suitable diameter and try to remove the bolt with a pair of pliers or by other means. **Note:**

The bolt must be coated with sealing compound (002989002010) during installation.

- Remove the four bolts in Fig. 1.17 from the inside of the timing housing. These are the bolts indicated by "A" in Fig. 1.23. The bolts are tightened to 1.8 kgm and a quarter of a turn during installation. An Allen key will be required.
- Slacken the cylinder head bolts in several stages in the reverse order to the one shown ion Fig. 1.23, i.e. start at No. 10 and work in order to No. 1, until all bolts have been slackened and can be removed by hand. A special wrench with the number 617 589 00 1 0 00 is used to slacken and tighten the cylinder head bolts.

Fig. 1.23 – Tightening sequence for the cylinder head. The bolts marked with (A) are located in the timing housing, shown in Fig. 1.21.

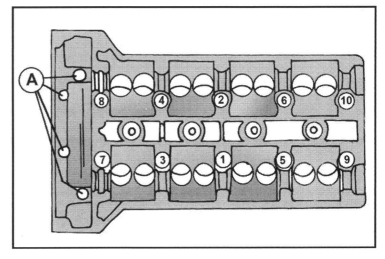

- Remove the two bolts securing the first bearing cap for the exhaust camshaft (looking onto the camshafts, this is the L.H. shaft) and remove the cap. In its place attach a lifting eye, similar as the one fitted to the opposite end of the cylinder head. As already mentioned, a "Torx" socket (size T40) will be required to remove and tighten the bolts.
- The cylinder head is now lifted off with a suitable lifting device, with ropes or chains attached to the two lifting eyes. Due to the weight of the head it may be rather difficult to lift the head off manually. A sticking head can be freed by hitting near the sealing face with a plastic or rubber mallet, at the same time operating the lifting device. Never try to separate the head from the block by inserting a sharp object (for example a screwdriver) into the sealing face gap. After removal place the head onto a work bench.
- Immediately check that the two guide pins are still in the cylinder block face. If they (or one) have come away with the head, remove them and re-insert them into the cylinder block before the head is fitted. Remove the cylinder head gasket.
- Clean the cylinder head and cylinder block faces of old gasket material. If the cylinder head gasket is being replaced due to failure, you will have to check the head sealing face for distortion as described later on. The cylinder head bolt bores in the cylinder block must be free of oil or water to prevent hydraulic locks during installation.

The installation is carried out in reverse order to the removal procedure. The following points refer mainly to the tightening torque values where applicable:

- Place the cylinder head gasket over the block face.
- Lower the cylinder head in position, using the lifting tackle as during removal. As already mentioned the two guide pins must be located in the cylinder block. Engage the pins with the cylinder head and fully lower it onto the block.
- Coat the thread and the underside of the bolt heads with oil.
- Screw the bolts into the threaded bores and tighten them in several stages in the order shown in Fig. 1.26 to a torque of 5.5 kgm (40 ft.lb).
- From the final position tighten each bolt in the order shown in Fig. 1.23 without torque spanner by one quarter of a turn (90°). And then a further quarter of a turn.

Engines

- Tighten the four bolts in the timing housing cover (A in Fig. 1.23) to 1.8 kgm (Allen key insert).
- Fit the camshaft sprocket and tighten the bolt to 2.0 kgm (14.5 ft.lb.) and from the final position a further quarter of a turn (90°).
- Unscrew the lifting bracket from the No. 1 camshaft bearing cap and refit the cap. Fit and tighten the two bearing cap bolts in several stages to 2.1 kgm (14.5 ft.lb.). A T40 torx-head insert is required to tighten the bolts.
- The remaining operations are now carried out in reverse order.

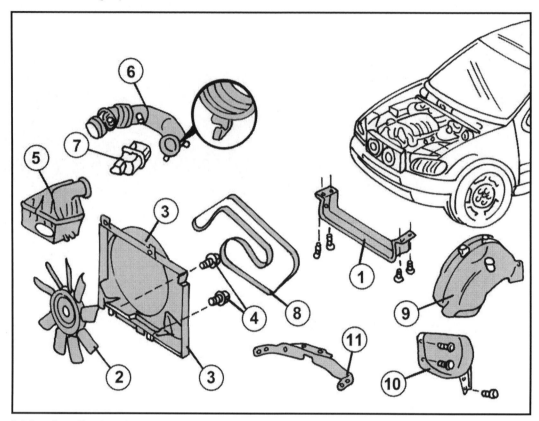

Fig. 1.24 – Details for the removal and installation of the M112 and M113 engine in series 163. The numbers are referred to in the text.

M112 and M113 engine in Series 163

The instructions are valid for models ML 320, ML350, ML 430 and ML 500 and are in general similar for all models. We try to refer to differences when applicable. Figs. 1.24 and 1.25 can be used during the removal.

Some special tools will be required during the removal which will be listed when necessary. Although the removal and installation may appear rather difficult, is can be carried out if you have some experience with engines. Proceed as follows. The specified numbers refer to Figs. 1.24 and 1.25 as applicable.

- Disconnect the battery and place the front end of the vehicle on chassis stands.
- In the case of an ML 430 remove the air guide (1).
- Drain the cooling system and remove the engine cover (trim cover).
- Remove the viscous fan (2), but not on all models. In the case of the ML 500 the electric fan must be removed.
- Remove the fan shroud (3). Secured with bolts (4) at the lower end.
- As an air condition system will be fitted you will have to insert a protective plate in front of the radiator and the condenser to prevent damage during removal of the engine. This can be made up of 1 mm thick plastic or metal sheet, but must have

a dimension of 400 x 680 mm (already mentioned during the removal of the engine).

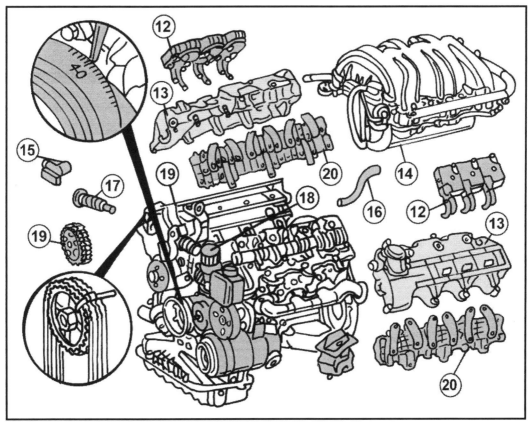

Fig. 1.25 – Details for the removal and installation of the M112 and M113 engine in series 163. The numbers are continued from Fig. 1.24.

- Remove the air cleaner housing (5).
- Remove the air intake tube (6) together with the resonance unit (7).
- Disconnect the fuel pipe from the fuel distributor. Attention – Fuel is under pressure – the workshop uses a special valve to reduce the pressure – Danger of fire.
- Remove the L.H. and R.H. ignition coil (12). Tighten the bolts to 0.8 kgm (6 ft.lb.) during installation.
- Remove the L.H. and R.H. cylinder head cover (13) as described below.
- Remove the inlet manifold (14) together with the fuel distributor.
- Unscrew the camshaft position sensor (15), if the R.H. cylinder head is removed.
- Remove the Poly V-belt (8) as described in a separate chapter.
- In the case of the ML 430 and ML 500 remove the panel inside the front wing (8), the protective cover (10) and the exhaust tube bracket (11). Support the exhaust system from below and separate the exhaust pipes from the manifold flanges. Tighten the flange connection to 2.0 kgm (14.5 ft.lb.) during installation.
- Remove the two camshafts as described later on. This includes the removal of the sprockets (19) and the bearing bridges (20). Also remove the chain tensioner (17).
- Remove the oil filter housing (18). In the case of the ML 430 and the ML 500 together with the oil/water heat exchanger.
- Remove the bolts (1) in Fig. 1.26. These secure the cylinder head to the timing housing cover.
- Slacken the cylinder head bolts in reverse order to Fig. 1.27 in several stages until all bolts are slack and can be removed. Note the differences between the L.H.

cylinder head (3) and the R.H. (4). The head can now be removed. A small crane and a chain can be used. Attach suitable lifting brackets to the cylinder head.

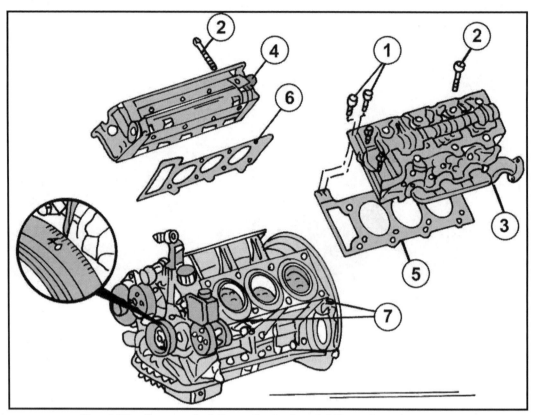

Fig. 1.26 – Removal of the cylinder head. V6 engine shown.

1 Bolts in timing housing
2 M11 bolts
3 L.H. cylinder head
4 R.H. cylinder head

5 L.H. cylinder head gasket
6 R.H. cylinder head gasket
7 Dowel sleeves

Fig. 1.27 – Tightening sequence for the cylinder head bolts in the case of a V6 engine. Similar on the V8 engine. Bolts (a) and (b) are fitted to the timing housing cover.

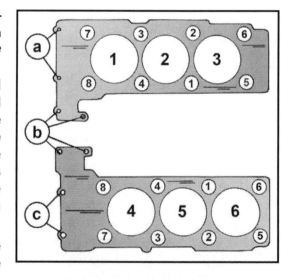

■ Remove the cylinder head gasket and immediately clean the cylinder head and cylinder block faces. If the guide pins remain in the cylinder head remove them and re-install them into the cylinder block face. If a new gasket is purchased quote the exact engine type as gaskets are different (for example in the cylinder bore diameter).

Although the installation is a reversal of the removal procedure, follow the points in the order given below:

• Check with a dealer if the cylinder head gasket can be re-machined.
• Check that the crankshaft is in the correct timing position, i.e. the 40° mark in the vibration damper must be aligned as shown in Fig. 1.26. In this position the pistons of cylinder No. 1 will be at TDC ignition timing point.
• Place the cylinder head gasket in position over the cylinder head. The dowel pins must engage. Use a rubber or plastic mallet to tap the head in position.

- Measure the length of the cylinder head bolts (M11 thread) between the end of the thread to the underside of the bolt head. New bolts have a length of 141.5 mm. From the measurement obtained you will see if new bolts must be fitted. The max. permissible length is 144.5 mm.
- Coat the underside of the bolt heads and the threads with engine oil and fit the bolts. Tighten them finger-tight.
- Tighten the cylinder head bolts in the sequence shown in Fig. 1.27 to 1.0 kgm (7 ft.lb.), i.e. starting with bolt (1). On both heads the bolt is located on the inside. A "Torx" head socket and a torque spanner is required. After all bolts have been tightened tighten them once more, but this time to 3.0 kgm (22 ft.lb.). The torque spanner is now removed.
- Now tighten all bolts in the order shown in Fig. 1.27 by a further quarter of a turn without torque spanner. After all bolts have been tightened in this manner re-tighten them again by a further quarter of a turn. The bolts in the inside of the timing housing cover are tightened to 2.0 kgm (14.5 ft.lb.).
- The remaining operations are carried out in reverse order. Finally check the engine oil level and correct if necessary.

Note: A further re-tightening of the cylinder head bolts is not necessary.

Cylinder Head Cover – Removal and Installation –M112/M113 Engines

Certain precautions must be observed when the cylinder head cover(s) is removed. Chapter "Ignition System" will refer to these. Remove as follows, referring to Fig. 1.28 for some of the details.

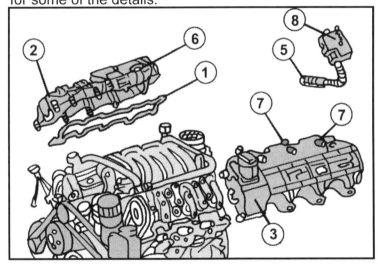

Fig. 1.28 – Details for the removal and installation of the cylinder head cover of a V6 engine. The numbers are referred to in the text.

- Remove the air cleaner housing.
- Withdraw the connecting plugs from the ignition coils. Mark them up if not sure where they are connected.
- Disconnect the spark plug connectors (5) from the spark plugs. The workshop uses a pair of pliers for this operation, i.e. a sort of double-sided open-ended spanner.
- Remove the ignition coils (8). Three bolts secure the coils. Tighten them to 0.8 kgm (6 ft.lb.) during installation.
- Remove the engine venting hose on the fitting (6) for the R.H. cylinder head cover. In the same manner disconnect the venting hose from the fitting (7) on the L.H. cylinder head cover.
- Remove the bolt securing the cylinder head cover on the oil dipstick tube (4). Rotate the dipstick tube to the side to free it of the cover.
- Remove the bolts securing the R.H. cylinder cover (2) and the L.H. cylinder cover (3). The bolts are tightened to 0.8 kgm (6 ft.lb.). The two covers can now be lifted off.

The installation is a reversal of the removal procedure.

Engines

Clean the sealing faces. The gasket (1) should always be replaced. Make sure that the gasket is correctly located in the sealing groove of the cylinder head cover, especially at the rear. Follow the tightening torques given above. Make sure that the ignition cables are connected to the correct cylinders.

Cylinder Head Removal – M272 Engine in Series 164

The L.H. and R.H. cylinder head cover can be removed as required. As in the case of the other V6 engine you will find that the operations are rather complicated, as you will have to located the various parts to be removed and/or disconnected. The description refers mainly to the tightening of the cylinder head bolts. The remaining operations are similar as described for the M112 and M113 engines.

Removal and Installation of the L.H. Cylinder Head

- Disconnect the battery earth cable as described earlier on.
- Place the front end of the vehicle on chassis stands or drive it onto a lift and remove the bottom engine compartment panelling.
- Drain the coolant from the radiator and the cylinder block.

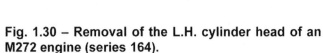

Fig. 1.29 – Details for the removal of the cylinder head of the M272 engine (series 164). First remove the parts shown as described below.

- Remove the following parts by referring to Fig. 1.29. Disconnect the two suction pipes (1) from the air cleaner housing (3) and remove the engine cover (2). To remove the cover lift it off the rubber bearings, disengage it from the air cleaner housing and pull it towards the front and out.
- Remove the fuel injection control unit.
- For the next operations refer to Fig. 1.30. Remove the hot film air mass meter (1) and the air cleaner housing (2). Disconnect the vacuum pipe for the brake servo unit (3) from the inlet manifold, the venting pipe (5) from the control valve (4) and a vacuum pipe (6) from the crankcase.

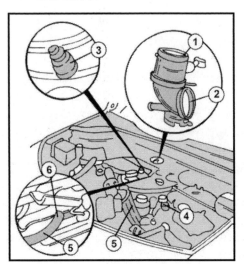

Fig. 1.30 – Removal of the L.H. cylinder head of an M272 engine (series 164).

1	Hot film air mass meter
2	Intake air housing
3	Vacuum pipe (brake servo unit)
4	Control valve
5	Venting pipe
6	Vacuum pipe

- Disconnect the electrical leads from the engine. Mark the connections if not sure where they are to be connected.
- On the cylinder head, near one of the coolant hoses, withdraw a cable connector plug from the temperature sensor for the coolant.
- Follow the fuel pipe and disconnect it from

the fuel distributor rail. Tighten the union nut to 2.0 kgm (14.5 ft.lb.) during installation.

- Remove the inlet manifold.
- Empty the steering fluid reservoir using a hand pump and disconnect the low pressure hose from the reservoir. Replace the hose clamp if necessary. The reservoir can now be removed. Tighten the bolts to 0.9 kgm (6 ft.lb.) to the front cover during installation.
- Remove the Poly V-belt and the belt tensioning device. Also remove the belt guide pulley from the water pump. The bolt is tightened to 3.5 kgm (25 ft.lb.) during installation.
- Remove the oil filter housing together with the oil/water heat exchanger. The removed bolts are tightened to 2.0 kgm (14.5 ft.lb.) during installation.
- Remove a shut-off valve and an intermediate flange from the L.H. cylinder head. Again all removed bolts are tightened to 2.0 kgm (14.5 ft.lb.).

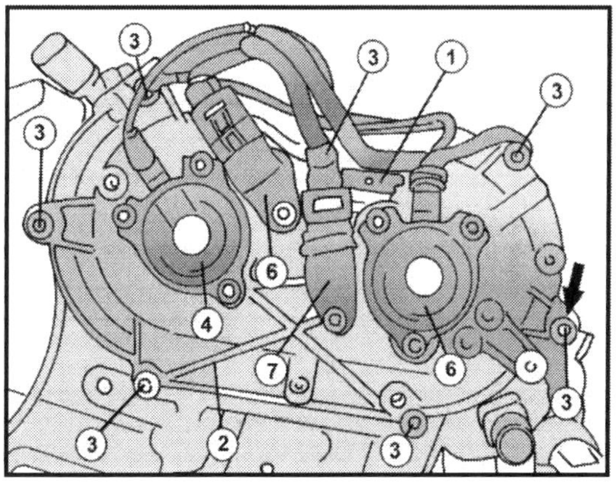

Fig. 1.31 – Details for the removal of the L.H. front cylinder head cover of an M272 engine (series 164). The numbers are referred to below.

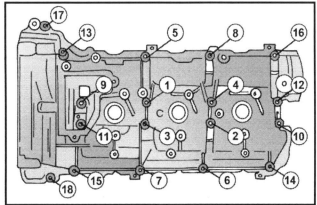

- Disconnect a coolant hose from the connection on the heat exchanger and a coolant pipe from the thermostat housing. The thermostat housing is now removed from the cylinder head. Refer to "Cooling System". Bolts are tightened to 2.5 kgm (18 ft.lb.).
- Remove the front cover from the cylinder head. The operations must be carrier by referring to Fig. 1.31. First disconnect the cable connector plug from the Hall sensor of the L.H. inlet camshaft (6) and the L.H. exhaust camshaft (7). Also disconnect the connector plug from the solenoid for the L.H. inlet camshaft (4) and the L.H. exhaust camshaft (5). Remove the bolts (3) out of the cover (2) and pull the cover towards the front. Note that dowel pins are inserted (arrow). During installation coat the cover face with "Loctite 5970" or a similar sealing compound. The bolts are tightened to 0.9 kgm, the Hall sensor and the solenoid valves with 0.8 kgm.

Fig. 1.32 – Tightening sequence for the securing bolts of the L.H. cylinder head cover. Slacken the bolts in reverse order.

- Remove the oil separator from the cylinder head cover. Tighten the bolts t 1.2 kgm (9 ft.lb.).
- Remove the ignition coils from cylinders Nos. 4 to 6. Tighten the coils with 0.9 kgm (6.5 ft.lb.) to the cylinder head cover.
- Remove the cylinder head cover. The cover is shown in Fig. 1.32. An earth cable must be removed from the cover. Also remove the L.H. rear lifting bracket. After slackening the bolts in the reverse order to Fig. 1.32 (No. 18 = 1), remove the cylinder head cover carefully. During installation apply a bead of "Loctite 5970" sealing compound (not wider than 1.0 mm) to the well cleaned sealing face.

Engines

Tighten the bolts in the order shown in Fig. 1.32 to 1.2 kgm (9 ft.lb.) and from the final position a further quarter of a turn.

- Rotate the engine in the direction of rotation by applying a socket to the crankshaft damper centre bolt until the engine is set to 40° after ignition top dead centre (as shown in Fig. 1.26). Check that the timing marks on the camshafts are in alignment.

- Remove the alternator. The bolts are tightened to 2.0 kgm (14.5 ft.lb.) to the timing housing cover.

- Remove the chain tensioner as described later on and remove the two camshaft adjusters. The operations are described later on in the connection with the timing mechanism.

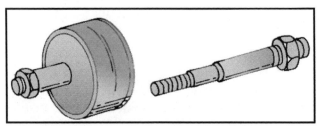

Fig. 1.33 – Tools to remove the slide rails bolts from the end of the L.H. cylinder head.

Remove the slide rail bolts from the end of the L.H. cylinder head. Again these operations are described in connection with the timing mechanism (also refer to the M111 four-cylinder engine). The tools shown in Fig. 1.33, i.e. an impact hammer and an extractor bolt are required. Two bolts must be removed, the position of which is shown with (3) in the cylinder head (1) in Fig. 1.34. Also in the illustration you can see the two camshaft adjusters (2). **Note:** The bolt must be coated with sealing compound "Loctite 5970" during installation.

Fig. 1.34 – View of the cylinder head (1) with the camshaft adjusters (2) and the two bearing bolts (3).

- Remove the bolts (9) in Fig. 1.35. These secure the cylinder head to the timing housing cover.

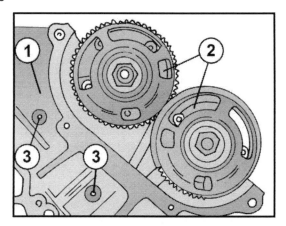

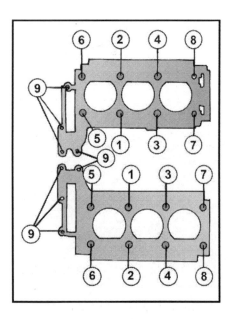

Fig. 1.35 – Tightening sequence for the cylinder head bolts (both cylinder heads).

- Slacken the cylinder head bolts in the reverse order shown in Fig. 1.35 in several stages until all bolts have been removed, noting the difference between the L.H. cylinder head and the R.H. cylinder head. The head can now be lifted off the cylinder block. A small hand crane or other suitable hoist should be used. Two suitable lifting brackets can be attached to the cylinder head.

- Take off the cylinder head gasket and immediately clean the cylinder head and cylinder block sealing faces. If the guide pins have come out together with the cylinder head transfer them back into the cylinder block. When ordering the new cylinder head gasket specify the vehicle type.

The installation of the cylinder head, although basically a reversal of the removal procedure, is carried out as follows:

- Check that the crankshaft is in the correct position, with the "40" in the vibration damper in line with the edge of the adjusting pointer, as shown in the circle in Fig. 1.26. The piston of No. 1 cylinder is now at top dead centre in its compression stroke.

- Place the cylinder head gasket and the cylinder head in position, engaging the dowel pins. Use a plastic or rubber mallet to tap the head well down until seated all round.

- Measure the length of each cylinder head bolt (thread diameter M11). Measure from the underside of the bolt head to the end of the bolt thread. All bolts longer than 172.0 mm must be replaced. New bolts have a length of 170.0 mm, i.e., from the dimension(s) obtained you will be able to tell the stretch of each bolt.

- Coat the underside of the cylinder head bolts and the threads with engine oil and insert them one after the other into their bores and tighten them finger-tight.

- Tighten the cylinder head bolts in the order shown in Fig. 1.35 to 2.0 kgm (14.5 ft.lb.), starting at bolt "1" (on both cylinder heads on the inside). A torx-head insert and a torque wrench must be used. After all bolts have been tightened, again using the torque wrench, tighten all bolts in the order shown to 4.0 kgm (29 ft.lb.). Then take off the torque spanner.

- Tighten each bolt in the order shown in Fig. 1.35 by a quarter of a turn (90°), using the tommy bar only. The tommy bar can, for example be arranged in longitudinal direction of the head and the bolt is tightened until the bar is across the head. After all bolts have been angle-tightened in the manner described, repeat the operation, again in the order shown. Tighten the bolts (9) securing the cylinder head to the timing case cover (2.5 kgm/18 ft.lb.).

- The remaining operations are carried out in reverse order. Check the oil level in the sump, irrespective if operations have been carried out on the engine or not. If the replacement of the cylinder head gasket was necessary because of a "blown" gasket, change the engine oil, as coolant will have entered the oil sump.

Final Note: An additional re-tightening of the cylinder head bolts is no longer necessary, as the bolts have their final torque setting due to the angle-tightening.

Removal and Installation of the R.H. Cylinder Head

Many of the operations are the same as described for the L.H. cylinder head and the relevant notes are given in the description.

- Carry out the operations described for the L.H. cylinder head until the inlet manifold has been removed.

- Unscrew the oil dipstick guide tube from the cylinder head.

- Remove the Poly V-belt and unscrew the belt guide pulley from the water pump. Tighten the bolt to 3.5 kgm (25 ft.lb.) during installation.

- Remove a shut-off valve from the R.H. cylinder head. All bolts are tightened to 1.4 kgm (10 ft.lb.).

- Remove the electric air pump (bolts are tightened to 1.4 kgm) and remove the pump switch-over valve.

- Remove the ignition coils for cylinders Nos. 1 to 3. Tighten the bolts to 0.9 kgm (6 ft.lb.) to the cylinder head cover.

- Remove the so-called centrifuge from the cylinder head cover. Tighten the cover bolts and the centrifuge to 0.6 kgm plus a quarter of a turn to the camshaft sprocket.

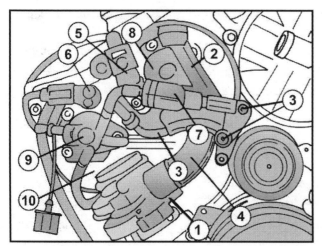

Fig. 1.36 – Details for the removal of the R.H. front cylinder head cover of an M272 engine (series 164). The numbers are referred to below.

• Remove the front cover from the cylinder head. The operations can be carried out with the help of Fig. 1.36. First withdraw the connector plug from the switch-over valve (1). Remove the two bolts (3) and remove the bracket (2) together with the air pump switch-over valve (7) and place the parts to one side. Disconnect the hose (4). Withdraw the connector plug from the Hall sensor of the R.H. inlet camshaft (5) and from the R.H. exhaust camshaft (6). Also withdraw the connector plug from the solenoid of the R.H. inlet camshaft (8) and the R.H. exhaust camshaft (9). Remove the 6 bolts from the cover and remove the cover towards the front. As in the case of the L.H. cylinder head cover you will find that dowel pins are inserted around the outside. During installation coat the cover face with "Loctite 5970" or a similar sealing compound. The bolts are tightened to 0.9 kgm, the Hall sensor and the solenoid valves with 0.8 kgm.

Fig. 1.37 – Tightening sequence for the securing bolts of the R.H. cylinder head cover. Slacken the bolts in reverse order.

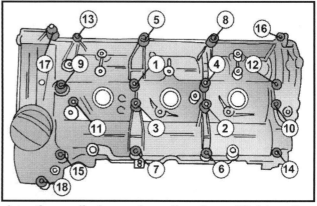

■ Remove the cylinder head cover. The cover is shown in Fig. 1.37. After slackening the bolts in the reverse order to Fig. 1.37 (No. 18 = 1), remove the cylinder head cover carefully. During installation apply a bead of "Loctite 5970" sealing compound (not wider than 1.0 mm) to the well cleaned sealing face. Tighten the bolts in the order shown in Fig. 1.37 to 1.2 kgm (9 ft.lb.) and from the final position a further quarter of a turn.

• Rotate the engine in the direction of rotation by applying a socket to the crankshaft damper centre bolt until the engine is set to 40° after ignition top dead centre (as shown in Fig. 1.26). Check that the timing marks on the camshafts are in alignment.

• Remove the alternator. Bolts are tightened to 2.0 kgm (14.5 ft.lb.).

• Remove the chain tensioner as described later on and remove the two camshaft adjusters. The operations are described later on in the connection with the timing mechanism.

• Remove the slide rail bolts from the end of the R.H. cylinder head. Again these operations are described in connection with the timing mechanism (also refer to the M111 four-cylinder engine). The tools shown in Fig. 1.33, i.e. an impact hammer and an extractor bolt are required. Two bolts must be removed, the position of which is shown with (3) in the cylinder head (1) in Fig. 1.34. Also in the illustration you can see the two camshaft adjusters (2), but note that the opposite side of the head is shown. **Note:** The bolt must be coated with sealing compound "Loctite 5970" during installation.

- Remove the bolts (9) in Fig. 1.35. These secure the cylinder head to the timing housing cover.
- Slacken the cylinder head bolts in the reverse order shown in Fig. 1.35 in several stages until all bolts have been removed, noting the difference between the L.H. cylinder head and the R.H. cylinder head. The head can now be lifted off the cylinder block. A small hand crane or other suitable hoist should be used. Two suitable lifting brackets can be attached to the cylinder head.
- Take off the cylinder head gasket and immediately clean the cylinder head and cylinder block sealing faces. If the guide pins have come out together with the cylinder head transfer them back into the cylinder block. When ordering the new cylinder head gasket specify the vehicle type.

The installation of the cylinder head, i.e. the tightening sequence of the cylinder head bolts are carried out in the manner described for the L.H. cylinder head. The tightening order is shown in Fig. 1.35.

1.4.0.3. Cylinder Head – Dismantling

The following text assumes that the cylinder head is to be replaced. If for example only the valves require attention, ignore the additional operations. Fig. 1.38 shows the V6 engine to give you an inside view of its construction. Similar valve parts are fitted to the other engines, as you can see in Fig. 1.39 on the next page for the V8 engine. The cylinder head must, of course, be removed.

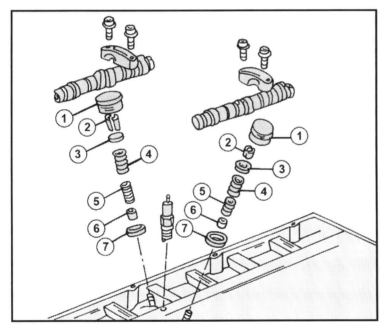

Fig. 1.38 – Valve details of a V6 engine. Similar parts are fitted to the four-cylinder engine.

1   Valve tappet
2   Valve cotter halves
3   Upper valve spring cup
4   Outer valve spring
5   Inner valve spring
6   Valve stem oil seal
7   Valve seat

- Remove the thermo switch, sender units, exhaust manifold, spark plugs, etc. from the cylinder head. Not all cylinder head are fitted with identical parts.
- Remove the camshafts as described under a separate heading.
- A valve spring compressor is required to remove the valves. Fig. 1.40 shows such a compressor. Valves are held in position by means of valve cotter halves. Compress the springs and remove the valve cotter halves (2) with a pair of pointed pliers or a small magnet (1).
- If a valve spring compressor is not available, it is possible to use a short piece of tube to remove the valve cotter halves. To do this, place the tube over the upper valve spring collar and hit the tube with a blow of a hammer. The valve cotter halves will collect in the inside of the tube and the components can be removed. The valve head must be supported from the other side of the cylinder head. Keep the hammer in close contact with the tube to prevent the cotter halves from flying out.

Engines

Fig. 1.39 – Valve details of a V8 engine.

1 Valve cotter halves
2 Upper valve spring cup
3 Valve spring
4 Valve stem oil seal
5 Lower valve spring seat
6 Cylinder head bolts
7 Cylinder head
8 Valve

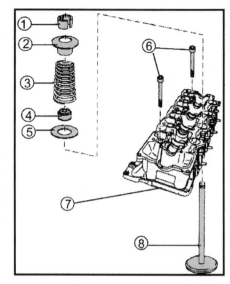

- Remove the valve spring collar and the valve spring. The valve springs (one spring or two springs per valve) are identified with a paint spot and only a spring with a paint spot of the same colour must be fitted. Remove the valves one after the other and keep them in their numbered order, writing the number in front of each valve.

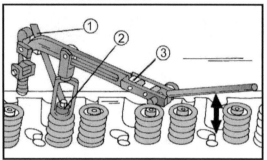

Fig. 1.40 – Removal of valves. Fit the valve spring compressor (3) as shown. The valve cotter halves (2) will be released and can be removed with a small magnet (1).

- Remove valve stem oil seals (1) in the L.H. view of Fig. 1.41 carefully with a screwdriver or a pair of pliers (2).
- Remove the valves one after the other out of the valve guides and pierce them in their fitted order through a piece of cardboard. Write the cylinder number against each valve if they are to be re-used.

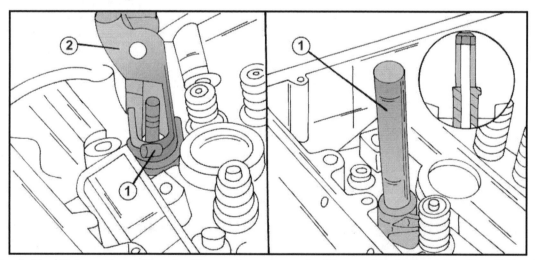

Fig. 1.41 – Valve stem oil seals (1) can be removed with a pair of pliers (2). The R.H. view shows the installation of an oil seal with a piece of tube (1).

1.4.0.4. Cylinder Head - Overhaul

We do not recommend the overhaul of the cylinder head. Instead take the head (or heads) to an engine shop to have it professionally overhauled, ready for installation. Below you will find a few useful hints before you decide to have the head overhauled. The cylinder head must be thoroughly cleaned and remains of old gasket material removed. The checks and inspections are to be carried out as required. Operations are similar on all engines.

Valve Springs: If the engine has a high mileage, always replace the valve springs as a set. To check a valve spring, place the old spring and a new spring end to end over a long bolt (with washer under bolt head) and fit a nut (again with a washer). Tighten the nut until the springs are under tension and measure the length of the two springs. If the old spring is shorter by more than 10%, replace the complete spring set.

The springs must not be distorted. A spring placed with its flat coil on a surface must not deviate at the top by more than 2 mm (0.08 in.).

Valve Guides:

Clean the inside of the guides by pulling a petrol-soaked cloth through the guides. Valve stems can be cleaned best by means of a rotating wire brush. Measure the inside diameter of the guides. As an inside micrometer is necessary for this operation, which is not always available, you can insert the valve into its guide and withdraw it until the valve head is approx. level with the cylinder head face. Rock the valve to and fro and check for play. Although no exact values are available, it can be assumed that the play should not exceed 1.0 - 1.2 mm (0.04 - 0.047 in.). Mercedes workshops use gauges to check the guides for wear.

Before a valve guide is replaced, check the general condition of the cylinder head and then decide if you have the guides replaced.

Valves must always be replaced if new valve guides are fitted. The valve seats must be re-cut when a guide has been replaced. If it is obvious that seats cannot be re-ground in the present condition, new valve seat inserts must be fitted. Again this is an operation for a specialist and the work should be carried out in a workshop.

Valve Seats:

Valve Seats: If the camshaft bearings are excessively worn, fit a new or exchange cylinder head. In this case there is no need to renovate the valve seats.

Check all valve seats for signs of pitting or wear. Slight indentations can be removed with a 45° cutter. If this operation is carried out properly, there should be no need to grind-in the valves. Use correction cutters to bring the valve seating area into the centre of the valve seat. Make sure that the valve seat width, given in Section 1.4.0.0. is obtained. This again is achieved by using cutters of different angles (for example 15° and 60°). Valve seat inserts can be fitted to the cylinder head. Replacement of valve seat inserts will require that the old seat insert is removed by machining. The machining must not damage the bottom face of the head recess. As this is a critical operation - we advise you to bring the cylinder head to your Mercedes Dealer or an engine shop who has the necessary equipment and experience to do the job. It may be possible to obtain a reconditioned cylinder head in exchange for the old one to avoid time delay. In this case remove all ancillary parts from the old head and refit them to the new head.

Valves can be ground into their seats in the conventional manner. To do this, coat the valve seat with lapping compound and use a suction tool, as shown in Fig. 1.42. Move the valve backwards and forwards. Ever so often, lift the suction tool, move it forward by ¼ of a turn and continue grinding. Work the seat until an uninterrupted ring is visible around the face of the valve. After grinding-in, clean the cylinder head, and even more importantly, the inside of the valve guide bores thoroughly. Any lapping paste inside the cylinder head will accelerate the wear of the new parts.

Use a pencil and mark across the valve seat closely spaced. Drop the valve into the respective valve guide and turn the valve by 90°, using the suction tool, applying slight pressure to the tool. Remove the valve and if the pencil marks have been removed from the entire circumference. The gap created will indicate the width of the valve seat and can be measured with a ruler or caliper. Otherwise repeat the grinding until this is the case.

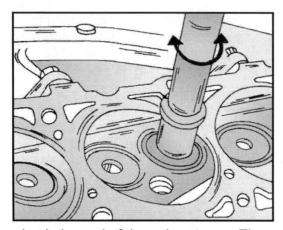

Fig. 1.42 – Grinding-in of valves.

Valves: The exhaust valves must not be discarded as ordinary scrap metal. They are filled with sodium, as is the case with other Mercedes engines. Never use such a valve as a drift – it may be tempting. Valves can be cleaned best with a rotating wire brush. Check the valve stem diameters and in this connection the inside diameters of the valve guides. If there is a deviation from the nominal values, it may be necessary to replace the valve guides (see above). Also check the end of the valve stems. There should be no visible wear in this area.

Sometimes it is only required to replace the exhaust valves, if these for example are burnt out at their valve head edges.

Cylinder Head: Thoroughly clean the cylinder head and cylinder block surfaces of old gasket material and check the faces for distortion. To do this, place a steel ruler with a sharp edge over the cylinder head face and measure the gap between ruler and face with feeler gauges. Checks must be carried out in longitudinal and diagonal direction and across the face. If a feeler gauge of more than 0.10 mm (0.004 in.) can be inserted, when the ruler is placed along or across the cylinder head, have the cylinder head face re-ground.

Camshaft: See separate heading.

1.4.0.5.　Cylinder Head - Assembly

The assembly of the cylinder head is a reversal of the dismantling procedure. Note the following points:

- Lubricate the valve stems with engine oil and insert the valves into the correct valve guides.
- Valve stem seals must be suitable for the engine in question. Make sure to order the correct seals. The repair kit contains fitting sleeves and these must be used to fit the seals (see last Section).
- The sleeves are fitted over the valve stem before the seal is pushed in position.
- Fit the valve spring and valve spring collar over the valve and use the valve lifter to compress the spring. Insert the valve cotter halves and release the valve spring lifter. Make sure that the cotter halves are in position by tapping the end of the valve stem with a plastic mallet. Place a rag over the valve end - just in case.
- Fit the camshaft(s) as described later on and carry out all other operations in reverse order to the dismantling procedure.

1.4.0.6.　Hydraulic Valve Clearance Compensation

The function of the hydraulic valve clearance compensating elements is to eliminate valve clearance, i.e. the dimensional changes in the valve train (valve lash) due to heat expansion and wear are compensated by the elements. The rocker arm is in constant contact with the cam. The compensating elements cannot be repaired, but can be checked for correct functioning as described below. Fig. 1.1 shows a sectional view of a valve with clearance compensation. You will also find a short description of the operation on the same page.

If the tappets are removed, note the following points:

- Always keep the tappets in an upright position, i.e. the open side towards the top.
- After removal of a tappet (see below), mark the cylinder number and the compensating element in suitable manner. Always fit original parts in their same locations.

Checking a hydraulic compensating element: As the elements are in continuous contact with the camshaft, you will rarely hear noises from the area of the hydraulic elements. If noises can be heard, check the elements as follows:
- Start the engine and run it approx. 5 minutes at 3000 rpm.
- Remove the cylinder head cover.
- Rotate the crankshaft until the cam for the tappet to be checked is pointing vertically towards the top.
- Use a drift and push the tappet towards the inside, or try to move the tappet with the fingers.
- If the tappet cannot be depressed or excessive clearance can be felt between the tappet and the back of the cam, replace the tappet. The tappet is supplied together with the hydraulic compensating element. Mercedes workshops can reset the tappet to its original position, but this operation is beyond the scope of the home mechanic.

Tappet Removal and Installation:
- Remove the camshafts as described later on.
- Use a suction tool to remove the tappets. Mark them, if they are to be refitted.
- Fit the tappets into their original bores, if re-used. Refit the camshaft as described and carry out all other operations in reverse order to the removal procedure.
- Fit the tappets into their original bores, if re-used. Refit the camshaft or the camshafts as described and carry out all other operations in reverse order to the removal procedure.

1.4.1. PISTON AND CONNECTING RODS
1.4.1.0. Technical Data
All dimensions are given in metric units.

Pistons
All dimensions are given in metric units.

Pistons
Available pistons: ....Standard and oversize (depending on engine)
Piston Running Clearance :
- Standard (new) – 111 engine:..0.025 – 0.035 mm
- Standard (new) – other engines:...0.04 mm
- Wear limit: ....0.08 mm
Max. weight difference of pistons in
  one engine:.. 4 grams (wear limit 10 grams)

Running clearance of piston pins :
- In connecting rod small end: ....0.007 – 0.017 mm
- In Piston: ....0.002 – 0.011 mm

Piston Ring Gaps (111 engine):
- Upper piston rings:.. 0.30 – 0.45 mm (wear limit 1.00 mm)
- Centre rings:.. 0.30 – 0.45 mm (wear limit 0.80 mm)

Engines

- Lower rings:...0.25 – 0.40 mm (wear limit 0.80 mm)
Piston Ring Gaps (112/113 engine):
- Groove 1: ....0.20 – 0.35 mm (wear limit 0.80 mm)
- Groove 2: ....0.20 – 0.40 mm (wear limit 0.80 mm)
Piston Ring Gaps (272 engine):
- Upper piston rings:..0.20 – 0.35 mm (wear limit 1.00 mm)
- Centre rings:..0.30 – 0.50 mm (wear limit 0.80 mm)
- Lower rings:..0.20 – 0.90 mm (wear limit 0.80 mm)

Side Clearance of Piston Rings in Piston (not all engines identical):
- Groove 1: ....0.030 – 0.075 mm (wear limit 0.10 mm)
- Groove 2: ....0.015 – 0.050 mm (wear limit 0.10 mm)

Note: The piston ring in groove 3 must not be removed.

Side Clearance of Piston Rings in Piston (272 engine):
- Groove 1: ....0.03 – 0.08 mm (wear limit 0.10 mm)
- Groove 2: ....0.02 – 0.06 mm (wear limit 0.10 mm)

Note: The piston ring in groove 3 must not be removed.

Side Clearance of Piston Rings in Piston (272 engine – ML350 models):
- Groove 1: ....0.03 – 0.07 mm (wear limit 0.10 mm)
- Groove 2: ....0.02 – 0.05 mm (wear limit 0.10 mm)
Note: The piston ring in groove 3 must not be removed.

Connecting Rods (as available)
Distance from centre small end bore to
  centre big end bore – 111 engines:........................ 145.0 mm +/- 0.05 mm
Distance from centre small end bore to
  centre big end bore – 112 engines:........................ 153.95 mm +/- 0.05 mm
Distance from centre small end bore to
  centre big end bore – 112/113: .... 148.450 mm +/- 0.05 mm
Width of con rod at big end bore – 111 engine: ....21.948 – 22.000 mm
Width of con rod at big end bore – 112/113 engine: .....19.948 – 20.000 mm
Basic bore diameter of big end bore – 111 engine:.........51.60 – 51.62 mm
Basic bore diameter of big end bore – 112/113 engine:.....55.600 – 55.614 mm
Basic bore diameter of small end bore – 111 engine: ....24.500 – 24.021 mm
Basic bore diameter of small end bore – 112/113 engine:............24.500 – 24.521 mm

Small End Bush:
- Inner diameter – all engines:...22.07 – 22.013 mm
Max. twist of connecting rods:.. 0.10 mm per 100 mm
Max. bend of connecting rods: .... 0.015 mm per 100 mm
Max. weight difference in same engine:...5 gram (per set)
Connecting rod bearing details:... See under "Crankshaft"

1.4.1.1.   Piston and Connecting Rods – Removal

Pistons and connecting rods are pushed out towards the top of the cylinder bores, using a hammer handle alter connecting rod bearing caps and shells have been removed. The engine must be removed to remove the connecting rod piston assemblies. The operations are not the same on all engines and will be summarised under separate headings below. If the pistons require replacement we suggest to have the work carried out in an engine shop.

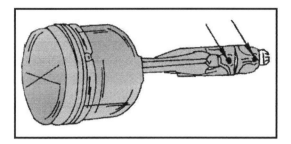

Fig. 1.43 – Big end bearing caps and connecting rods must be marked at opposite points as shown before removal.

Three piston rings are fitted to each piston. The two upper rings are the compression rings, i.e. they prevent the pressure above the piston crown to return to the crankcase. The lower ring is the oil scraper ring. Its function is to remove excessive oil from the cylinder bore, thereby preventing the entry of oil into the combustion chamber. The three rings are not the same in shape. The upper ring has a rectangular section, the centre ring has a chamfer on the inside and the lower ring is chrome-plated on its outside. Only the correct fitting of the piston rings will assure the proper operation of the piston sealing. Before removal of the assemblies note the following points:

*   Pistons and cylinder bores are graded in three diameter classes within specified tolerance groups and marked with the letters or numbers. The class number is stamped into the upper face of the cylinder block, next to the particular cylinder bore. If the cylinder block has been re-bored, you will receive the block with the correct pistons.

Fig. 1.44 - Cut-out in the piston pin bore allows to insert a screwdriver blade to remove the piston pin securing ring.

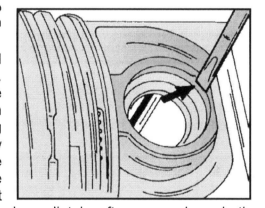

*   Mark each piston and the connecting rod before removal with the cylinder number. This can be carried out by writing the cylinder number with paint onto the piston crown. Also mark an arrow, facing towards the front of the engine (the arrow in the piston crown will be covered by the carbon deposits). When removing the connecting rod, note the correct installation of the big end bearing cap. Immediately after removal mark the connecting rod and the big end bearing cap on the same side. This is best done with a centre punch (cylinder No. 1 one punch mark, etc., see Fig. 1.43).
*   Mark the big end bearing shells with the cylinder number.

Fig. 1.45 – Removal or installation of piston rings.

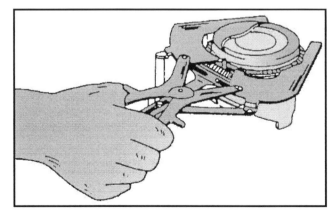

*   Big end bearing journals can be re-ground to four undersizes (in steps of 0.25 mm between sizes). Corresponding bearing shells are available.
*   Remove the bearing caps and the shells and push the assemblies out of the cylinder bore. Any carbon deposits on the upper edge of the bores can be carefully removed with a scraper.

- Remove the piston pin snap rings. A notch in the piston pin bore enables a pointed drift to be inserted, as shown in Fig. 1.44, to remove the rings.
- Press the piston pins out of the pistons. If necessary heat the piston in boiling water.
- Remove the piston rings one after the other from the pistons, using a piston ring pliers if possible (Fig. 1.45). If the rings are to be re-used, mark them in accordance with their pistons and position.

The above instructions apply to the pistons of an M111 engine. The following information apply to the removal of the pistons of an M112, M113 and M272 engine in series 163 and 164. Fig. 1.46 shows the attachment of pistons to the crankshaft.

M112 and M113 engines in ML320, ML350 and ML430 – Series 163
M113 engine in ML500 – Series 164

- Remove the engine and separate the automatic transmission from the engine.
- Remove the upper part of the oil sump, the cylinder head and the oil pump. When removing the oil pump push the chain tensioner to one side and lift off the drive chain.

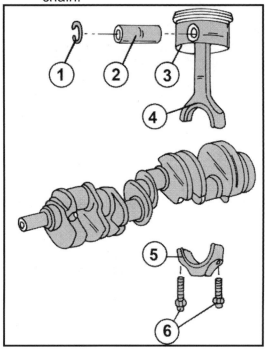

Fig. 1.46 – Piston and connecting rod of a V8 engine (M113).
1 Circlip
2 Piston pin
3 Piston
4 Connecting rod
5 Big end bearing cap
6 Bearing cap bolts

- The removal of the piston(s) is carried out as described for the M111 engine (either on the L.H. or R.H. cylinder bank). Fig. 1.46 shown the attachment of a piston to the crankshaft.

M272 engine in ML350 – Series 164
- Remove the engine.
- Remove the lower part of the oil sump and then the complete oil sump. Also remove the oil pump.
- Remove the splash shield at the bottom of the crankcase.

- Remove the inlet manifold and the two cylinder heads as described for the M272 engine.
- The removal of the piston(s) on the L.H. or R.H. cylinder bank is now carried out as described for the M111 engine. Do not interchange L.H. and R.H. pistons/connecting rods. Fig. 1.46 shows the attachment of a piston to the crankshaft.

1.4.1.2.   Measuring the Cylinder Bores

An inside caliper is necessary to measure the diameter of the cylinder bores. We strongly recommend to have the bores measured in an engine shop. If the cylinder block must be re-bored, the shop will also replace the pistons.

1.4.1.3.   Checking Pistons and Connecting Rods

All parts should be thoroughly inspected. Signs of seizure, grooves or excessive wear requires the part to be replaced. Check the pistons and connecting rods as follows:

Fig. 1.47 – Checking the side clearance of the piston rings in the grooves of the piston.

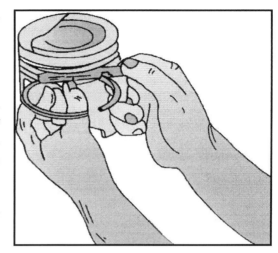

- Check the side clearance of each piston ring in its groove by inserting the ring together with a feeler gauge, as shown in Fig. 1.47. The grooves must be thoroughly cleaned before the check. If the wear limit exceed the values in the technical data is reached, either the rings or the piston are worn.
- Check the piston ring gap by inserting the ring from the bottom into the cylinder bore. Use a piston and carefully push the piston ring approx. 1 in. further into the bore. This will square it up. Insert a feeler gauge between the two piston ring ends to check the ring gap, as shown in Fig. 1.48. Refer to Section 1.4.1.0. for the wear limits. Rings must be replaced, if these are exceeded. New rings should also be checked in the manner described.

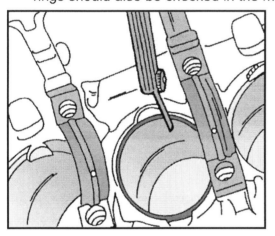

Fig. 1.48 – Checking the piston ring gaps, using a feeler gauge. The gap "A" must be measured.

- Piston pins and small end bushes must be checked for wear or seizure. One individual connecting rod can be replaced, provided that a rod of the same weight group is fitted. Connecting rods are marked with either one or two punch marks (arrow, Fig. 1.49), indicating the weight category, and only a rod with the same mark must be fitted.

- Connecting rod bolts must have a certain length. Just in case they have stretched previously we recommend to replace the bolts.

Fig. 1.49 – The arrow shows the weight category marking of the connecting rods.

- Connecting rods should be checked for bend or twist, particularly when the engine has covered a high mileage. A special jig is necessary for this operation and the job should be carried out by an engine shop.

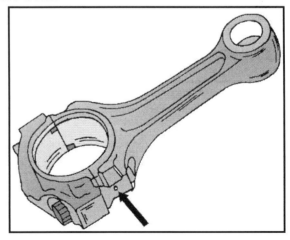

The following information concern the connecting rods:
- Connecting rods which were over-heated due to bearing failure (blueish colour) must not be refitted.
- Connecting and bearing caps are matched to each other and must be fitted accordingly.
- New connecting rods are supplied together with the small end bearing bush and can be fitted as supplied.

Engines

- If the piston pin has excessive clearance in the small end bush, a new bush must be fitted. Again this is best left to an engine shop, as the bush must be reamed out to the correct diameter to obtain the correct running clearance for the piston pin.

1.4.1.4.   Piston and Connecting Rods - Assembly

If new pistons are fitted, check the piston crown markings to ensure the correct pistons are fitted. If the original pistons are fitted, arrange them in accordance with the cylinder number markings.

- If connecting rods have been replaced check the bottom of the big end bearing caps. Either one or two punch marks are stamped into the centre of the cap, as shown in Fig. 1.49.
- Insert the connecting rod into the piston and align the two bores. Make sure that the arrow in the piston crown is facing the front of the engine.
- Generously lubricate the piston pin with engine oil and insert it into the piston and connecting rod, using thumb pressure only. Never heat the piston to fit the piston pin. Fit the circlips to both sides of the piston, making sure of their engagement around the groove.
- Using a pair of piston ring pliers (Fig. 1.45), fit the piston rings from the top of the piston, starting with the bottom ring. The two compression rings could be mixed up. Under no circumstances mix-up the upper and lower compression rings. Fig. 1.50 and 1.51 show the rings and are to be fitted accordingly. Under no circumstances mix-up the upper and lower compression rings. The rings are marked with "Top" or the name of the manufacturer. The ring gaps of the compression rings must be spaced 120° to each other. The oil scraper ring is fitted in accordance with the L.H. top view in Fig. 1.50.

1.4.1.5.   Pistons and Connecting Rods – Installation

- Generously lubricate the cylinder bores with oil. Markings on connecting rods and bearing caps must be opposite each other. The arrows in the piston crowns must face towards the front of the engine. We would like to repeat again:

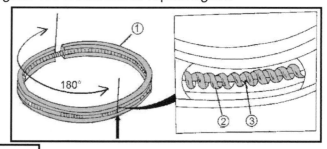

Fig. 1.50 – Correct installation of the multi-part oil control ring (applies to all engines).
1 Chamfered piston ring with spring insert
2 Round spring
3 Spring insert

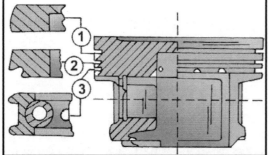

Fig. 1.51 – Sectional view of the pistons and piston rings (all engines).
1 Upper compression ring
2 Second compression ring
3 Multi-part oil control ring

- Arrange the piston rings at equal spacing of 120° around the circumference of the piston skirt and use a piston ring compressor to push the rings into their grooves. Check that all rings are fully pushed in. Check that the marking "Top" or the name of the manufacturer can be read from above after installation. Arrange the multi-part oil control ring (scraper ring) so that the spring ends are offset by

180°. Study Fig. 1.50 before further assembly. Fig. 1.51 shows the section of the piston rings, again as fitted to all engines. Make sure that all rings are fitted as shown.

• Rotate the crankshaft until two of the crankpins are at the bottom.

• Place a piston ring compressor around the piston rings as shown in Fig. 1.52 and push the piston from above into the cylinder bore as shown in the illustration. The cylinder block can be placed on its side to guide the connecting rod. The big end bearing shell should be in the big end bearing.

Fig. 1.52 – Fitting a piston with a piston ring compressor. Push the piston into the bore with a hammer handle.

• Insert the second bearing shell into the connecting rod bearing cap, with the locating tab and fit the assembly over the connecting rod. Check that connecting rod/cap marks are facing each other.

• Coat the contact areas for the cap bolts with engine oil and fit and tighten the bolts as follows:

• Tighten the connecting rod bolts to 0.5 kgm (3.5 ft.lb.) and then again to 2.5 kgm (18 ft.lb.) – 2.0 kgm (14.5 ft.lb.) in the case of the 272 engine, in several stages. From this position tighten each bolt by a further 90° (1/4 of a turn) without using the torque wrench. It is assumed that the stretch bolts have been replaced.

• Rotate the crankshaft until the remaining crankpins are at bottom dead centre and fit the two other piston/connecting rod assemblies in the same manner.

• Check the pistons and connecting rods once more for correct installation and that each piston is fitted to its original bore, if the same parts are refitted.

• With a feeler gauge measure the side clearance of each big end bearing cap on the crankpin. The standard value is between 0.11 – 0.23 mm. The wear limit is 0.50 mm.

• All other operations are carried out in reverse order.

1.4.2.   CYLINDER BLOCK

The cylinder block consists of the crankcase and the actual block with the cylinder bores. Special attention should be given to the cylinder block at each major overhaul of the engine, irrespective of whether the bores have been re-machined or not.

Thoroughly clean all cavities and passages and remove all traces of foreign matter from the joint faces. If any machining of the bores has taken place, it is essential that all swarf is removed before assembly of the engine takes place.

Measurement of the cylinder bores should be left to an engine shop, as they have the proper equipment to measure cylinder bores. It is, however, feasible to check the cylinder block face for distortion, in a similar manner as described for the cylinder head. The max. permissible distortion is 0.05 mm.

1.4.3.   CRANKSHAFT AND BEARINGS

1.4.3.0.   Technical Data

All dimensions in metric units. Data as available.
Max. run-out of main journals*:
Journals Nos. 2 and 4 – 4-cyl: 0.07 mm

Engines

Journals Nos. 2 and 5 – 6-/8-cyl.:	0.07 mm
Journal No. 3 – 4-cyl.:	0.10 mm
Journals Nos. 2, 4, 5 – 6-/8-cyl.:	0.10 mm
Max. out-of-round of journals:	0.005 mm
Max. taper of main journals:	0.010 mm
Max. taper of crankpins:	0.015 mm

* Crankshaft placed with end journals in "V" blocks.

Main Bearing Journal Diameter – M111 engine:
Nominal: .... 57.950 – 57.965 mm
1st repair size: .... 57.700 – 57.715 mm
2nd repair size: .... 57.450 – 57.465 mm
3rd repair size: .... 57.200 – 57.215 mm
4th repair size: .... 56.950 – 56.965 mm
Main Bearing Journal Diameter – M112/M113 engines:
Nominal: .... 63.940 – 63.945 mm
Repair sizes: .... Refer to engine workshop
Crankpin Diameter – M111 engine
Standard. .... 47,955 – 47,965 mm
Repair size .... Four available
Crankpin Diameter – V6/V8 engines:
Standard. .... 55.600 – 55.614 mm
Repair size: .... Refer to engine workshop
Bearing Running Clearances:
Main bearings – M111 engine: .... 0.031 - 0.053 mm
Main bearings – M112/M113 engines: .... 0.026 - 0.050 mm
Main bearings – M272 engine: .... 0.022 - 0.048 mm
Big end bearings – M111 engine: .... 0.025 - 0.065 mm
Big end bearings – M112/M113 engines: .... 0.022 - 0.067 mm
Big end bearings – M272 engine: .... 0.022 - 0.066 mm
Wear limit (all engines): .... 0.080 mm
Bearing End Float:
Main bearings (M111 engine): .... 0.10 - 0.24 mm
Main bearings (remaining engines): .... 0.10 - 0.266 mm
Big end bearings (all engines): .... 0.12 - 0.23 mm
Wear limit - Main bearings: .... 0.30 mm
Wear limit - Big end bearings: .... 0.50 mm

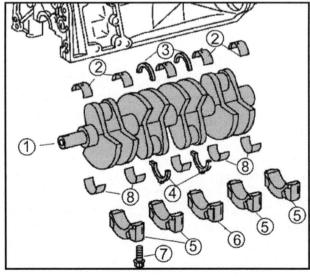

Fig. 1.53 – Crankshaft and bearing parts (V6 engine).
1   Crankshaft
2   Bearing shells in crankcase
3   Thrust washers
4   Thrust washers in bearing caps
5   Main bearing caps
6   Fitted bearing cap
7   Bearing cap bolt, M11
8   Bearing shells in bearing caps

1.4.3.1.   Crankshaft - Removal and Installation

The engine must be removed to take out the crankshaft. The operations are similar on all engines, but a different number of main bearings are fitted, depending on the engine. 1.53 shows the crankshaft of the M111 engine, Fig, 1.54 shows the parts of a V6 engine. Fig. 1.55 shows the parts you will find after a V8 engine has been dismantled. The instructions are given in general for all engines.

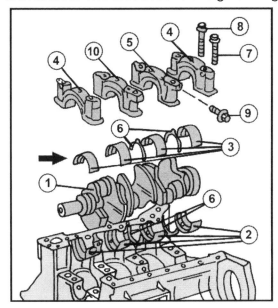

Fig. 1.54 – Crankshaft and bearing parts (V6 engine).
1 Crankshaft
2 Bearing shells in crankcase
3 Bearing shells in main bearing caps
4 Crankshaft bearing cap (end caps)
5 Fitted bearing cap
6 Thrust washers
7 Bearing cap bolt, M8 x 75 mm
8 Bearing cap bolt, M10 x 90 mm
9 Bearing cap side bolt, M8 x 40 mm
10 Crankshaft bearing caps

• After removal of the engine take off the oil sump and the oil pump as described for the engine in question, remove the rear oil seal carrier, the cylinder head and the timing case cover. Piston and connecting rods can remain in the cylinder block or can be removed as already described. If the pistons remain in the engine mark the big end bearing caps and remove them together with the bearing shells. Always keep caps and shells together.

• Counterhold the flywheel in suitable manner and evenly slacken the clutch securing bolts. Use a centre punch and mark the clutch and flywheel at opposite points. Lift off the clutch plate and the driven plate. Immediately clean the inside of the flywheel and unscrew the flywheel.

Fig. 1.55 – Crankshaft and bearing parts (V8).
1   Crankshaft
2   Bearing shells in crankcase
3   Bearing shells in main bearing caps
4   Crankshaft bearing cap (end caps)
5   Fitted bearing cap
6   Thrust washers
7   Bearing cap bolt, M8 x 75 mm
8   Bearing cap bolt, M10 x 90 mm
9   Bearing cap side bolt, M8 x 40 mm
10   Crankshaft bearing caps

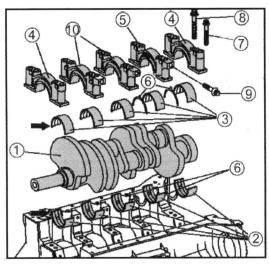

• Remove the drive plate for a torque converter of an automatic transmission in the same manner.

• With the flywheel still locked, remove the crankshaft pulley bolt and remove the crankshaft pulley/damper as described later on.

• The crankshaft end float should be checked before the crankshaft is removed. To do this, place a dial gauge with a suitable holder in front of the cylinder block and place the gauge stylus against the end flange of the crankshaft, as shown in Fig. 1.56. Use a screwdriver to push the crankshaft all the way to one end and set the gauge to "0". Push the shaft to the other side and note the dial gauge reading. The resulting value is the end float. If it exceeds 0.30 mm (0.012 in.) replace the thrust washers during assembly, but make sure to fit washers of the correct width.

Engines

These are located left and right at the centre bearing. Note that only two washers of the same thickness must be fitted.

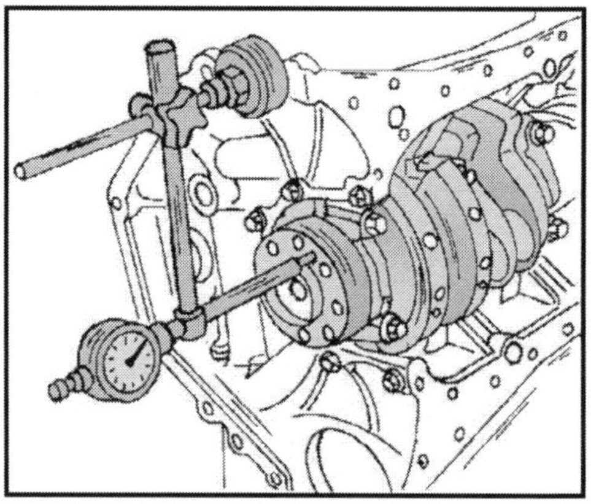

Fig. 1.56 – Checking the crankshaft end float with a dial gauge.

The crankshaft is now removed as follows:

Four-cylinder (M111 engine)
Fig. 1.53 shows details of the shaft and the bearing assembly.

- Remove the engine from the transmission. Take care not to distort the clutch drive shaft when the transmission is lifted off.
- Unscrew the main bearing bolts (7) in Fig. 1.53 evenly across. The bearings caps are marked with the numbers 1 to 5. The numbers are stamped into the centre of the caps. No. 1 cap is located at the crankshaft pulley side.
- Remove the bearing shells (8) from the bearing journals (they could also stick to the caps) and immediately mark them on their back faces with the bearing number. Also remove the thrust washers (4). Again mark their fitted position.
- Lift the crankshaft (1) out of the cylinder block and remove the remaining thrust washers (3) from the centre bearing location and the remaining bearings shells (2). Keep the shells together with the lower shells and the bearing caps. These shells have an oil bore and a groove and must always be fitted into the crankcase when the crankshaft is installed.

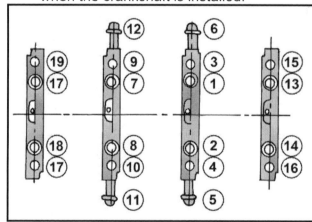

Fig. 1.57 – Tightening order for the crankshaft bearing cap bolts (V6). Note the different diameters and bolt length.

V6 and V8 Engines (M112 and M113)
The operations are similar on both types of engine. The instructions are given for the V6 engine (see Fig. 1.54, but Fig. 1.55 shows the respective parts for a V8 engine.

Fig. 1.58 – Tightening order for the crankshaft bearing cap bolts (V8). Note the different diameters and bolt length.

- Unscrew the main bearing bolts in reverse order to the numbering in Fig. 1.57 in the case of a V6 engine or Fig. 1.58 in the case of a V8 engine. Note that bolts of different diameter and length are used.

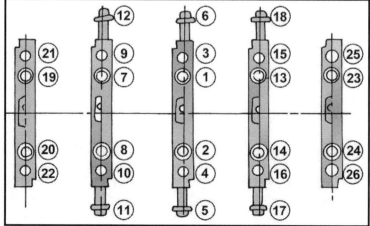

Each bearing cap is secured with two bolts on either side from above and the side of each cap is additionally secured by a bolt inserted from the side. Mark each bearing cap and its position on the crankcase.

- Remove the crankshaft bearing caps (4), the bearing cap (10) and the fitted bearing cap (5). Cap (10) and (5) have a tight fit and must be levered out carefully. Remove the bearing shells (2) from the bearing journals (they could also stick to the caps) and immediately mark them on their back faces with the bearing number. The numbers refer to illustration of the crankshaft for the V6 engine.

- Lift the crankshaft (1) out of the cylinder block and remove the remaining thrust washers (6) from the centre bearing location and the remaining bearings shells. Keep the shells together with the lower shells and the bearing caps. These shells have an oil bore and a groove and must always be fitted into the crankcase when the crankshaft is installed.

1.4.3.2. Inspection of Crankshaft and Bearings

Main and crankpin journals must be measured with precision instruments to find their diameters. All journals can be re-ground up to four times, depending on the engine, and the necessary bearing shells are available, i.e. repair size shells can be fitted. For this reason we strongly recommend to take the removed crankshaft to an engine shop to have the measurements carried out and, if required, the bearing shells replaced.

1.4.3.3. Crankshaft - Installation

Four-cylinder Engines (M111)

- Thoroughly clean the bearing bores in the crankcase and insert the shells with the drillings into the bearing bores, with the tabs engaging the notches. Fit the thrust washers to the centre bearing, with the oil grooves towards the outside.

Fig. 1.59 – Fitting the main bearing cap together with the thrust washer.

- Use the two forefingers as shown in Fig. 1.59 to hold the thrust washers against the bearing cap and fit the cap in position.

- Lift the crankshaft in position and fit the bearing caps with the inserted shells (again shells well oiled and locating tabs in notches). Fit the two thrust washers to the centre bearing cap, again with the oil groove towards the outside. Place this cap in position, guiding the two thrust washers in order not to dislodge them. Use the forefingers to hold the washers (Fig. 1.59).

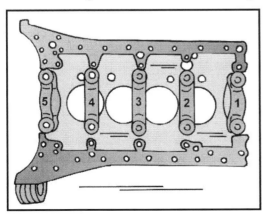

Fig. 1.60 – Bearing caps are marked in the centre as shown.

- Check the numbering of the bearing caps in accordance with Fig. 1.60 and fit them in position, with the shells inserted. Use a plastic mallet to tap them down. Caps can only be fitted in one position, but the bearing cap numbers must be observed.

- Tighten the bolts from the centre towards the outside in several steps to a torque reading of to 5.5 kgm (39.5 ft.lb.) and from this position a further 90° (quarter of a turn).

- Rotate the crankshaft a few times to check for binding.
- Re-check the crankshaft end float as described during removal. Attach the dial gauge to the crankcase as shown in Fig. 1.56. The remaining operations are carried out in reverse order to the removal procedure. The various sections give detailed description of the relevant operations, i.e. piston and connecting rods, rear oil seal flange, timing mechanism, flywheel and clutch or drive plate, oil pump, oil sump and cylinder head.

V6 and V8 Engines

Again the instructions are given for the V6 engine. If the operations are carrier out on a V8 engine refer to Fig. 1.55 as the only difference is the additional main bearing cap.

- Thoroughly clean the bearing bores in the crankcase and fit the bearing cap (4), bearing cap (10), fitted bearing (5) and the bearing shells in crankcase (2) as well as the bearing shells (3) in the crankcase with engine oil.
- Insert the shells with the drillings into the bearing bores, with the tabs engaging the notches. Fit the thrust washers (6) to the centre bearing, with the oil grooves towards the outside. The numbers refer to Fig. 1.54.
- Use the two forefingers as shown in Fig. 1.59 to hold the thrust washers against the bearing cap and fit the cap in position.
- Lift the crankshaft in position and fit the bearing caps with the inserted shells (again shells well oiled and locating tabs in notches). Fit the two thrust washers to the centre bearing cap, again with the oil groove towards the outside. Place this cap in position, guiding the two thrust washers in order not to dislodge them. Use the forefingers to hold the washers (Fig. 1.59).
- Fit the remaining bearing caps in a accordance with their numbering and tap them in position, using a plastic or rubber mallet. The caps can only be fitted in one position, but the cap numbers must be correct.

The bolts are now tightened in accordance with Fig. 1.58 (V6) or Fig. 1.59 (V8), but note the length and the diameter of the bolts.

- Tighten the M8 bolts (7) to 2.0 kgm (14.5 ft.lb.) and from the final position by a further 90° (quarter of a turn).
- Fit the M8 bolts to the side of the bearing cap and tighten it to 3.0 kgm (22 ft.lb.).
- The M10 bolts (8) are tightened in three stages. First tighten them to 0.5 kgm (3.6 ft.lb.) and then to 3.0 kgm (22 ft.lb.). From the final position tighten the bolts a further quarter of a turn. The correct tightening is only possible if the correct position of the bolts is located by referring to Figs. 1.54 or 1.55.
- Rotate the crankshaft a few times to check for binding.
- Re-check the crankshaft end float as described during removal. Attach the dial gauge to the crankcase as shown in Fig. 1.56. The remaining operations are carried out in reverse order to the removal procedure. The various sections give detailed description of the relevant operations, i.e. piston and connecting rods, rear oil seal flange, timing mechanism, flywheel and clutch or drive plate, oil pump, oil sump and cylinder head.

1.4.3.4.   Flywheel or Drive Plate (Automatic)

The flywheel or the drive plate for an automatic transmission model can be removed without removal of the crankshaft. The engine can also remain in the vehicle. Fig. 1.60 shows the attachment and the driven plate for reference. Note that two washers are used on the flywheel, one in front and one behind the flywheel in the case of a ML 230 model, not as shown in the illustration. The drive plate, however, is only fitted with one washer on the outside of the drive plate (V6 and V8 models). Only the instructions for the flywheel apply to the M111 engine (ML 230). The remaining models have a drive plate. Remove the part in question as follows:

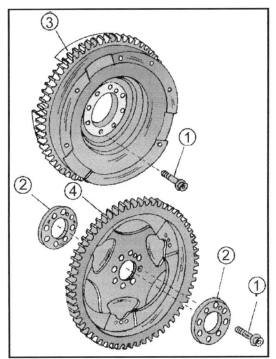

Fig. 1.61 – View of flywheel and driven plate. Refer to the information in the text above.
1 Securing bolt, always replace
2 Distance washer, drive plate or flywheel
3 Flywheel, manual transmission
4 Drive plate, automatic

- Remove the transmission (Section 3.1.) or the automatic transmission. Remove the clutch in the case of a manual transmission.
- Remove the plastic cover at the rear end of the oil sump and remove the two bolts below.
- Counterhold the flywheel in suitable manner and remove the clutch after having marked its relationship to the flywheel. Remove the drive plate in a similar manner. 8 bolts are used to secure the flywheel. A dowel pin is fitted into the crankshaft flange to guide the flywheel or driven plate during installation.

Fig. 1.62 – Pressing the guide bearing into the inside of the flywheel (2). A press mandrel (1) must be used.

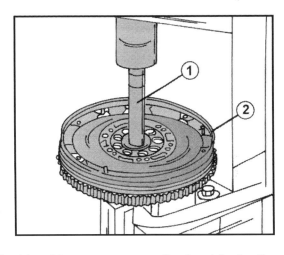

- Remove the flywheel or the drive plate. Distance washers are used as explained above, which can also be removed. The securing bolts can be discarded, as they must be replaced. If a new flywheel or driven plate is to be fitted, quote the engine type and vehicle model.
- If the flywheel or the starter ring looks worn, take the wheel to your dealer to have the flywheel re-machined and/or the ring gear replaced.
- Fit the flywheel or drive plate as applicable. Always use new flywheel bolts if a dual-mass flywheel is fitted.

Engines for manual transmissions are fitted with a ball bearing inside the flywheel. The bearing must be pressed out of the flywheel, i.e. you will have to have access to a press. Place the flywheel onto a press table as shown in Fig. 1.62, insert the bearing and press the bearing in position. Grease the bearing after installation.

Six-cylinder and eight cylinder engines

- Fit the drive plate with the dowel pin engaged. Fit a distance washer on top of the drive plate.
- Fit the bolts and tighten them evenly across to 4.5 kgm (32.5 ft.lb.). From this position tighten the bolts a further 90°. The angle is important to give the stretch bolts their correct tension. Fig. 1.63 demonstrates the angle-tightening in the case of a flywheel. The same applies to the driven plate.

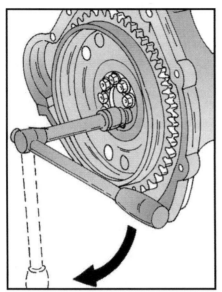

Fig. 1.63 – Apply the socket and extension as shown and tighten the bolts by 90° (quarter of a turn).

Installation of flywheel or drive plate of a four-cylinder engine

• The length of the bolts must be measured from the end of the thread to the underside of the bolt head before they are re-used. Either long bolts or short bolts are used. There is no need to measure the long bolts (approx. 2 in.). If the short bolts are longer then 22.5 mm, replace them.

• Fit the flywheel or the drive plate with the dowel pin engaged. Fit a distance washer underneath and on top of the drive plate (see Fig. 1.61 and explanation).

• Fit the bolts and tighten them evenly across to 4.5 kgm. From this position tighten the bolts a further 90° as shown in Fig. 1.63. Note that Torx-head bolts are used on some engines.

1.4.3.5. Crankshaft Pulley and Vibration Damper

Four-cylinder engine M111

The engine is fitted with a one piece crankshaft pulley/vibration damper assembly. The damper is located on the end of the crankshaft by means of a Woodruff key and secured by the central bolt in the end of the shaft. Fig. 1.64 shows the front end of the engine with the location of some of the parts.

Remove the parts as follows, noting that a puller may be necessary to withdraw the hub:

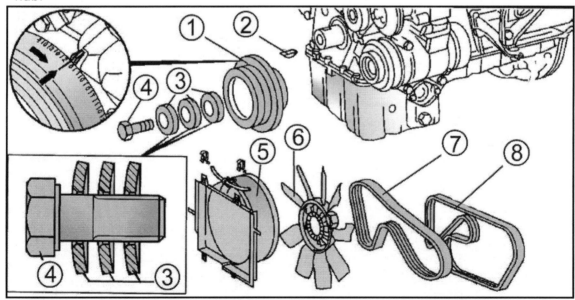

Fig. 1.64 – Parts to be removed in the case of a four-cylinder engine.

1 Pulley and damper	4 Centre bolts	7 Compressor drive belt
2 Woodruff key	5 Fan shroud	8 Poly V-belt
3 Dished washers	6 Cooling fan	

• Remove the fan clutch (if fitted) and the fan shroud (5) (section "Cooling System").

• Remove the compressor drive belt (7) if air conditioning is fitted and remove the Poly V-belt (8) (section "Cooling System").

- Rotate the engine (crankshaft) until the piston of No. 1 cylinder is at the TDC position, i.e. the long line in the crankshaft pulley must be opposite the pointer as shown in the upper, L.H. corner of the illustration.
- Engage a gear and apply the handbrake to lock the engine against rotation. In the case of a vehicle with automatic transmission remove the starter motor and lock the starter motor ring gear in suitable manner. The same can be carried out when a manual transmission is fitted and the bolt cannot be removed by engaging a gear.
- Unscrew the crankshaft pulley/vibration damper bolt (4) in Fig. 1.63 and take off the washer (3). The bolt is tightened to a very high torque (30 kgm/216 ft.lb.), i.e. a suitable socket is required.
- Remove the dished washers underneath the bolt, but note how they are fitted. All three bolts are curved and the curved side must be facing towards the outside.
- Withdraw the assembly from the end of the crankshaft. A tight vibration damper can be removed with a suitable puller. You can also try two tyre levers, applied at opposite points of the damper.

The installation of the crankshaft pulley and the vibration damper is carried out as follows:
- Rotate the crankshaft until the Woodruff key is visible and slide the crankshaft pulley/vibration damper with the key way over the key and the shaft. Make sure that the Woodruff key has engaged and has not been dislodged.
- Place the three washers over the centre bolts as mentioned above, lubricate the bolts thread, fit the bolt and tighten it to the value given above. The crankshaft must still be locked against rotation.
- Fit the drive belt and all other items as described later on.
- The remaining operations are carried out in reverse order.

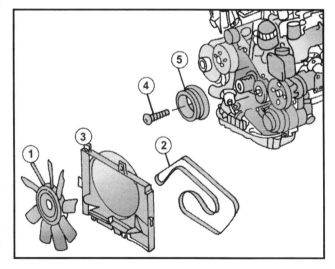

Fig. 1.65 – Removal and installation of the crankshaft pulley in the case of an M112 engine.

1   Viscous clutch and fan
2   Poly V-belt
3   Fan shroud
4   Centre bolt (30 kgm)
5   Damper/crankshaft pulley

V6 and V8 Engines (M112, M113, M272)

Although the operations are not the same on all engines, they can be combined. Fig. 1.65 shows the parts to be removed in the case of the M112 engine, Fig. 1.66 shows a front view of the M272 engine as fitted to model ML 350 of series 164.

- Remove the sound-proofing panel from underneath the engine compartment.
- Remove the engine trim panel to gain access to all parts.
- Remove the viscous fan (1). The fan shroud (3) and the Poly V-belt (2).
- Engage a gear and apply the handbrake to lock the engine against rotation. In the case of a vehicle with automatic transmission remove the starter motor and lock the starter motor ring gear in suitable manner. The same can be carried out when a manual transmission is fitted and the bolt cannot be removed by engaging a gear.

Engines

- Unscrew the crankshaft pulley/vibration damper bolt (4) and remove. The bolt is tightened to a very high torque (20 kgm/145 ft.lb.), i.e. a suitable socket is required.

Fig. 1.66 – Removal and installation of the crankshaft pulley in the case of an M272 engine.
1 Vibration damper/pulley
2 Centre bolt (20 kgm)
3 Woodruff key
4 Crankshaft oil seal

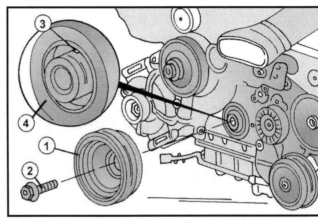

- Withdraw the assembly from the end of the crankshaft. A tight vibration damper can be removed with a suitable puller. You can also try two tyre levers, applied at opposite points of the damper.

The installation of the crankshaft pulley and the vibration damper is carried out as follows:

- Rotate the crankshaft until the Woodruff key is visible and slide the crankshaft pulley/vibration damper with the key way over the key and the shaft. Make sure that the Woodruff key has engaged and has not been dislodged.
- Lubricate the bolts thread, fit the bolt and tighten it to the value of 20 kgm, (145 ft.lb.) and from the final position a further 95° (M112 and M113 engines) or 90° (other engines). The crankshaft must still be locked against rotation.
- Fit the drive belt and all other items as described later on.
- The remaining operations are carried out in reverse order.

1.4.3.6. Rear Crankshaft Oil Seal and Oil Seal Carrier

Four-cylinder engines

The rear crankshaft oil seal is located inside a flange, which is bolted to the rear of the crankcase. Two dowels, one on each side of the cover, locate the flange correctly in relation to the crankshaft centre. The flange is secured by means of six bolts, as shown in Fig. 1.67 and is fitted with sealing compound ("Loctite").

Fig. 1.67 – The arrows show the oil seal carrier securing bolts.

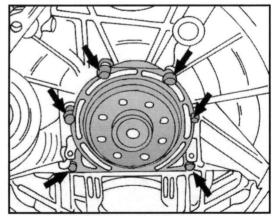

Transmission and flywheel and/or drive plate must be removed to replace the oil seal. If only the oil seal needs replacement, lever it out carefully with a screwdriver, without damaging the flange. If the oil seal carrier is to be removed, remove the bolts around the outside edge and two bolts from below. Apply two screwdrivers underneath the lugs on each side of the cover, as shown in Fig. 1.68. and carefully lever the carrier off the crankcase. The oil seal can now be removed from the inside.

Clean the carrier and crankcase faces and fit a new oil seal to the carrier (removed or still fitted). The sealing lip of the new oil seal is offset to prevent it from running on the same crankshaft area. Fill the space between the sealing lip and the dust protection lip with grease.

Fig. 1.68 – To remove the oil seal cover insert two screwdrivers carefully underneath two lugs shown by the arrows.

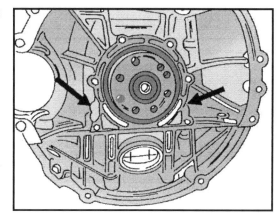

Coat the carrier face with sealing compound and fit it to the block, with the dowel pins engaged. Slightly tap the carrier in position. Great care must be taken during installation in order not to damage the oil seal.

Fit the bolts. First tighten the two lower bolts and then the other bolts. The torque is 1.0 kgm (7.2 ft.lb.).

Carry out all other operations in reverse order.

Fig. 1.69 – Removal and installation of the rear oil seal cover together with the oil seal. The faces marked with the arrows must be coated with "Loctite".

1 Cover with oil seal
2 Fitting sleeve (normally in repair kit)
3 Oil seal in cover
4 Crankshaft
5 Screws, inserted from front, 0.9 kgm
6 Screws, inserted from below, 0.9 kgm

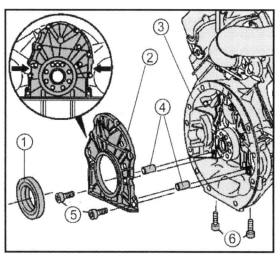
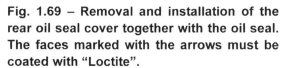

V6 and V8 Engines

Read the note below before commencing the removal. The oil seal carrier is attached in similar manner as in the case of the four-cylinder engine. Fig. 1.69 shows the attachment at the rear of the crankcase. The removal and installation is carried in a similar manner as described for the four-cylinder engine, with the difference that the oil seal carrier must be removed before the seal can be removed. Never remove the seal with the flange fitted. The same applies to the installation. First fit the flange and then drive the seal in position, using a piece of suitable tube.

Note the tightening torque values and the order of tightening: Fit the bolts. First tighten the two lower bolts (6) and then the other bolts (5). The torque for the lower bolts depend on the thread diameter. M6 bolts to 0.9 kgm (7 ft.lb.), M8 bolts to 2.0 kgm (14.5 ft.lb.).

Important Note: On some engines the rear sealing ring cannot be replaced (end cover of M272 engine in model ML 350, Series 164, is always replaced when a new seal is required). In the case of the remaining engines require at your dealer, quoting the engine type, model year, etc.

1.4.3.7. Front Crankshaft Oil Seal

The front crankshaft oil seal is located in the timing cover and can be replaced with the cover fitted. Oil leaks at this position can also be caused by a leaking timing cover gasket. Check before replacing the oil seal.

The crankshaft pulley/vibration damper as already described before the oil seal can be replaced. The seal can be carefully removed with a screwdriver (see Fig. 1.70). Screw a self-tapping screw into the outside of the seal and apply the screwdriver plate under the screw head. It is also possible to unscrew the oil seal cover to replace the seal.

Engines

Thoroughly clean the surrounding parts. Burrs on the timing cover bore can be removed with a scraper. Also clean the cylinder block face.

Fill the space between sealing lip and dust protection lip with grease and carefully drive a new oil seal into the timing cover and over the crankshaft until the ring outer face is flush. Fit the two bolts from below and then the remaining bolts. All bolts are tightened to 1.0 kgm (7.2 ft.lb.).

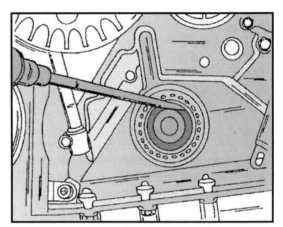

Fig. 1.70 – Removal of the front crankshaft oil seal if the seal is fitted to the timing cover.

Refit the vibration damper as described and carry out the remaining operations in reverse order.

1.4.3.8. Replacing Welsh Plugs in the Crankcase

Welsh plugs are fitted into the side of the cylinder block. These plugs will be "pushed" out if the coolant has been allowed to freeze and can be replaced with the engine fitted, provided the special tool 102 589 07 15 00 can be obtained.

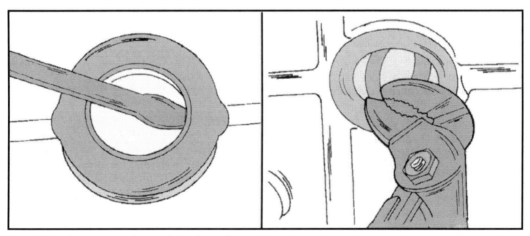

Fig. 1.71 – Removal of a welsh plug. Operation 1 on the left, operation 2 on the right.

Welsh plugs can be replaced as follows:
* Drain the cooling system and remove all parts obstructing the welsh plug in question, i.e. transmission, intermediate flange, injection pump, etc.
* The removal of a welsh plug is carried out in two stages. First place a small chisel or strong screwdriver blade below the lip of the welsh plug, as shown in Fig. 1.71 on the L.H. side and push the screwdriver in the direction of the arrow until it has swiveled by 90°. Then grip the plug with a pair of pliers, as shown in Fig. 1.71 on the right and remove it.

Thoroughly clean the opening in the cylinder head from grease and coat the locating bore with "Loctite 241" (obtain from a dealer if possible). Fit the large new welsh plug with the special tool mentioned above or use a drift of suitable size and drive it in position until flush with the cylinder block face.

Refit all removed parts and allow the vehicle to stand for at least 45 minutes before the cooling system is filled and the engine is started. Then start the engine and check for coolant leaks.

1.4.3.9. Replacing the Pilot Bearing in the Crankshaft

Engines for manual transmissions are fitted with a ball bearing in the end of the crankshaft, sealed off with a sealing ring.

Fig. 1.72 – Removal of the pilot bearing with a two-arm puller.

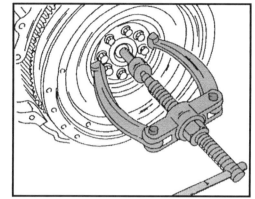

The sealing ring must be removed to withdraw the ball bearing with a suitable puller, as shown in Fig. 1.72. The pilot bearing can be replaced with the engine fitted to the vehicle, but the transmission and the clutch must be removed. Then apply the extractor as shown in the illustration. The sealing ring will come away with the bearing. Coat the new bearing with heat-resistant grease and drive it into the end of the crankshaft, using a drift of suitable diameter as shown in Fig. 1.62. The ball bearing must be driven against its stop. Fit a new oil seal in a similar manner, taking care not to damage it.

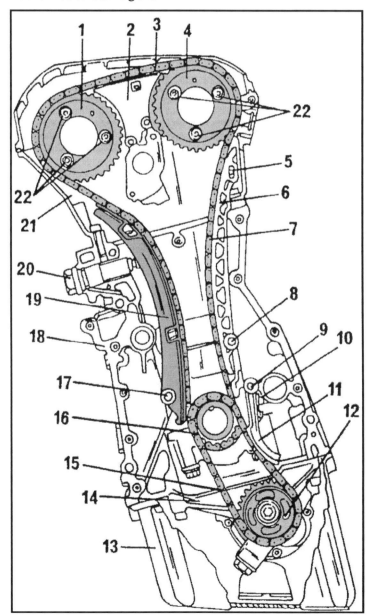

Fig. 1.73 – Timing chain and drive chain for the oil pump in fitted position.

1. Exhaust camshaft sprocket
2. Retainer
3. Guide rail
4. Inlet camshaft sprocket
5. Bearing bolt for guide rail
6. Guide rail
7. Double roller chain
8. Stud, 10 x 40
9. Stud, 8 x 60
10. Swivel spring
11. Tensioning rail
12. Oil pump drive sprocket
13. Oil sump
14. Oil pump
15. Single roller chain
16. Crankshaft
17. Stud, 10 x 40
18. Cylinder block
19. Tensioning rail
20. Timing chain tensioner
21. Cylinder head
22. Shouldered bolts, replace

1.4.4. TIMING MECHANISM – M111 Engine (ML 230)

The following description deals with the timing mechanism of the engine. The endless timing chain is engaged with the camshaft sprockets and the crankshaft sprocket. The chain is guided by slide rails. The tension of the chain is ensured

Engines

by means of a hydraulic chain tensioner, which is located in the timing cover and pushes onto a tensioning rail. The camshaft sprockets are fitted by means of a bolt and located by a Woodruff key. A second, smaller chain is used to drive the oil pump. The chain is fitted around a second sprocket on the crankshaft and around the pump drive sprocket and has its own chain tensioner. Fig. 1.73 shows the parts of the timing mechanism seen from the front end.

1.4.4.0.   Chain Tensioner – Removal and Installation

The chain tensioner is fitted into the R.H. side of the cylinder head as shown in Fig. 1.73 with item (20). The tensioning force of the chain tensioner is a combination of the fitted compression spring and the pressure of the engine oil. The oil contained inside the tensioner also absorbs shock loads from the timing chain. A chain tensioner cannot be repaired, i.e. must be replaced if suspect.

Important Note: If the chain tensioner has been slackened for any reason, it must be removed completely and refitted, as the internal mechanism will prevent tightening.

The chain tensioner (1) can be removed as follows. The cylinder head cover must be removed (page 27):

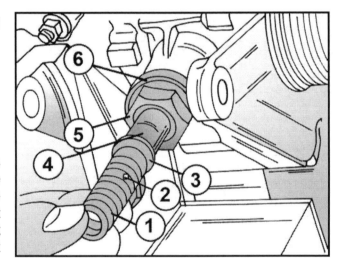

Fig. 1.74 – Details for the removal and installation of the chain tensioner.
1   Filler pin
2   Pressure spring
3   Locking spring
4   Pressure pin
5   Tensioner housing
6   Sealing ring

- Rotate the crankshaft as already described to set the piston of No. 1 cylinder to the top dead centre position. Insert the timing pin into the exhaust camshaft to prevent the shaft from rotating.
- Cover the alternator with a thick rag.
- Slacken the chain tensioner plug by approx. 1 turn and then remove it completely. The tensioner is now installed as follows:
- Unscrew the closing plug with the sealing ring and remove the filler pin and the pressure spring. Details are shown in Fig. 1.74. The pressure pin and the locking spring are removed out of the chain tensioner housing.
- Fit the chain tensioner housing with the oil seal and tighten the housing to 8.0 kgm (58 ft.lb.).
- Fit the pressure pin with the locking spring, the pressure spring and the filler pin into the chain tensioner housing.
- Fit the closing plug with a new sealing washer into the chain tensioner housing and tighten the plug to 4.0 kgm (29 ft.lb.).
- Check the oil level in the sump and correct if necessary. Check for oil seals around the chain tensioner.

1.4.4.1.   Timing Chain – Removal and Installation

We cannot recommend the replacement of the timing chain as a DIY operation when the engine is fitted to the vehicle. Apart from special tools, to separate the chain links, fitting a new chain, etc. which cannot be substituted by make-shift tools and a hand grinding machine, you will need the experience to deal with timing chains of a two-camshaft Mercedes-Benz engine. The timing chain has a long service life and may not need replacing.

If the engine is removed you can replace the chain in accordance with the instructions given, as the new chain is placed in position over the various sprockets in accordance with Fig. 1.73. The remaining operations can be taken from the various operations described in this section.

1.4.4.2.   Timing Housing Cover

Various preparatory operations must be carried out before the timing cover can be removed. Some of the following operations mentioned below are described in detail under different headings. Remember that the two camshafts must be locked in position after the crankshaft has been rotated into the required timing position. Details for the removal and installation are shown in Fig. 1.75. The cooling system must be drained.

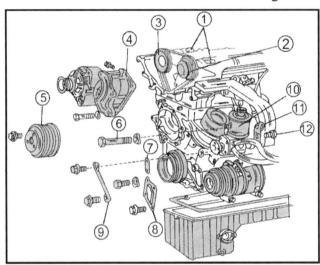

Fig. 1.75 – Details for the removal and installation of the timing housing cover.
1 Timing pins in rear of camshafts
2 Camshaft timing gearwheel
3 Camshaft timing gearwheel
4 Bracket and alternator
5 Crankshaft pulley
6 Bolt
7 Spacer plate
8 Gasket
9 Lock plate
10 Reservoir
11 Bracket
12 Bolt

- Remove the viscous clutch for the cooling fan.
- Remove the upper timing cover as described below.
- Release the drive belt tensioner and take off the drive belt (Section "Cooling System").
- Remove the water pump.
- Remove the oil filter cartridge. The oil contained in the filter housing will flow back into the oil sump.
- Remove the oil sump securing bolts near the timing cover and then remove the remaining oil sump bolts to separate the sump from the crankcase.
- Remove the alternator and the alternator mounting bracket.
- Remove the steering pump pulley. The pulley must be prevented from rotating when the bolts are slackened. Remove the bolts (12) in the illustration and take off the bracket (11). The shape of the bracket is not the same on models without and with A/C system. Remove the bolts opposite the steering pump pulley and remove the pump without disconnecting the hoses (place the pump to one side).
- Rotate the crankshaft pulley until the long line is opposite the pointer, as shown in Fig. 1.19. The piston of No. 1 cylinder is now at TDC.
- The two camshafts are now locked in their position with the timing pins from the rear as already shown in Fig. 1.20. If you do the operation without the timing pins, you will have to make absolutely sure that the shafts cannot rotate during the subsequent operations.

Engines

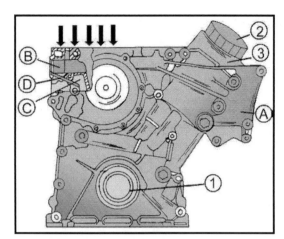

Fig. 1.76 – Timing cover seen from the outside. Take care not to damage the cylinder head gasket in the area shown by the arrows.
1 Oil seal, crankshaft
2 Oil filter over, plastic
3 Oil filter housing
A Steering pump mounting bracket
B Threaded bore for chain tensioner
C Oil chamber for chain tensioner
D Oil drilling to chain tensioner

- Mark the two camshaft gearwheels and the timing chain at opposite points with a spot of paint.
- Remove the chain tensioner as previously described for the four-cylinder engine.
- Prevent the exhaust camshaft from rotating and slacken and remove the centre bolt for the timing gear. Withdraw the timing gear. Carry out the same operation on the inlet camshaft. If fitted remove the camshaft adjuster.
- Remove the upper bearing bolt for the chain guide as described during the removal of the cylinder head. The bolt must be coated with sealing compound during installation.
- Remove the four bolts inside the timing cover (bolts "A" in Fig. 1.17). Tighten the bolts to 2.1 kgm during installation.
- Remove the vibration damper (crankshaft pulley) as already described.
- Remove the timing cover securing bolts and remove the cover. The cover is guided by means of two dowel pins and must be carefully detached. Take care not to damage the cylinder head gasket at the position shown by the arrows in Fig. 1.76. Tighten the bolts to 2.5 kgm during installation. Not all bolts are of the same length and it will help to mark where they are inserted.
- Immediately check the condition of the oil seal in the cover and replace it if necessary.

Fig. 1.77 – Details for the removal and installation of the upper timing cover.
1 Thermostat housing
2 Combi bolt, M8 x 35
3 Cover
4 Dowel pins
5 Sealing ring
6 Combi bolt, M6 x 22
7 Cylinder head cover

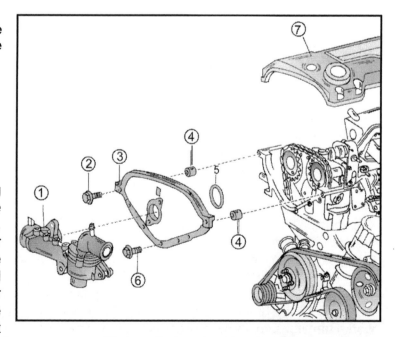

The installation of the timing cover is a reversal of the removal procedure. Thoroughly clean the cover face and the face on the cylinder head. The two oil seals in the rear of the cover must be replaced. Coat the sealing face with "Omnifit FD10" sealing compound. Take care not to fill the oil chamber for the chain tensioner "C" in Fig. 1.76. The tightening torques have already been given above. The two camshaft timing gears are tightened to 2.0 kgm + 90° ("Torx" wrench T40 required).

1.4.4.3. Upper Timing Cover – Four-cylinder Engine M111

Fig. 1.76 shows details for the removal and installation of the cover, shown for the M111 engine. To remove the upper timing cover, the cylinder head cover and the thermostat housing must be removed first. The cover closes the chain housing at the upper end and is fitted with sealing compound Omnifit FD10, or a similar compound used locally i.e. you will have to obtain some of the compound before you start the removal. Fig. 1.77 shows the parts to be removed. Fig. 1.78 shows a view of the cover from the front.

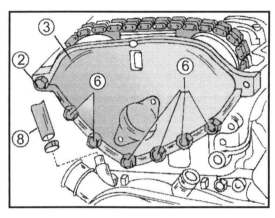

Fig. 1.78 – View of the upper timing cover from the outside. The numbers are the same as given in Fig. 1.76. Additionally the coolant hose (8) is shown.

In the inside of the timing cover you will find a coolant pipe (1, Fig. 1.79) which is sealed off by an oil seal (2) and enters into a groove in the cylinder head. Remove the cover after removal of the cylinder head cover and the thermostat housing as follows:

- On the outside left, seen from the front, remove a bolt and then remove the remaining bolts of the cover.

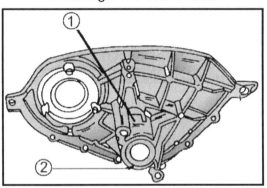

Fig. 1.79 – View of the upper timing cover from the inside. The oil seal (2) in the cover (1) must be replaced.

- Remove the timing cover. It is fitted to two dowel sleeves (4) in Fig. 1.77 and must be separated from the sleeves.
- Thoroughly clean the timing cover and cylinder head sealing faces and coat the cover face with the sealing compound mentioned above. The "O" sealing ring (2) in Fig. 1.79 must always be replaced if the cover has been removed. Tighten the M6 bolts to 0.9 kgm and the M8 bolts to 2.1 kgm.

1.4.4.4. Chain Tensioning Rail – Removal and Installation

The engine must be removed from the vehicle to replace the tensioning rail. To reach the tensioning rail in the inside of the timing chain housing, you will have to expose the front end of the engine. The cylinder head must also be removed. The operations to remove the various components, i.e. cylinder head, camshafts, camshaft sprockets, etc. have already been described and must be followed. In Fig. 1.75 you will see some of the parts to be removed.

The tensioning rail is fitted to the lower end by means of a bearing bolt, which must be extracted from the crankcase in the same manner as described during the removal of the cylinder head. In Figs. 1.22 and Fig. 1.33 you will see the arrangement of extractor bolt and impact hammer to remove such a bearing bolt.

The plastic liner of the tensioning rail is retained with clips and can be replaced separately without replacing the complete rail. We advise you to enquire in a Mercedes workshop, if the replacement of the liner is sufficient.

The installation of the tensioning rail is a reversal of the removal procedure. The instructions to fit the camshaft sprockets, upper and lower timing cover, cylinder head, etc. must be followed.

Engines

1.4.4.5. Guide Rail in Cylinder Head – Removal and Installation

The guide rail is located between the two camshaft sprockets below the upper timing chain cover, i.e. the latter must be removed to gain access. The rail is held in position by two bolts.

• Remove the upper timing chain cover as already described.

• Rotate the crankshaft until the vibration damper is in the position shown in Fig. 1.19. The tips of the cams for No. 1 cylinder must be facing upwards.

• Lock the two camshafts in position as shown in Figs. 1.16 and 1.17.

• Remove the chain tensioner as described earlier on and remove the guide rail after unscrewing the two bolts.

The installation is a reversal of the removal procedure. Tighten the two guide rail bolts to 1.0 kgm (7.2 ft.lb.).

1.4.6. CAMSHAFTS – Four-cylinder Engine – M111
1.4.6.0. CHECKING THE CAMSHAFT TIMING POSITION

As already mentioned: Camshafts and associated parts can only be removed when the camshafts are in their basic timing position. The cylinder head cover must be removed as described on page 27:

• Rotate the crankshaft until the setting shown in Fig. 1.19 has been obtained.

• From the rear of the camshaft gearwheels insert the timing pins (No. 111 589 01 15 00) through the holes of the camshaft bearing cap No. 1 and No. 6 into the camshaft flanges, as shown in Fig. 1.80. If the timing pins cannot be obtained you may try suitable bolts/pins to lock the camshafts.

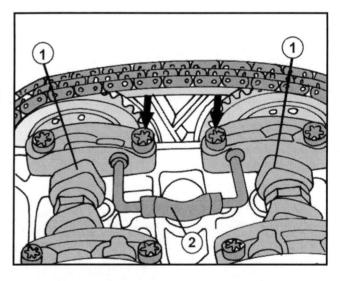

Fig. 1.80 – The two camshaft sprockets (1) are locked in position by inserting the timing pins (2) as shown from the rear of the camshaft caps as described.

1.4.6.1. Adjusting the Camshaft Timing Position

In order to set the two camshafts to the basic timing position they can be rotated without the danger of the pistons hitting the valves, provided that the piston of No. 1 cylinder is in the top dead centre position as already described (see also Fig. 1.19). If a new adjustment is required:

• Remove the upper timing cover and remove the chain tensioner as already described.

• Remove the exhaust camshaft timing gear and lift the timing chain from the inlet timing sprocket.

• Rotate the camshafts into their correct position and lock them by inserting the timing pins (Fig. 1.80) as described in the previous section.

• Place the timing chain over the inlet camshaft sprocket, engage the exhaust camshaft sprocket with the chain and fit the sprocket to the camshaft. The bolts must always be replaced. Tighten them to 2.0 kgm (14 ft.lb.) and then a 60°.

• Refit the chain tensioner and then proceed as described in Section 1.4.6.0 to set the camshafts to their basic timing position.

1.4.6.2. Camshafts – Removal and Installation

Fig. 1.81 shows the camshafts with details of the removal and installation. Remove the camshafts as follows:

Fig. 1.81 – Details for the removal and installation of the camshafts (M111).

1 Open-ended spanner
2 Exhaust camshaft sprocket
3 Exhaust camshaft
4 Inlet camshaft sprocket
5 Inlet camshaft
6 Timing chain
7 Camshaft bearing cap
8 Bolts, 2.1 kgm
9 Sprocket bolt

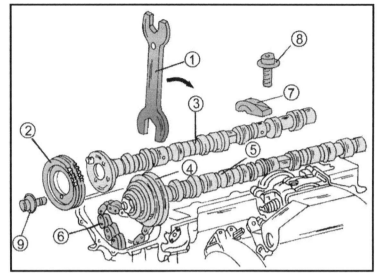

* Remove the upper timing cover as already described and remove the slide rail from the cylinder head.

* Set the crankshaft to the TDC position as already mentioned above. Refer to Fig. 1.19. In this position the piston of No. 1 cylinder will be approx. 30° after TDC and the camshafts can be rotated without contact between pistons and valves.

* Using a spot of paint, mark the two chain sprockets and the timing chain at opposite points. Allow the paint to dry before proceeding.

* Remove the chain tensioner.

* Remove the exhaust camshaft sprocket from the camshaft. This is the L.H. shaft when looking at the front of the engine. Disengage the sprocket from the timing chain. In the same manner remove the inlet camshaft sprocket.

* Apply an open ended spanner (1, in Fig. 1.81) and rotate the shafts until the cam heels (the round part) are resting against the tappets. This will release the tension from the camshaft bearings.

* Slacken the camshaft bearing cap bolts in several stages until they are free and can be removed.

* The two camshafts can now be removed from the cylinder head. If required, remove the hydraulic valve tappets (mark installation position).

The installation of the camshafts is carried out as follows:

* Lubricate the tappets and insert them into their correct bores.

* Lubricate the camshaft bearing journals and place the shafts into the bearing bores. Rotate the shafts until the cam heels are against the tappet faces. You must obtain the best position, as not all cams will be in contact with the tappet surfaces.

* Place the camshaft bearing caps in position in accordance with their numbers. Caps and cylinder head are marked with corresponding numbers.

* Fit the bearing cap bolts and tighten them gradually and evenly from the centre towards the outside to a final torque of 2.1 kgm and from the final position a further 60°. A T40 torx head wrench is necessary. The camshaft must be held against rotation by applying the spanner to the hexagon on the shaft.

* Place the timing chain over the sprocket of the inlet camshaft (5) in Fig. 1.81 and place the upper guide rail in position. Check the paint mark on chain and sprocket. Now place the exhaust camshaft sprocket into the chain, against observing the paint marks and fit the sprocket to the exhaust camshaft (3).

Engines

- Tighten both camshaft sprocket bolts (must be replaced) to 2.0 kgm and from the final position by a further 60°. The camshafts must be prevented from rotating by using the open-ended spanner (1) on the hexagons on the shaft.
- Refit the chain tensioner.
- After installation check the basic position of the camshafts as described earlier on. Section 1.4.6.0. describes the checking of the basic position, if adjustment is necessary refer to section 1.4.6.1.

Camshafts – Important Notes

The identification number of the camshaft is engraved at the position shown in Fig. 1.82 into the camshaft. As the valve timing is controlled by the camshafts, only shafts with identical identification must be fitted. Camshafts must only be removed in the manner described as they are sensitive to damage.

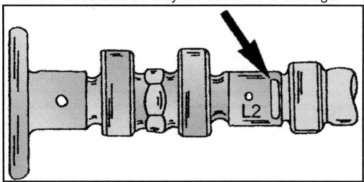

Fig. 1.82 – The location of the camshaft identification.

The bearing bores are marked from 1 to 10 and are marked in the bearing caps and the cylinder head. During installation follow the numbering. The inlet camshaft can be removed with or without timing gear and/or camshaft adjuster.

1.4.6.3. Crankshaft Sprocket – Removal and Installation

- Remove all parts to gain access to the front of the engine. The oil sump must be removed. After removal the view shown in Fig. 1.83 will be obtained.

Fig. 1.83 – Detail for the removal and installation of the crankshaft timing gear.

1   Crankshaft sprocket
2   Woodruff key
3   Oil pump drive chain
4   Tension lever (oil pump drive chain)
5   Timing chain
6   Special puller

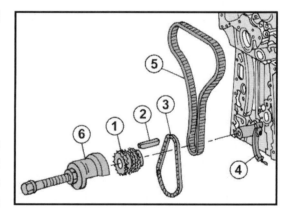

- Push the tensioning arm (4) against the tension of the spring downwards and lift off the oil pump drive chain (3). The chain must be replaced if no longer in usable condition.
- Lift the timing chain (5) from the crankshaft timing gear (1). To remove the sprocket a puller, identified with (6) or a similar puller can be used. The tensioning arm (4) can be pushed downwards to facilitate the removal.
- Check the condition of the Woodruff key in the crankshaft end. The same applies to the Woodruff key for the crankshaft pulley hub.

Refit the crankshaft sprocket as follows:

- Fit the key (1) into the crankshaft. The flat area must be parallel with the crankshaft face.
- Drive the sprocket (1) over the crankshaft end, using a suitable piece of tube. Check that the key has engaged.

- Rotate the engine a few times and check that the timing marks at the upper end of the camshafts are in line.
- Refit the oil pump drive chain tensioning arm (5), the timing cover and the cylinder head cover.
- All other operations are carried out in reverse order.

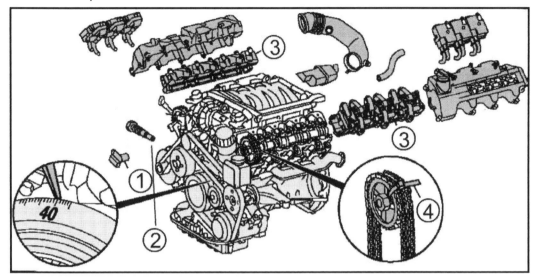

Fig. 1.84 – Details for the removal and installation of the upper timing cover of a V6 or V8 engine, shown on the example of the M112 engine. The illustration legend is given in the description.

1 Camshaft Hall sensor   3 Camshaft bearing bridge
2 Chain tensioner   4 Tie strap

1.4.7. CAMSHAFTS – Six and Eight Cylinder – V6 and V8
1.4.7.0. Checking the Camshaft Timing Position

As already mentioned: Camshafts and associated parts can only be removed when the camshafts are in their basic timing position. The workshop uses a locating plate which is inserted into a groove in the camshaft, but by carefully turning the crankshaft this can be avoided. The cylinder head cover must be removed. Fig. 1.84 shows the parts to be removed in the case of the V6 engine M112. Proceed as follows:

Fig. 1.85 – Alignment of the balance shaft.

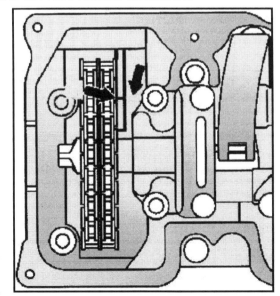

- Rotate the crankshaft until the 40° mark in the vibration damper (pulley) is opposite the pointer, as shown in the circle on in the illustration at the L.H. bottom (after TDC of cyl. 1). Only turn the engine in direction of rotation.
- Check with Fig. 1.85 that the pin on the crankcase and a notch in the balancing weight are aligned as shown (V6 engine).

1.4.7.1. Adjusting the Camshaft Timing Position

In order to set the two camshafts to the basic timing position they can be rotated without the danger of the pistons hitting the valves, provided that the piston of No. 1 cylinder is in the top dead centre position as already described (see also Fig. 1.84 and Fig. 1.85) If a new adjustment is required:

- Remove the chain tensioner and the camshaft Hall sensor.
- Remove the R.H. and L.H. camshaft timing gears (sprockets). The camshafts are prevented from rotating with an open-ended spanner. Lift the timing chain from two timing sprockets. Do not allow the chain to drop into the timing cover (tie it up).
- Rotate the camshafts into their correct position as described in the previous section.
- Place the timing chain over the two camshaft sprockets and fit the sprockets to the camshafts. The bolts must always be replaced. Tighten them to 5.0 kgm (37 ft.lb.) and then a further quarter of a turn.
- Refit the Hall sensor and the chain tensioner and then proceed as described in Section 1.4.10.1 to set the camshafts to their basic timing position.

1.4.7.3. Camshafts – Removal and Installation

The removal of a camshaft involves the removal of the bearing bridge before the camshaft(s) can be removed. After removal of the bearing bridge in question, the camshaft is lifted out.

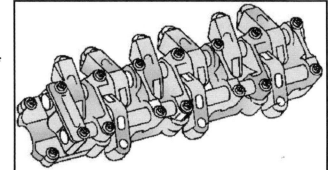

Fig. 1.86 – One of the camshaft bearing bridges.

Removal and Installation of Bearing Bridges

Fig. 1.86 shows one of the bearing bridges. The difference between the engine is an additional bridge in the case of the V8 engine. The following should be noted:

- Lubricate the camshaft bearings before installation. The camshafts must not be replaced individually.
- *If the bearing bridge is damaged, replace the cylinder head with the camshaft bearing bridge.* The M7 bolts must always be replaced. Tighten the bolts in accordance with the diagrams shown in Fig. 1.87 and 1.88.

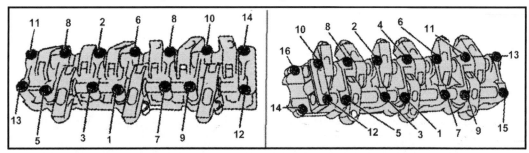

Fig. 1.87 – Tightening sequence for the camshaft bearing bridges of a V6 engine. Note the different number of bolts used on the L.H. and R.H. bridge.

The removal of a bearing bridge is carried out after removal of the cylinder head cover. Set the No. 1 cylinder to top dead centre position (40° after ignition timing point, explained above, see also Fig. 1.84). After removal of the chain tensioner slacken the bolts in reverse order to the sequence shown in Figs. 1.86 or 1.87, depending on the engine (V6 or V8). Note that some bolts are 45 mm long, others 84 mm. Mark where they have been removed from.

The installation is a reversal of the removal procedure. Insert the bolts in accordance with the length and tighten them, using the diagrams shown in Figs. 1.87 or 1.88, depending which of the bridge has been removed. Note that one bridge has 14 bolts and the other one 16 bolts (V6) or 18 and 20 bolts (V8). Count the number of bolts and use the diagram accordingly. The 45 mm long bolts are tightened to 1.5 kgm (11 ft.lb.), the 84 mm long bolts are tightened to 1.0 kgm (7.2 ft.lb.) and then a further 90° (quarter of a turn).

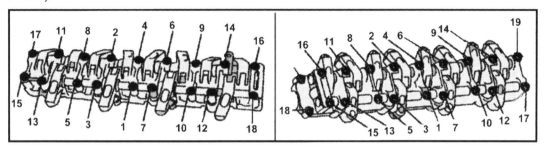

Fig. 1.88 – Tightening sequence for the camshaft bearing bridges of a V8 engine. Note the different number of bolts used on the L.H. and R.H. bridge.

Removal and Installation of Camshafts

• Remove the camshaft sprockets of the L.H. and R.H. camshaft. An open-ended spanner is used to prevent the camshaft from rotating. Use a piece of wire or metal strap to attach the timing chain to the sprockets, as shown by (4) in Fig. 1.84 and remove the sprockets from the camshafts.

• Remove the bearing bridges in the manner described above and lift out the camshaft(s). If necessary replace both camshafts. It is not possible to replace camshafts individually.

The installation is a reversal of the removal procedure. Tighten the camshaft sprocket bolts to 5.0 kgm (36 ft.lb.) and from the final position a further quarter of a turn without torque wrench.

1.4.8. TIMING MECHANISM (includes balance shaft – V6)

1.4.8.0. Chain Tensioner – Removal and Installation

The chain tensioner is fitted to the timing cover, seen from the front end of the engine on the L.H. side of the pulley group. The viscous fan, the fan shroud, the V-belt and the alternator must be removed to unscrew the chain tensioner. A sealing ring underneath the tensioner must be replaced during installation. Tighten the tensioner to 8.0 kgm (58 ft.lb.) during installation. The alternator bolts are tightened to 5.7 kgm (41 ft.lb.).

1.4.8.1. Timing Chain – Removal and Installation

We cannot recommend the replacement of the timing chain as a DIY operation when the engine is fitted to the vehicle. Apart from special tools, to separate the chain links, fitting a new chain, etc. which cannot be substituted by make-shift tools and a hand grinding machine, you will need the experience to deal with timing chains of a two-camshaft Mercedes-Benz engine. The timing chain has a long service life and you may not need replacing.

If the engine is removed you can replace the chain in accordance with the instructions given, as the new chain is placed in position over the various sprockets. The remaining operations can be taken from the various operations described in this section.

1.4.8.2. Balance Shaft – Removal and Installation

Fig. 1.89 shows details for the removal and installation of the balance shaft, fitted to the V6 engine. The engine must be removed to remove and install the balance shaft. Proceed as follows:

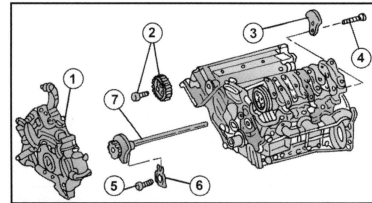

Fig. 1.89 – Details for the removal and installation of the balance shaft. The numbers are referred to in the text.

- Remove in the following order the flywheel, the end cover, the oil sump and the timing cover (1) as described earlier on.
- Set the engine to the top dead centre position. The alignment of the balance shaft must be as shown in Fig. 1.85.
- Remove the R.H. camshaft sprocket (2) as described during the removal of the camshafts. Use a piece of wire to attach the timing chain to the sprocket (4 in Fig. 1.84). The engine must not be rotated with the sprocket removed. The sprocket bolt is tightened to 5.0 kgm + 90°.
- Remove the bolt (4) at the rear end of the engine, securing the counterweight to the shaft. A hole in the counterweight enables you to insert a drift to prevent the shaft from rotating. Withdraw the counterweight (3). The bolt is tightened to 2.0 kgm (14.5 ft.lb.) and then a further quarter of a turn.
- At the front of the engine remove the bolt (5), take off the locking plate (6) and remove the shaft towards the front. The bolt is tightened to 1.5 kgm (10 ft.lb.) during installation.

The installation is a reversal of the removal procedure. After installation check the timing alignment with Fig. 1.85. The markings of the pin on the crankcase (2) and the notch (1) in the balance weight must be aligned.

1.4.9. Timing Mechanism/Camshafts – M272 V6 Engine – ML 350

The removal of the camshafts of this engine is practically impossible for the ordinary D.I.Y. enthusiast various items, known as centre valves (for inlet and exhaust camshaft), pulse wheels (for inlet and exhaust camshaft), camshaft adjusters (for inlet and exhaust camshaft), a so-called centrifuge (a cover is fitted over it) and other items. For this reason we cannot give you any further information.

1.5. Tightening Torque Values

The tightening torques for the various engines are given in the instructions to remove and install the various parts. We have tried to list every possible item you may have to tighten during the installation.

1.6. Lubrication System

The lubrication system is a pressure-feed system. A gear-type oil pump is driven via the crankshaft timing sprocket by means of a separate single roller chain and is kept under tension with its own chain tensioner with torsion spring.

The oil filter is fitted in vertical position on the side of the cylinder block. The filter element is held in the filter housing by means of a screw cap, fitted to the top of the filter housing. The workshop uses a special wrench to undo this cap. The filter consist of the lower part and a throw-away oil filter. An oil pressure switch is fitted to the side of the filter lower housing.

The engine is fitted with a light-metal oil sump, containing an oil level sensor. The oil sump can be removed with the engine fitted to the vehicle. Note that the oil sump can consist of one parts or two parts, depending on the engine. Operations to remove and install the oil sump and oil pump are different and are described under separate headings.

1.6.0.   TECHNICAL DATA

Oil Capacities: ....See Page 8
Oil pressure at idle speed:... Workshop operation
Oil pressure at 3000 rpm:.. Workshop operation

1.6.1.   OIL SUMP – REMOVAL AND INSTALLATION

M111 Engine (ML 230)

The oil sump can be removed with the engine fitted. A one piece sump is fitted. Various parts must be removed and can be found at the positions shown in Fig. 1.90. The engine must be lifted out of its mounting, i.e. a suitable lifting device must be available. The battery must be disconnected.

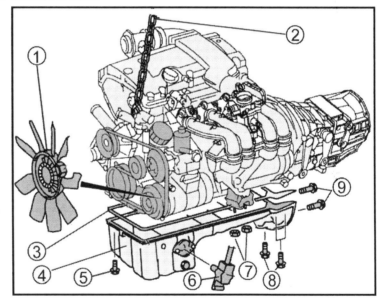

Fig. 1.90 – Details for the removal of the oil sump, showing parts to be disconnected or removed (see text).

*   Remove the bottom section of the sound-proofing panel.
*   Drain the engine oil. Make sure the container collecting the oil is large enough for the oil in the engine. Refit the drain plug with a new sealing ring and tighten it to 3.0 kgm (22 ft.lb.).
*   Remove the viscous fan.
*   Remove the coolant expansion tank after removal of the two securing bolts from the bulkhead (do not disconnect the coolant hoses).
*   Remove the bolts (7) from the two engine mountings at the positions shown.
*   Raise the engine with a suitable chain (2) and a lifting device, without damaging any of the parts.
*   Disconnect the connector plug from the oil level sensor (6).
*   Remove the bolts (5), (8) and (9) out of the oil sump. Immediately check the length and the diameter of the bolts. Bolts are inserted from below and two more are fitted to the gearbox side. Tighten the M6 bolts with 1.0 kgm and the M8 bolts with 2.5 kgm during installation. The bolts securing the oil sump to the transmission are tightened to 4.0 kgm (29 ft.lb.). The oil sump (4) is taken out

towards the bottom. The crankshaft may have to be rotated slightly to clear all parts. An automatic transmission may have to be pushed to one side.

Then installation is a reversal of the removal procedure. Most of the tightening torque values are already given above. Also note the following points:

- Always replace the oil sump gasket. Use some sealing compound and stick the gasket to the oil sump sealing face.
- Self-locking nut and bolts must be replaced.
- When tightening the engine mountings lower the engine onto the mountings and then fit the nuts. Fully lower the engine and tighten the nuts to 3.5 kgm (25 ft.lb.).
- Fill the engine with oil, start the engine and allow it to run for a while. Check the connections oil sump/crankcase for oil leaks.

1.6.2. OIL SUMP – REMOVAL AND INSTALLATION – M112/M113

The following instructions the V6 engine (for example ML 320) and the V8 engine (for example ML 430). The oil sump can be removed with the engine fitted to the vehicle, but the engine must be lifted out of its mountings to remove the engine mountings on the L.H. and R.H. sides, i.e. a suitable lifting device must be available. The oil sump consists of an upper part and a lower part, as shown in Fig. 1.91. The following instructions describe the removal of the complete oil sump. The lower part can be removed without removing the upper part, if necessary (for example if the oil pump is to be removed). The removal of the lower sump part can be carried out without lifting the engine. If necessary follow the instructions given below. The engine oil should be drained immediately whichever operation is carried out.

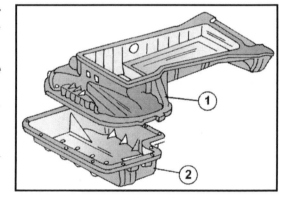

Fig. 1.91 – The oil sump consists of an upper part (1) and a lower part (2). Both can be removed individually as required.

Removal and Installation of the complete Oil Sump

- Remove the lower parts of the oil sump as described below.
- At the side of the oil sump disconnect a connector plug for the oil level sensor and remove the adjacent oil pipe from the oil dipstick tube. Replace the oil seal. The bolt is tightened to 0.8 kgm.

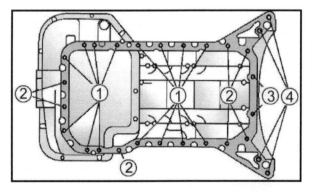

Fig. 1.92 – The location of the various oil sump bolts (M112/M113 engines).
1   Bolts, M6 x 20 mm
2   M6 x 40 mm
3   M6 x 90 mm
4   M8 x 30 mm

- Unscrew the upper oil sump part from the crankcase and remove the sump in the direction of drive towards the front. The crankshaft may have to be rotated to clear all parts. Bolts are not of the same length and diameter. Fig. 1.92 shows the inserted bolts around the oil sump. The ends of the oil sump must be flush with the transmission face. Fit the different bolts in accordance with the illustration and tighten them. M6 bolts are tightened to 0.9 kgm, M8 bolts to 2.0 kgm. Tighten all bolts evenly around the circumference.

• Fit the well cleaned oil drain plug and tighten it to 3.0 kgm (22 ft.lb.). Finally fill the engine with the correct quantity of oil (Page 8).

Removal and Installation of the lower oil sump part

The following operations are carried out by referring to Fig. 1.93.

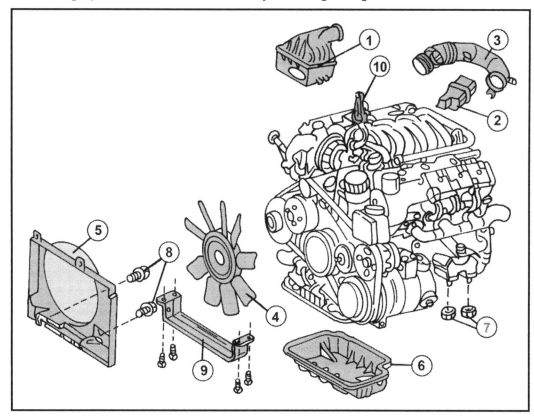

Fig. 1.93 – Details for the removal of the oil sump lower part in the case o an M112 and M113 engine.

1 Air cleaner housing	4 Viscous fan	7 Nuts
2 Resonance unit	5 Fan shroud	8 Bolts
3 Resonance pipe	6 Oil sump lower part	9 Air guide panel

• Remove the viscous fan (4) (section "Cooling System"). **Attention:** The bolts has a R.H. thread. In the case of models ML 320 and ML 350 remove the fan shroud (5). To do this remove the bolts (8) at the bottom. In the case of the ML 430 model removal the air guide (9).
• Remove the panelling underneath the engine compartment and drain the engine oil.
• Remove the engine mounting nuts (7) from the front axle carrier. Tighten them to 3.5 kgm (25 ft.lb.) during installation. Before detaching the L.H. mounting free fluid pipe for the power steering out of its bracket.
• In the case of all V6 engines and in the case of the V8 engine in models ML 430 and ML 500 remove the resonance pipe (3) together with the resonance unit (2). The pipe is held in position at the rear of the inlet manifold by means of a plastic plate. Withdraw the connector plug from the hot film air flow meter and unscrew the resonance pipe from the cylinder head cover.
• Raise the engine out of the engine mountings with the help of a chain attached to the front lifting eye (1) without damaging any of the parts.
• Unscrew the bottom part of the oil sump.

The installation is a reversal of the removal procedure. Before installation clean the sealing faces of the sump and crankcase. The sealing faces in Fig. 1.94 must be coated with "Loctite 5970" sealing compound and the sump must be fitted within 10 minutes. The bead of the sealing compound must not exceed 2.0 mm and not "flattened". The illustration shows a V6 engine, but the V8 engine is similar.

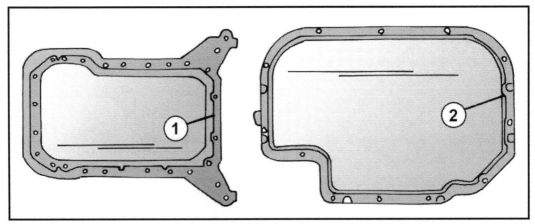

Fig. 1.94 – Application of the sealing compound. In the L.H. view for upper parts of the oil sump (1), in the R.H. view for the lower part (2). Follow the instructions given below.

Tighten all oil sump bolts evenly to 1.4 kgm (10 ft.lb.). Fit the oil drain plug, tighten it to 3.0 kgm (22 ft.lb.) and fill the engine with the correct amount of oil.

1.6.3. OIL SUMP – 272 ENGINE – In Model ML 350 – Series 164

The removal and installation is carried out in a similar manner as described in the last section, i.e. the engine must be lifted as described in order to remove the engine mountings. Additionally the air filter housing, the hot film air flow meter and the air duct housing must be removed to gain access to all parts. Again a two-part oil sump (upper and bottom section) is fitted and both can be removed individually. The M6 bolts securing the oil sump are tightened to 0.9 kgm (7.2 ft.lb.). The M8 bolts are tightened to 2.0 kgm (14.5 ft.lb.). Torx-head bolts are used.

1.6.4. OIL SUMP – 113 ENGINE – In Model ML 500 – Series 164

The oil sump consists of an upper part and a lower part. The removal of the sump is rather complicated – you have been warned.

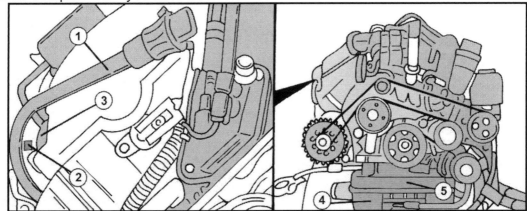

Fig. 1.95 – Details for the removal of the oil sump in the case of the M113 engine (V8) in model series 164. The numbers are referred to in the text. (4) and (5) show the oil sump.

Removal of complete oil sump
- Referring to Fig. 1.95 remove the oil dipstick guide tube (1) from the bracket (3). Unscrew the bolt (2) out of the bracket (3) and withdraw the guide tube (1) towards the top. Push it to one side.

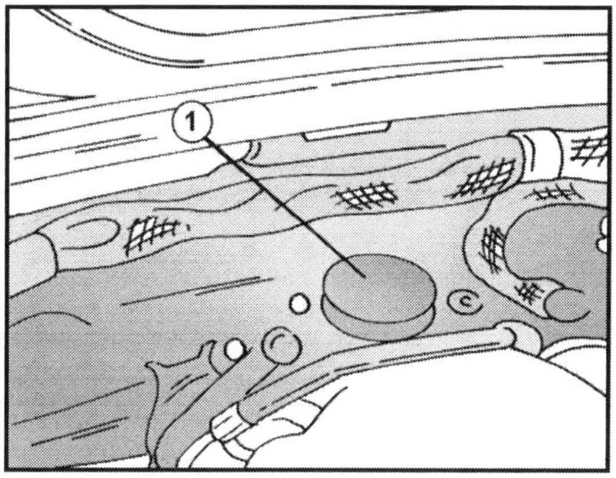

Fig. 1.96 – The hot film air mass meter (1) can be found at the position shown.

- Remove the hot film air mass meter, situated at the position shown in Fig. 1.96.
- Place the front end of the engine onto secure chassis stands and remove the panelling underneath the engine. In total 11 bolts must be removed.
- Drain the engine oil. Remember that 8.5 litres must be collected. The drain plug is tightened to 3.0 kgm (22 ft.lb.).
- Remove the complete exhaust system.
- Remove the bottom part of the oil pump as described below.
- Remove the oil pump. Refer to heading below.
- Locate a bolt on the vent pipe for the transfer box, remove the bolts and take off the bracket.
- Remove the bolt securing the oil cooler pipe to the bracket on the oil sump. The bolt is tightened to 0.9 kgm.

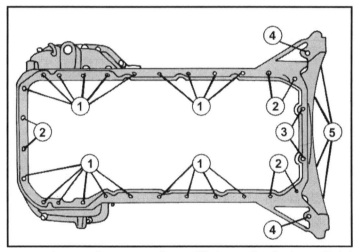

Fig. 1.97 – Location of the oil sump bolts of an M113 engine in model series 164.

1   Bolt, M6 x 20 mm
2   Bolt, M6 x 40 mm
3   Bolt, M6 x 90 mm
4   Bolt, M8 x 30 mm
5   Bolt, M10 x 45 mm

- Remove the bolt (4) of the double clamp in Fig. 1.12 on the alternator mounting bracket (5). Tighten the clamp to 0.8 kgm.
- Remove the bolts securing the engine mountings. Tighten the bolts to 5.3 kgm (38 ft.lb.) during installation.
- Lift the engine in the manner shown in Fig. 1.90 or 1.93 without damaging any parts in the engine compartment.
- Unscrew the upper parts of the oil sump from the crankcase and withdraw the oil sump in the direction of drove towards the front. The crankshaft may have to be rotated to clear all parts. The bolts are not all of the same length and diameter and Fig. 1.97 must be referred to for the location of the various bolts.

Note the following during the installation of the oil sump:

- Coat the sealing faces shown in Fig. 1.94 with "Loctite 5907" sealing compound. The oil sump must be fitted within 10 minutes of applying the sealing compound. The bead of the compound must not exceed 2.0 mm.
- The end of the oil sump must be aligned flush with the transmission face. Fit the various bolts in accordance with Fig. 1.97 and tighten them evenly. M6 bolts are tightened to 0.9 kgm, M8 bolts to 2.0 kgm.
- Fit the clean oil drain plug and tighten it to 3.0 kgm (22 ft.lb.). Finally fill the engine with the correct amount of engine oil.

Lubrication System

Removal of the oil sump lower part

- Place the front end of the engine onto secure chassis stands and remove the panelling underneath the engine. In total 11 bolts must be removed.
- Drain the engine oil. Remember that 8.5 litres must be collected. The drain plug is tightened to 3.0 kgm (22 ft.lb.).

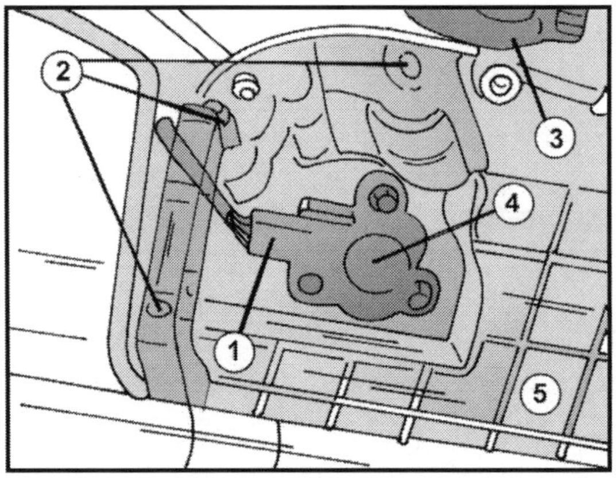

Fig. 1.98 – Details for the removal and installation of the lower oil sump part of an M113 engine in series 164. The numbers are referred to in the text.

- Remove the bolts securing the mounting clamps of the stabiliser bar on both side and remove the clamps. There is no need to remove the stabiliser bar – just pull it downwards. The bolts are tightened with 11.0 kgm (79 ft.lb.) to the front axle carrier.
- Next remove the bottom part of the oil sump by referring to Fig. 1.98. Withdraw the connector plug (1) from the sensor (4) for the oil level, temperature, etc. Undo the bolts and remove the sensor from the lower oil sump part. Tighten the bolts to 1.0 kgm during installation.
- Remove the bolts securing the bracket for the steering pump fluid pipe (3). Tighten the bolts with 1.0 kgm to the oil sump during installation.
- Remove the bolts (2) and take off the bottom part of the oil sump.

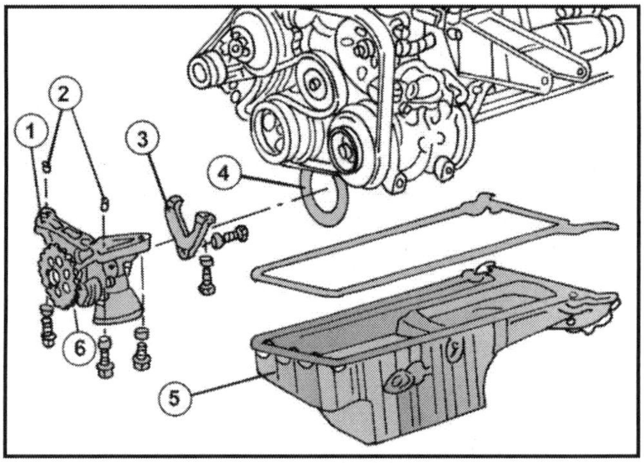

Fig. 1.99 – Attachment of oil pump and oil sump (M111 engine).
1 Oil pump assembly
2 Dowel sleeves
3 Reinforcement bracket
4 Oil pump drive chain
5 Oil sump
6 Oil pump sprocket

The installation is carried out in reverse order, noting the following points:

- Coat the sealing faces shown in Fig. 1.94 with "Loctite 5907" sealing compound. The oil sump must be fitted within 10 minutes of applying the sealing compound. The bead of the compound must not exceed 2.0 mm.

Fig. 1.100 – View if the fitted oil pump drive.
1 Chain tensioner blade
2 Torsion spring
3 Bolt and washer
4 Drive chain

- Tighten the bolts securing the lower oil sump part to the upper part to 1.3 kgm (9.5 ft.lb.).
- Fit the clean oil drain plug and tighten it to 3.0 kgm (22 ft.lb.). Finally fill the engine with the correct amount of engine oil.

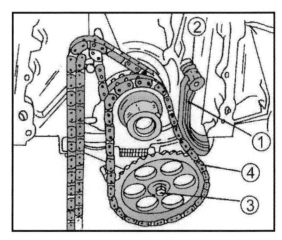

1.6.5. OIL PUMP - REMOVAL AND INSTALLATION

M111 Engine

Fig. 1.99 shows the attachment of the pump.

- Remove the oil sump as described in Section 1.6.1.
- Undo the bolt (3) in Fig. 1.100 securing the pump chain sprocket and remove together with the washer. Remove the oil pump sprocket together with the drive chain (4) from the crankshaft. The bolt is tightened to 3.2 kgm (20 ft.lb.) during installation.
- When removing the sprocket you will notice that one side is curved. This side must face the oil pump during installation. Fig. 1.101 shows this side with the arrow. The oil pump sprocket can only be fitted in one position.

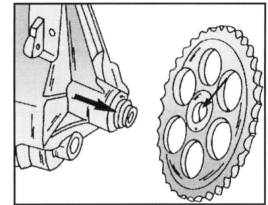

Fig. 1.101 – Attachment of the oil pump sprocket to the oil pump shaft. Engage as shown.

- Remove the pump securing bolts from the bottom of the crankcase (Torx-head socket required) and remove together with the washers. The mounting bracket (3) in Fig. 1.99 will also come away. The pump is now withdrawn towards the bottom. Note that two dowels locate the pump.

Pump sprocket and drive chain can be replaced as a set. An overhaul of the pump is not possible.

The installation is a reversal of the removal procedure. Observe the following points:

- Fill the pump with engine oil before installation. Fit it to the crankcase, ensuring that the dowels (2) in Fig. 1.99 engage. Fit and tighten the bolts to 2.5 kgm (18 ft.lb.). Fit the bracket (3), if fitted, and tighten the two bolts to 1.0 kgm (7.2 ft.lb.).
- Fit the oil pump sprocket in accordance with Fig. 1.101. Fit the bolt with the washer and tighten the bolt to 3.2 kgm (23 ft.lb.).
- The remaining operations are now carried out in reverse order. After releasing the chain tensioner (1) in Fig. 1.100 the chain will be correctly tensioned.

M112 and 113 Engines

After removal of the oil sump bottom parts as already described remove the oil pimp from the crankcase. The following points should be noted during installation:

- Clean the suction filter before installation. Fill then pump with engine oil to ensure immediate lubrication.
- Fit the pump to the crankcase and fit the bolts. Tighten them to 2.0 kgm (14.5 ft.lb.).
- Finally fill the engine with the correct amount of engine oil. After running the engine for a while check the area around the oil sump/crankcase for signs of oil leaks.

M272 Engine (ML 350) – Series 164

The complete oil sump must be removed to gain access to the oil pump. As the operations to remove the upper part of the oil sump has not been described for this engine, you will have the pump replaced in a workshop. If the engine has been removed you will quickly see which parts must be removed to take out the oil pump.

1.6.6. OIL PUMP - REPAIRS

Oil pumps should not be dismantled and/or repaired. If a new pump is fitted check the drive chain and the chain sprocket to prevent fitting a new pump together with new drive components.

1.6.7. OIL LEVEL SENDER UNIT – REMOVAL AND INSTALLATION

The oil level sender unit in the side of the oil sump can be replaced with the engine fitted. After draining the engine oil withdraw the cable connector plug from the sender unit (switch) and remove the two screws. Remove the oil seal below the sender unit (always replace).

Install in reverse order. Tighten the screws to 1.2 kgm (9 ft.lb.). Finally fill the engine with oil.

1.6.8. OIL PRESSURE SWITCH – REMOVAL AND INSTALLATION

The switch is located at the front end of the engine, L.H. side above one of the belt pulleys. The switch can be removed after withdrawing the cable connector. The switch is tightened to 2.0 kgm (14 ft.lb.).

1.6.9. OIL FILTER – REMOVAL AND INSTALLATION

The filter element is removed with a special filter wrench. The workshop uses a special tool, shown in Fig. 1.102, which is placed over the screw cap at the top of the filter and engages with the ribs.

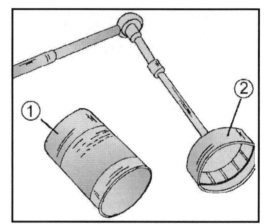

Fig. 1.102 – The screw cap on top of the oil filter (1) is removed with the special tool (2) as shown. Alternatively follow the description below.

A suitable socket, extension and ratchet complete the arrangement. Some engines have an oil cooler fitted, which reduced the oil temperature by about 15°C.

Fig. 1.103 shows where the oil filter is located. The following text describes the removal and installation of the filter and is valid for all engines. We would like to point out that a special filter wrench is used in the workshop, as already mentioned. The hexagon fitted to the top of the oil filter cover on earlier and similar engines has now been removed. If you intend to carry out regular servicing of your vehicle we recommend to obtain such a filter wrench, available under Parts No. 103 589 02 09 00. Otherwise it may be possible to use a large pair of pliers or grips, but remember that access is limited. Remove the filter as follows:

- On all models use a filter chain wrench and unscrew the screw cap (1) in Fig. 1.103 (unless you have the special tool 103 589 02 09 00). Fully unscrew the screw cap and remove it. The filter element (2) will be attached to the cap (catch dripping oil) and can be carefully knocked off with a small drift, applied to the centre rod. Take off the sealing ring (3).

Fig. 1.103 – Fitted oil filter (all engines).
1 Filter screw cap, 2.5 kgm
2 Filter insert (element)
3 Sealing ring

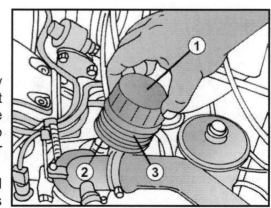

- Fit the new filter element (2) to the screw cap, replace the sealing ring (3) and fit the cap to the filter housing. Tighten the cap to 2.5 kgm (18 ft.lb.). You will have to estimate the torque without the filter wrench.

- Check the oil level in the engine and correct if only the oil filter element has been replaced. Otherwise fill the engine with the correct amount of oil.

• Start the engine and allow it to run for a while. Then switch off and check the filter surrounding for oil leaks.

1.6.10. ENGINE OIL COOLER

M272 Engine – ML 350 (Series 164)
On this engine the oil cooler is fitted to the side of the oil filter as shown in Fig. 1.104.
The removal is fairly complicated, if not comprehensive:

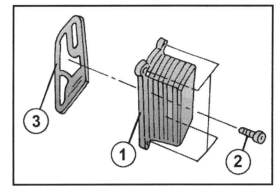

Fig. 1.104 – Oil cooler installation in the case of the M272 engine.
1 Oil cooler (heat exchanger)
2 Bolts, 1.2 kgm
3 Seal

• Place the front end of the vehicle on secure chassis stands and remove the protective panel underneath the engine compartment. Drain the cooling system.

• Remove the front engine covering panel as described in section "Engines" (see also Fig. 1.29).

• Remove the L.H. air intake tube.

• Remove the steering fluid reservoir from the front engine cover.

• Remove the bolts (2) and withdraw the oil cooler (1) from the oil filter housing. The sealing ring (3) must always be replaced.

The installation is a reversal of the removal procedure. The bolts are tightened to 1.2 kgm (9 ft.lb.).

M112 and M113 Engines – Series 163
The parts to be removed are shown in Fig. 1.105. The cooling system must be drained, as it will be necessary to disconnect the two coolant hoses (4) and (5) from the oil cooler (6). The bolts (8) must be tightened to 1.1 kgm (8 ft.lb.) during installation.
The installation is a reversal of the removal procedure. Finally fill the cooling system.

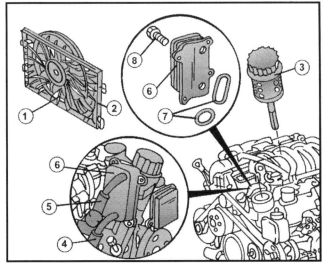

Fig. 1.105 – Details for the removal and installation of the oil cooler (heat exchanger) in the case of the M112 and M113 engine.
1 Electric fan
2 Fan shroud
3 Oil filter screw cap
4 Coolant hose
5 Coolant hose
6 Oil cooler (heat exchanger)
7 Sealing rings
8 Bolts, 1.1 kgm

1.6.11. ENGINE OIL CHANGE

The engine oil should be changed in accordance with the recommendations of the manufacturer. Remember that there are a few litres of engine oil to handle and the necessary container to catch the oil must be large enough to receive the oil. Dispose of the old oil in accordance with the local laws. You may be able to bring it to a petrol station. **Never discharge the engine oil into a drain.** Drain the oil as follows, when the engine is fairly warm:

- Jack up the front end of the vehicle and place the container underneath the oil sump. Unscrew the oil drain plug (ring spanner or socket). Take care, as the oil will "shoot" out immediately. Remove the oil filler cap to speed-up the draining.
- Check the plug sealing ring and replace if necessary. Clean the plug and fit and tighten to 3.0 kgm (22 ft.lb.).
- Fill the engine with the necessary amount of oil.
- Refit the oil filler cap and drive the vehicle until the engine operating temperature is reached. Jack up the vehicle once more and check the drain plug area for oil leaks.

1.6.12.   ENGINE OIL PRESSURE

The oil pressure can only be checked with an oil pressure gauge, which is fitted with a suitable adapter in place of the oil pressure switch. We recommend to leave the oil pressure check to a workshop. Low oil pressure can also be caused through a low oil level in the sump.

1.7.   Cooling System

The cooling system operates with an expansion tank, at the R.H. side of the engine compartment. A coolant level indicator is fitted into the expansion tank. If the level drops below the "Min" mark for any reason, the switch contacts will close and light up a warning light in the instrument panel. A check of the coolant level is therefore redundant.

The water pump is fitted to the front at the bottom of the cylinder block, is sealed off by means of an "O" sealing ring and secured by means of bolts. The pump cannot be repaired. The thermostat is mentioned later on.

1.7.0.   TECHNICAL DATA

Type: ....Water pump-assisted thermo-siphon system with
impeller-type water pump

Anti-freeze amount:...See Section 1.7.1.0

1.7.1   COOLANT - DRAINING AND REFILLING

Although there are differences within the model/engine range the following applies in general to all vehicles.

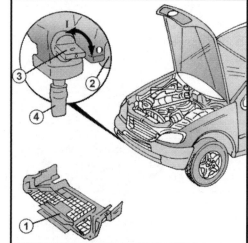

Fig. 1.106 – Draining the cooling system (general view).
1   Front sound-proofing panel
2   Radiator
3   Drain tap
4   Drain hose
- If the engine is hot open the expansion tank cap to the first notch and allow the pressure to escape. The coolant must have a temperature of less than 90° C. but we recommend to wait until the temperature has dropped to 50° C. In all cases use a thick rag to cover the expansion tank cap to protect your hand.

Fig. 1.107 – The arrow shows the small connection where the hose can be connected before the drain plug (1) is opened.

- Remove the noise dampening panel from underneath the vehicle.
- Unscrew the coolant drain plug at the bottom of the radiator. You can push a hose over the nipple Fig. 1.106 (shown in general) and guide the hose into a container to drain and collect the coolant. Fig. 1.107 shows a view from below. The hose is pushed over the nipple (1). If the anti-freeze solution is in good condition, your can re-use it. Poke a piece of wire into the bore of the drain hole to dislodge sludge, if the coolant flow is restricted.

To ensure that the cooling system is filled without air lock, proceed as follows when filling with the coolant. Refer to Section 1.7.1.0 for the correct anti-freeze amount to be added. Anti-freeze marketed by Mercedes-Benz should be used, as this has been specially developed for the engine.

- Set both heater switches to the max. heating capacity, by moving the controls. If an automatic climate control system is fitted, press the "DEF" button.
- Fill the pre-mixed anti-freeze solution into the expansion tank filler neck until it reaches the "Cold" mark. Do not fit the expansion tank cap at this stage.
- Start the engine and run it until the operating temperature has been reached, i.e. the thermostat must have opened. Fit the cap when the coolant has a temperature between 60° to 70° C. A thermometer can be inserted into the radiator filler neck to check the temperature.
- Check the coolant level after the engine has cooled down and correct if necessary.
- Refit the noise dampening panel underneath the vehicle.

1.7.1.0.   Anti-freeze Solution

The cooling system is filled with anti-freeze when the vehicle leaves the factory and the solution should be left in the system throughout the year. When preparing the anti-freeze mixture, note the following ratio between water and anti-freeze solution. We recommend to use the anti-freeze supplied by Mercedes-Benz. It may cost you a little more, but your engine will thank you for it. The following amounts should be observed:

To –37° C:
111 engine – 5.25 litres anti-freeze
112 engine – 5.5 litres anti-freeze
113 engine – 6.00 litres anti-freeze
272 engine – 5.00 litres anti-freeze
To –45° C:
111 engine – 5.75 litres anti-freeze
112 engine – 6.0 litres anti-freeze
113 engine – 6.50 litres anti-freeze
272 engine – 5.50 litres anti-freeze

1.7.2.   RADIATOR AND COOLING FAN

1.7.2.0.   Checking Radiator Cap and Radiator

The cooling system operates under pressure. The expansion tank cap is fitted with a spring, which is selected to open the cap gasket when the pressure has risen to value engraved in the cap. If the cap is replaced, always fit one with the same marking, suitable for the models covered.

To check the radiator cap for correct opening, a radiator test pump is required. Fit the pump to the cap and operate the pump until the valve opens, which should take place near the given pressure (1.4 kg/sq.cm). If this is not the case, replace the cap. Fig. 1.108 shows the working principle of such a test pump.

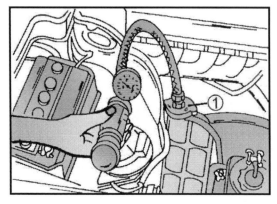

Fig. 1.108 – A radiator test pump (1) is used to check the cooling system for leaks and the expansion tank cap for correct opening. The pump is connected to the expansion tank.

The same pump can also be used to check the cooling system for leaks. Fit the pump to the expansion tank filler neck and operate the plunger until a pressure of 1.0 kg/sq.cm. is indicated. Allow the pressure in the system for at least 5 minutes. If the pressure drops, there is a leak in the system.

1. 7.2.1.   Radiator – Removal and Installation

Different radiators are fitted depending on the model. When the radiator is replaced make sure you obtain the correct one. Note the differences of the different engines, depending if the model in question belongs to the 163 or 164 range of models.

The parts shown in Fig. 1.109 are on the example of the M111 engine in model ML 230 must be initially removed before access is possible to the radiator. The removal and installation is, however, similar on all models.

* Drain the cooling system as described.
* Remove the cooling fan (see later on).
* Remove the clamps (2) from the fan shroud (3). These are attached by means of bolts from below. The shroud can then be removed. **Note:** If a new cooler is fitted it may be different (integral cooler for the power steering fluid). In this case a new fan shroud will also be necessary.

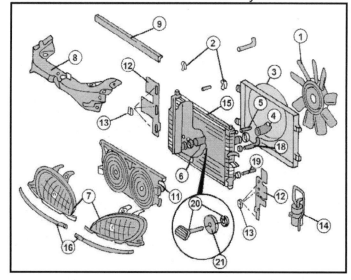

Fig. 1.109 – Details for the removal of the radiator as fitted to the ML 230 (M111 engine). The numbers are referred to in the text.

* Remove the coolant pipes (4) and (6). The hose clamps are tightened with a hexagon socket (6 or 7 mm). Also disconnect the coolant pipe (5) from the radiator.
* Remove the covers (16) and the headlamps (7).
* Remove the upper crossmember for the radiator (8) and the rubber insert (9).

* If the vehicle is produced after May 1998 disconnect the return pipe for the steering fluid (18) and the feed pipe (19).

- Remove the fan shroud (11) after disconnecting the connector plug.
- If air conditioning is fitted remove the condenser without disconnecting any of the pipes. On these vehicles also separate the fluid container (14) from the radiator (15). Push the assembly to one side.
- Remove the attachment parts (20) and the rubber damper (21). During installation it is possible that the rubber damper drops down. Take care.
- Detach the air guides (12), secured by mounting clips. The clips (13) should be replaced. Lift out the radiator (15).

The installation is a reversal of the removal procedure. The guide pins at the bottom of the radiator must enter the locating bores in the lower radiator crossmember. Finally fill the cooling system and start the engine. Check all connections for leaks. The headlamp setting must be checked (workshop recommended).

1.7.3.   WATER (COOLANT) PUMP

M111 engine (ML 230)

Fig. 1.110 shows the water pump and its attachment. The description refers to the numbers in the illustration.

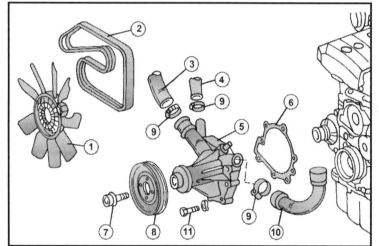

Fig. 1.110 – Parts to be removed during the removal of the water pump. The numbers are referred to in the text.

To remove the water pump proceed as follows:

- If fitted remove the viscous clutch (1) (see below).
- Drain the coolant from the radiator and the cylinder block.
- Disconnect the coolant hoses (3), (4) and (10) after slackening the hose clamps (9). Replace hoses and/or clamps if necessary.
- Remove the water pump pulley bolts (7) together with the washers and withdraw the water pump pulley (8). Tighten the bolts to 1.0 kgm (7.3 ft.lb.) during installation.
- Remove the Poly V-belt (2).
- Remove the bolts (11) and take off the water pump (5). The gasket (6) is not fitted to all engines.

The installation is a reversal of the removal procedure. Thoroughly clean the sealing faces. If no gasket (6) is fitted, coat the pump sealing face with sealing compound. Tighten the water pump securing bolts to 1.0 kgm (M6 bolts) or 2.5 kgm (M8 bolts).

M112 and M113 Engine (ML 320, ML350, ML430, ML500)

Details for the removal are shown in Fig. 1.111. The numbers are referred to in the description. Any parts (numbers) not mentioned are not fitted to ML models.

- Place the front end of the vehicle on secure chassis stands.
- Remove the viscous clutch (1). Not fitted to all engines, for example not in the case of the ML 500.
- Remove the fan shroud (3). In the case of the ML 500 remove the cooling fan.
- Drain the cooling system as described earlier on.
- Remove the Poly V-belt (2).

Cooling System

Fig. 1.111 – Removal and installation of water pump in the case of a V6 or V8 engine (M112 and M113).

1 Viscous fan
2 Poly V belt
3 Fan shroud
4 Coolant hose
5 Coolant hose
6 Coolant hose to oil/water heat exchanger
7 Water pump pulley
8 Water pump
9 Water pump gasket

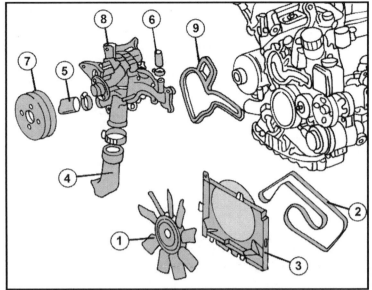

- Remove the water pump pulley (7). Hold the pulley against rotation by inserting a screwdriver blade between one of the bolts and the centre hub and remove the bolts securing the water pump pulley and withdraw the pulley. Tighten the pulley bolts to 0.9 kgm (7 ft.lb.) during installation.

- Remove the coolant hoses (4) and (5) in Fig. 1.111 and a further hose (6), the latter from the oil-water heat exchanger, after undoing the hose clamps from the water pump.

- Unscrew the water pump (8) from the timing case and remove it towards the bottom. Note the length of the different bolts.

The water pump cannot be overhauled.

The installation is a reversal of the removal procedure. Make sure that the sealing faces of coolant pump and timing case cover are free of oil or grease. Attach the new gasket (9) with two or three spots of sealing compound to the water pump housing. Tighten the M6 bolts securing the pump to the timing case to 1.4 kgm (10 ft.lb.) and the M8 bolts to 3.5 kgm (25 ft.lb.). The water pump pulley is tightened to 0.9 kgm.

Finally refill the cooling system, start the engine and check all parts belonging to the cooling system for leaks.

1.7.4.   DRIVE BELTS AND DRIVE BELT TENSION

A single drive belt, also known as poly V-belt, is fitted to the front of the engine, but the layout of the belt is not the same on all engines and depends on if fitted with an air conditioning system or a vehicle without A/C system. If a compressor is fitted it will also be driven by the same belt. The same belt drive system is, however, fitted to all engines and is held in its correct tension by means of an automatic tensioning device.

Different is also the length of the belt in the case of engines without A/C system or in the case of a fitted A/C system. If a new belt is fitted make sure your obtain the correct one.

The removal of the belt requires a drift or pin of 4 mm diameter or a 4 mm drill, the use of which is described in the following instructions. After the front of the engine has laid bare of all obstructing parts remove the belt as follows.

Four-cylinder Engines (M111)

The tensioning device of these engines is shown in Fig. 1.112. The housing (1 and the tensioning arm (2) are made of light-metal alloy. The tensioning force onto the tensioning arm is obtained by a spring between the housing and the arm. The spring is pre-tensioned. The tensioning device cannot be dismantled. Remove the belt as follows:

Fig. 1.112 – Details for the removal and installation of the drive belt. Also shown are the component parts of the tensioning device (four-cylinder, M111).

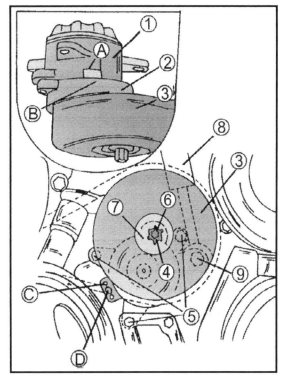

1 Tensioner housing
2 Tensioning arm
3 Tensioning roller
4 "Torx" head bolt
5 Bolts, tensioner to timing cover, 2.5 kgm
6 M11 nuts, roller to tensioning arm
7 Plastic cap
8 Damper
9 Bolt, damper to tensioning arm, 2.5 kgm
A Range of tensioner
B Marks
C Alignment bore
D Alignment bore

- Remove the viscous clutch as described later on.

- Before the belt is removed insert a pin or drift of 6 mm in diameter into the two bores "C" and "D" in Fig. 1.123. The tensioning arm (2) must be turned as far as possible towards the right to enable the pins/drift to be inserted.

- Rotate the tensioning arm (2) together with the tensioning roller (3) in anti-clockwise direction by applying a "Torx" head key into the head of screw (4). The belt can now be lifted off the various pulleys.

- When purchasing a new belt quote the engine capacity and the engine code. Fit the belt in the numbered order of Fig. 1.113, i.e. commence at the tensioning roller.

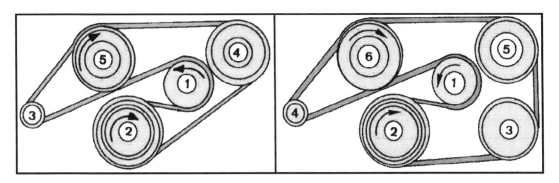

Fig. 1.113 – The layout of the drive belt of a four-cylinder engine (M111). On the left for vehicles without A/C system, on the right with A/C system.

On the left::
1 Tensioning roller
2 Crankshaft pulley
3 Alternator pulley
4 Steering pump pulley
5 Water pump pulley

On the right:
1 Tensioning roller
2 Crankshaft pulley
3 Compressor pulley
4 Alternator pulley
5 Steering pump pulley
6 Water pump pulley

- Reset the tensioning arm into its original position. Check the adjustment with the help of marks "A" and "B". Correctly adjusted the mark "B" must be within the adjustment range "A".

V6/V8 Engines (M112/M113)

Fig. 1.114 shows details of the installation of the belt.

Fig. 1.114 – Details for the removal and installation of the Poly V-belt.
1   Poly V-belt
2   Tensioning device
3   Pin or drift, 4 mm diameter
4   Belt tensioning roller

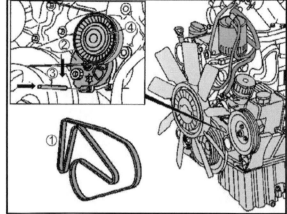

- Disconnect the battery earth cable.
- Refer to the L.H. view of Fig. 1.115 and turn the front part (1) of the pulley tensioning device against the spring force, i.e. turn it in the direction of the arrow. Then refer to the R.H. view and insert the pin (2) of 5 mm diameter (or drift, or drill shank) into the holes, positioned in line in the front part and in the housing (3) in order to lock the tensioning pulley (4) in this position. The V-belt can now be removed from the various pulleys.

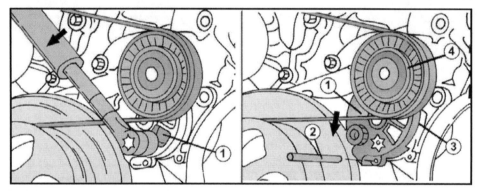

Fig. 1.115 – Removal of the Poly V-belt of a V6/V8 engine.

The installation is carried out as follows:
- Check the removed V-belt for damage and traces of wear before installation. Replace the belt if necessary, fitting the correct belt.
- Fit the V-belt (1) in Fig. 1.114, in all cases first over the tensioning pulley (4). Then depending on the version fit it over the remaining pulleys shown in Fig. 1.116. Make sure the belt engages with the grooves in the pulleys.

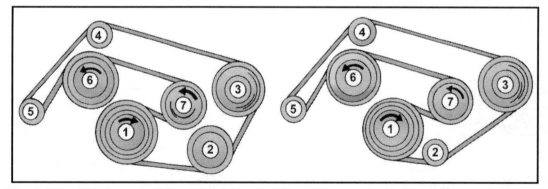

Fig. 1.116 – The layout of the drive belt of a V6 or V8 engine. On the left for models without A/C system, on the right with A/C system. Note the different pulleys (cont. next page).

On the left::
1   Crankshaft pulley
2   Guide pulley 3
3   Steering pump pulley

On the right:
1   Crankshaft pulley
2   Compressor pulley, A/C
3   Steering pump pulley

4 Guide pulley 1
5 Alternator pulley
6 Water pump pulley
7 Tensioning roller

4 Guide pulley 1
5 Alternator pulley
6 Water pump pulley
7 Tensioning roller

•   Refer to Fig. 1.117 and turn the front part (1) of the tensioning device sufficiently against the force of the spring (direction of the arrow, R.H. view) until it is possible to withdraw the inserted pin (2) or drift/drill bit, depending what has been used out of the holes in the front part (1) and the housing (3) of the tensioning device (3).

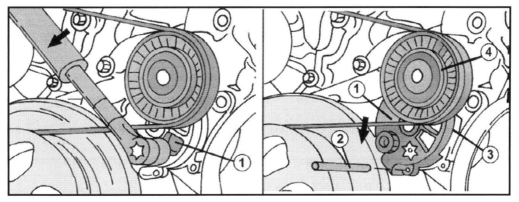

Fig. 1.117 – Details for the installation of the poly V-belt of a V6/V8 engine. The numbers refer to the description.

•   Slowly turn the front part (1) of the tensioning device in the L.H. view in the direction of the arrow until the V-belt is automatically tensioned by the force of the spring. The belt is now tensioned and no further operations are necessary. Rotate the crankshaft a few times before and re-check the belt drive before the removed parts are refitted.

272 Engine in ML 350 (Series 164)

The removal is fairly straight-forward. Pull out the front engine cover upwards and out of the mountings. Study the layout of the pulleys. Seen from the front you will see two larger pulleys. The bottom one belongs to the A/C compressor, the one immediately above to the power steering pump. Fig. 1.118 shows a view of the pulleys.

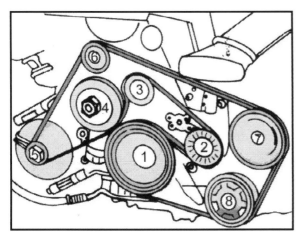

Fig. 1.118 – The layout of the drive belt of a 272 engine.
1   Crankshaft pulley
2   Tensioning pulley
3   Guide pulley
4   Water pump pulley
5   Alternator pulley
6   Guide pulley
7   Steering pump pulley
8   Compressor pulley (A/C)

The smaller pulley in the centre is the tensioning pulley (2). This pulley must be rotated in an anti-clockwise direction by applying a socket to the hexagon located under the pulley. Remove the Poly V-belt as soon as it is slack, but remember the routing.

1.7.5.   THERMOSTAT

The thermostat of a four-cylinder engine is fitted into a cover, where the large cooling hose is connected, as can be seen in Fig. 1.119. It should be noted that the thermostat cannot be removed from its cover, i.e. a new thermostat means that a complete cover must be fitted. The thermostat of a V6 or V8 engine is also fitted into a cover, where the large cooling hose is connected. The removal is in general for all engines.

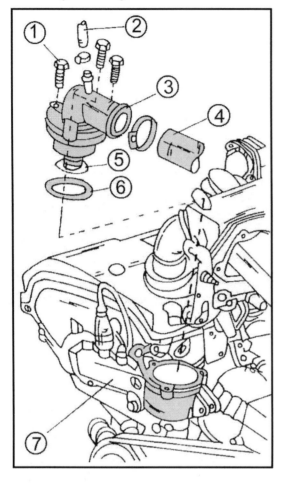

Fig 1.119 – Details for the removal and installation of the thermostat (M111, four-cylinder). Similar parts are fitted to the other engines, but note the differences given below.
1   Cover screw
2   Hose to expansion tank
3   Thermostat housing cover
4   Hose to radiator
5   Thermostat
6   Sealing ring
7   Thermostat housing

The thermostat can be removed after draining the cooling system. Disconnect the hoses (2) and (4) from the housing cover (3) after slackening the hose clamps. The cover can now be removed together with the thermostat..

Special notes for M272 Engine

To gain access to the thermostat is will be necessary to remove the Poly V-belt and the guide pulley (3) in Fig. 1.118 after the coolant hose has been disconnected from the coolant thermostat housing. Push the hose to one side. Underneath the thermostat housing you will find a connector plug (for a "three-disc thermostat valve") which must be withdrawn. Unscrew the bolts securing the thermostat housing and remove the housing with the integrated thermostat. Replace the "O" sealing ring (6) in Fig. 119 and the gasket In the case of the M272 engine.

The installation is a reversal of the removal procedure. Note the tightening torques: Thermostat housing V6 and V8 = 1.4 kgm (10 ft.lb.), M111/271 engine = 0.9 kgm (7 ft.lb.), 272 engine = 2.5 kgm (18 ft.lb.). On this engine tighten the V-belt guide pulley to the coolant pump to 3.5 kgm (25 ft.lb.).

The thermostat cannot be repaired and must be replaced as specified above.

1.7.6.   VISCOUS FAN CLUTCH – REMOVAL AND INSTALLATION

The clutch is maintenance-free and should have a trouble-free operation. To remove and install the clutch you will need a few special tools which can be seen in Fig. 1.120 and the tools must either be obtained or similar tools must be used. The same applies for the removal of the water pump as this requires the removal of the clutch.

Four-cylinder Engine (M111)

Remove the clutch as follows, referring to Fig. 1.120:

•   Set the bonnet into the vertical position and disconnect the battery.
•   Unscrew the nut (3) at the rear of the visco-clutch clockwise, as the nut has a left-hand thread. This will require the spanner shown in the illustration. This will require the special tool (1) which is inserted into the belt pulley. The tool is a peg spanner which is inserted with its pegs into the pulley. You may try to prevent the

pulley from rotating by pressing onto the belt. The nut is tightened to 4.0 kgm (29 ft.lb.) during installation.

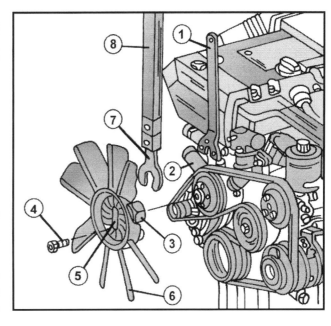

Fig. 1.120 – Details for the removal and installation of the visco-clutch of a four-cylinder M111 engine. Note how the special tools are used.
1 Counter-holding tool
2 Belt pulley
3 Nut, 4.0 kgm
4 Allen head bolt
5 Fan visco-clutch
6 Fan blades
7 Bolt to hold large nut
8 Extension for torque wrench

• Remove the clutch (5). If required remove the three bolts (4) securing the fan blades and take off the blades. The fan blades can only be fitted in one position. Bolts are tightened to 0.9 kgm (7 ft.lb.).

• During installation prevent the pulley from rotating as shown and tighten the nut. If the torque wrench (8) is not used you will have to estimate the torque.

V6/V8 Engines

The removal and installation of the viscous fan clutch (fluid coupling) presents no particular problems after access to the front of the engine has been created. The fan clutch is secured fan clutch is attached in a similar manner as, shown in Fig. 1.120, with one important difference – i.e. the nut (3) has RIGHT-HAND thread. The workshop uses a special open-ended spanner to apply to the securing nut to enable the application of a torque wrench, as shown in Fig. 1.120. Otherwise you will have to estimate the torque during installation. Proceed as follows:

Fig. 1.121 – The water pump pulley can be prevented from rotating as shown with the special counter-holder (1).

• Disconnect the battery earth cable, observing the necessary precautions.

• Counterhold the water pump pulley in suitable manner. The workshop uses as special counter holder which has two pin and can be inserted into two holes in the pulley, as shown in Fig. 1.121.

• Undo the union nut at the rear of the viscous fan as shown in Fig. 1.120 in the normal manner, as it has a R.H. thread and lift out the fan wheel (4) out of the engine compartment.

• If necessary remove the screws and take the fan wheel off the fluid clutch.

The installation is a reversal of the removal procedure. The installation position relative to the viscous fan clutch is fixed by the rib on the fan wheel. Attach the fan wheel with 1.0 kgm to the clutch and tighten the nut to 4.5 kgm (32.5 ft.lb.). The water pump drive wheel must again be prevented from rotating as described above.

1.8. Petrol Fuel Injection System

Different fuel injection systems are fitted to the engines covered in the manual. The four-cylinder M111 engine is fitted with a fuel injection system known as "HFM". The system operates in conjunction with the ignition system. The V6 and V8 engines are fitted with a fuel injection system known as "ME-SF5". An "ME-SF1" system can also be fitted. All systems operates in conjunction with the ignition system. The latter systems either have six or eight injection valves, which inject the fuel during starting speed up to 600 rpm and during acceleration at the same time into all cylinders. Both systems are made by Bosch.

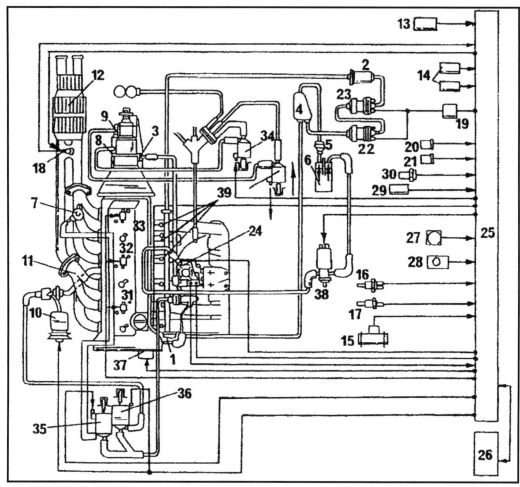

Fig. 1.122 – Schematic functional diagram of the injection system (four-cylinder).

1 Pressure regulator	11 Hot film air mass meter	21 ABS control unit
2 Fuel filter	12 Sensor, coolant temperature	22 Resistor, ECU
3 Vacuum element	13 Sensor, intake air temperature	23 CO potentiometer
4 Fuel tank	14 Lambda probe	24 Starter motor switch
5 Vent valve	15 Relay, fuel pump	25 Ignition coil (cyl. 1 and 4)
6 Charcoal filter	16 Sensor, crankshaft position	26 Ignition coil (cyl. 2 and 3)
7 Inlet manifold	17 Sensor, camshaft position	27 Switch-over valve (A/T)
8 Catalytic converter	18 Fuel pump	28 Solenoid valve
9 Compressor (A/C system)	19 Idle speed regulator	29 Injection valves
10 Sensor, anti-pinking	20 HFM control unit	

1.8.1. INJECTION SYSTEM - General

Fig. 1.122 shows the major component parts of the "HMF" system as fitted to four-cylinder engine. Fig. 1.123 shows a diagram of a V6 engine.

The system has four injection valves, which inject the fuel during starting speed up to 600 rpm and during acceleration at the same time into all four cylinders. As soon as the engine speed exceeds 600 rpm, two of the cylinders, i.e. No. 1 and 4 or No. 2 and 3 are supplied with the injected fuel at the same time. Special notes for the "HFM" system are given when applicable.

The electronic control unit calculates the duration of the injection in accordance with the operating conditions of the engine. The injected amount of fuel depends therefore on the opening time of the injection valves, which can be between 1.5 seconds and 130 milli-seconds. The vacuum in the inlet manifold, the engine speed, the coolant temperature and the intake air temperature are factors which contribute to the injection amount.

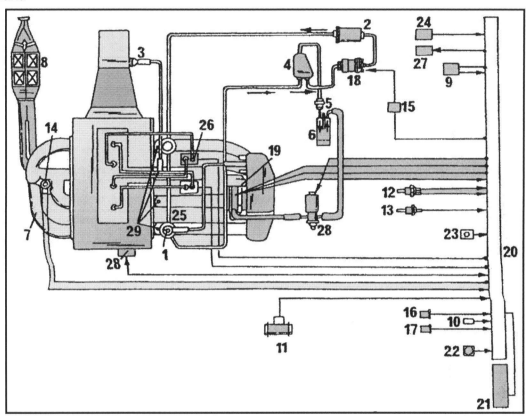

Fig. 1.123 – Schematic functional diagram of the HMF injection (V6 engine).

1 Pressure regulator	14 Detonation sensor	28 CO potentiometer
2 Fuel filter	15 Hot film air mass meter	29 Switch
3 Vacuum element	16 Sensor, coolant temperature	30 Overload switch
4 Fuel tank	17 Sensor, inlet air temperature	31 Ignition coil, cyl. 2 and 5
5 Vent valve	18 Heated Lambda probe	32 Ignition coil, cyl. 3 and 4
6 Charcoal filter	19 Relay, fuel pump	33 Ignition coil, cyl. 1 and 3
7 EGR valve (if fitted)	20 Sensor, crankshaft position	34 Switch-over valve (A/T)
8 Vacuum valve	21 Sensor, camshaft position	35 Switch-over valve (EGR)
9 Vacuum element	22 Fuel pump	36 Switch-over valve
10 Air injection pump	23 Fuel pump	37 Electro-magnetic unit
11 Exhaust manifold	24 Idle speed regulator	38 Switch-over valve
12 Catalytic converter	25 HMF control unit	39 Injection valve
13 Compressor (A/C)	26 ABS control unit	
	27 Hot film reference unit	

The engine speed is controlled by a speed limiter. If the engine speed exceeds 5650 rpm, the fuel is cut-off to the cylinders. The control unit will detect when the top gear is engaged by comparing the driving speed with the engine speed.

The fuel supply is also interrupted when the vehicle is coasting, i.e. the engine speed is higher than specified by the fitted gearbox, the idle speed switch is closed and a cruise control system (if fitted) is switched off. When the engine speed is again above 1100 rpm, fuel supply will resume and the fuel is injected once more into the two cylinders mentioned above.

General Note: Any work on the component parts of the injection system will require special instruments and equipment to adjust, measure and check important values. It is therefore recommended to leave any work to a dealer. The following description should be considered for information only. Not all items are mentioned.

Temperature Sender Unit
Fitted to the inlet manifold and monitors the intake air temperature.

Engine Speed Sensor
Monitors the engine speed for the ignition and injection parts of the system. Also informs the control unit of the crankshaft position and recognises the cylinder (see below).

Cylinder Identification Sensor, also camshaft position sensor
Informs the control unit which of the cylinders is being injected and is firing. Influenced by the automatic transmission, ABS control unit, cruise control system, Lambda probe, idle speed regulation and A/C system amongst them.

Injection valves
Fig. 1.124 shows the shape of an injection valve. The R.H. view shows a sectional view. The valves consist of the valve body (4) and the magnetic core (3). Located

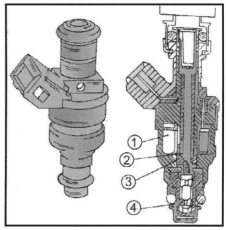

Fig. 1.124 – View of an injection valve on the left. The R.H. view shows a sectional view.
1   Electro-magnetic coil
2   Pressure spring
3   Magnet
4   Injection valve

inside the valve body are the electro-magnetic coil (1) and the guide bore for the valve needle. If the magnetic coil does not receive any current, the spring (2) will push against the valve needle against its seat and closes the fuel supply.

As soon as current flows through the magnetic coil, the valve needle will lift by the action of the magnetic core (3) pushing against the spring (2). The fuel is now injected through the two bores in the centre of the valve and enters the inlet valves of the engine.

Fuel Distribution Rail
Supplies all injection valves with fuel. Also serves as fuel reservoir and prevents pressure variation. Fuel inlet connection with filter and fuel return connection are also connected to the distribution rail.

Fuel Pressure Regulator
The regulator is situated at the rear of the fuel distribution rail and keeps the system pressure at a constant value.

Hot Film Air Mass Meter
This item is fitted to the "HFM" system from which is also receives its name, i.e. **H**ot **F**ilm **M**otor regulation. Fitted to the inlet tube between the air cleaner and the throttle valve part.

1.8.2. PRECAUTIONS WHEN WORKING ON THE SYSTEM

Always note the points listed below when carrying out any operations on the injection system and in this connection on the ignition system:

Attention: We advise that persons with a heart pacemaker should not work on the injection system.

*   Always switch off the ignition and disconnect the battery. When we refer to disconnecting the battery, always disconnect the negative cable and push it well away.
*   Never touch any connections, cable, leads, etc. when the engine is running, even when the engine is switched off, but the ignition is on.
*   Never disconnect or connect any electrical cables when the engine is running.

8.1.3. WORK TO BE CARRIED OUT ON THE M111 ENGINE

All work on the injection system should be left to a dealer or a workshop dealing with the injection system in question, as some special tools are required for most operations.

Some of the operations are described below and can be carried out with some knowledge.

In all cases read the instructions before commencing with the work.

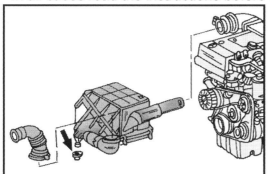

Fig. 1.125 – Installation of the air cleaner.

Air Cleaner and Air Cleaner Element

The installation of the air cleaner is shown in Fig. 1.125 on the example of the M111 engine. The air cleaner element should be replaced every two years. Removal and installation can be carried out by referring to the illustration. The air intake can be removed from the engine compartment, if required. If the air cleaner housing has been removed make sure that the guide pins at the bottom engage with the bores in the body. The hot film air mass meter must be removed in the case of the "HFM" system before the filter can be removed.

Fuel Distribution Rail – Removal and Installation

Fig. 1.126 shows a general view of parts to be removed.

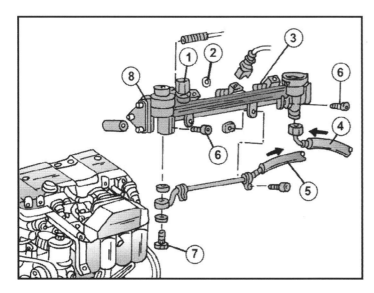

Fig. 1.126 – Removal and installation of the fuel distribution rail.
1   Service valve
2   "O" sealing rings
3   Injector valve
4   Fuel feed pipe
5   Fuel return pipe
6   Securing bolts
7   Banjo bolt
8   Distribution rail

As the system is under pressure, the necessary precautions must be taken to reduce the pressure. The workshop used a special service valve to reduce the pressure in the fuel rail which is screwed at position (1) into the rail. The distribution rail (8) can be removed after removal of the securing bolts (6). The "O" sealing rings must always be replaced. Oil them with oil before installation.

Disconnect the fuel feed line (4). Take care as fuel may splash out. The union nut is tightened to 2.4 kgm (18 ft.lb.). Also remove the banjo bolt (5) and unscrew the pipe. The two sealing rings must be replaced.

Installation is carried out in reverse order.

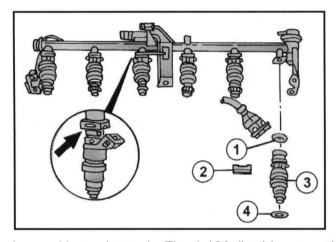

Fig. 1.127 – View of the fuel distributor rail together with the injection valves.
1 "O" sealing ring
2 Locking tab
3 Injection valve
4 "O"M sealing ring

Injection valves – Removal and Installation

The injection valves are removed together with the fuel distribution rail as described above. After removal you will see the valves at the positions shown in Fig, 1.126 (in this case shown on a six-cylinder engine). The valves are secured by means of a locking tab (2) which must be removed. The "O" sealing rings (1) and (4) must always be replaced.

Inlet Manifold – Removal and Installation

Obviously a comprehensive operation, but it may be necessary to remove the manifold in order to carry out other operations. Fig. 1.128 shows details and will help. The battery must be disconnected.

- Remove the fuel distribution rail and the injection valves as already described.
- Disconnect all vacuum pipes/hoses and electrical leads from the engine. Mark their connections if necessary.
- Withdraw the connector plug from the crankshaft position sensor and any other plug you may feel is in the way.

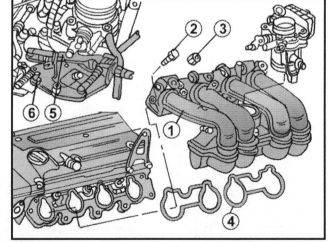

Fig. 1.128 – Details for the removal and installation of the inlet manifold (M111 engine)
1 Inlet manifold
2 Bolt
3 Nut
4 Gaskets
5 Connecting linkage
6 Bolt

- Disconnect the cables from the starter motor.
- Remove the throttle operating unit from inlet manifold. To do this remove the bolts (6) and unclip the throttle valve cable. The connecting linkage (5) must be separated.
- Remove the bolts (2) and the nuts (3) and take off the manifold (1). Check the gaskets (4) and replace them if necessary.

The installation is a reversal of the removal procedure. Nuts and bolts are tightened to 2.0 kgm (14.5 ft.lb.).

Important Note: If possible have the work carried out in a workshop.

8.1.4. WORK TO BE CARRIED OUT ON THE V-ENGINES

With some experience you may be able to carry out the following operations. We suggest to read the instructions before commencing with any of the jobs. The instructions apply to the M112 and M113 engines.

Lambda Probes

The workshop uses a special wrench (No. 000 589 71 03 00) to remove the Lambda probes (oxygen sensors). This is a long socket with a cut on one side which can be guided over the cable connection. Each catalytic converter has two probes, one before the converter and one behind it. Remove them as follows (battery disconnected).

- Follow the cable run to the connection on the Lambda probe and withdraw the connector plugs. Four plugs must be withdrawn (if all sensors are to be removed).
- Unscrew the Lambda probe(s) with the wrench mentioned above or with an open-ended spanner which can be applied to the hexagon. Withdraw the sensor.
- Coat the new Lambda probe with a heat-resistant grease (you may be able to obtain some in a workshop). The sensors are tightened to 4.5 kgm (32.5 ft.lb.). No problem if the special wrench is used, as a torque spanner can be applied. Otherwise the torque must be estimated.
- The remaining operations are carried out in reverse order.

Fuel Distribution Rail – Removal and Installation

 Fig. 1.129 shows the parts to be removed. As the system is under pressure, the necessary precautions must be taken to reduce the pressure. The workshop used a special service valve to reduce the pressure in the fuel rail which is screwed at position (1) into the rail. The actual removal presents no problems, but it may be more difficult to locate the various parts. The following description will try to pin-point the location. The description assumes that the engine is seen from the side, with the oil filler cap on the R.H. side.

- Disconnect the battery.
- Remove the air cleaner housing.

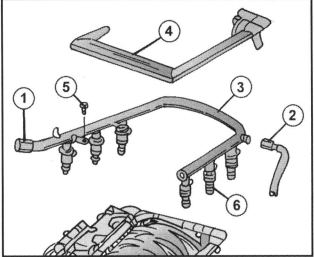

Fig. 1.129 – Details for the removal and installation of the fuel rail, shown here in the case of a V6 engine. The numbers are referred to in the text.

- Remove a clamp screw and disconnect the air intake hose from the air mass meter.
- Disconnect the fuel pipe (2). The union nut is tightened to 3.8 kgm (27 ft.lb.).
- Remove the connector plug from the ignition coil (L.H. side of engine).
- Disconnect the vent hose from the L.H. and R.H. cylinder head cover.
- Withdraw the connector plug from the camshaft Hall sensor. Looking at the engine, you will find the sensor at the left, lower end. In the same area there is another plug. Also withdraw it.
- Cut a cable binder at the distribution pipe (3) – always replace it.

Injection System

- Remove the plastic cover (4) from the distribution pipe.
- Remove the bolts (5) securing the pipe to the inlet manifold (1.0 kgm) and remove the pipe together with the injection valves (6) towards the top. Withdraw the connectors from the valves and take out the pipe. If a new distributor pipe is to be fitted you can transfer the injection valves to the new pipe.

The installation is a reversal of the removal procedure, noting the specified tightening torques.

Injection Valves – Removal and Installation

The injection valves are secured by clips. The fuel distribution pipe must be removed to replace an injection valve. The remaining instructions refer to Fig. 1.130.

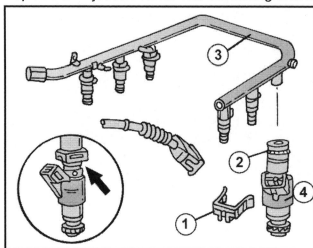

Fig. 1.130 – Removal and installation of injection valves of an M112 or M113 engine. Shown is a V6 engine.
1 Securing clip
2 Sealing washer
3 Fuel distribution pipe
4 Injection valve

After removal of the clip (1) the injection valve (4) can be withdrawn out of the distribution pipe (3). The sealing washer (2) at the end of the injection valve must always be replaced. Oil the new sealing rings and push the valve or valves into the bore. The securing clip must engage into a cut-out into the injection valve (marked with arrow).

Inlet manifold – Removal and Installation

A time consuming operation. As the inlet manifold must be removed to carry out other operations we will give you a short description. Fig. 1.131 shows the attachment of the manifold and will help you during removal and installation. The battery must be disconnected. The system must be free of pressure.

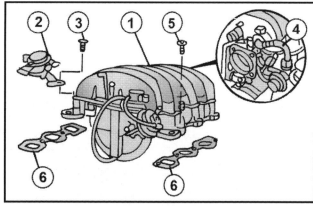

Fig. 1.131 – Attachment of the inlet manifold in the case of a V6 engine.
1 Inlet manifold
2 Shut-off valve
3 Bolt
4 Fuel line, 3.8 kgm
5 Bolt, 2.0 kgm
6 Manifold gaskets

As the fuel distribution pipe and the injection valves must be removed refer to the instructions already given. Also remove the hot film air mass meter, the air intake pipe and all pipes connected to the manifold.

The inlet manifold can now be removed by referring to Fig. 1.131. The bolts are tightened to 2.0 kgm (14.5 ft.lb.), the gaskets (6) must always be replaced.

Air Cleaner and Air Cleaner Element

The removal and installation as carried out as described in a similar manner as described for the M111 engine. The air intake hose can be removed after slackening the clamp screw on the air cleaner housing.

1.9. Ignition System

Although the ignition system operates together with the injection system, there are some details which will be given in short below.

The ignition part of the injection system fitted to the M111 engine corresponds basically to the known "EZL" system, but the high tension distributor has been replaced by two of the respective number of the required ignition coils. Depending on the engine you will find the coils at the positions shown in Figs. 1.132 and 1.133.

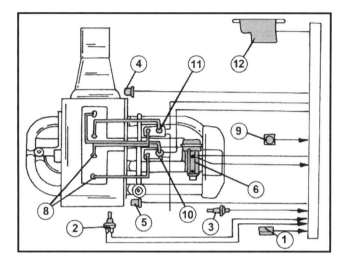

Fig. 1.132 – Functional diagram of the ignition system as fitted to a four-cylinder M111 engine.

1 Detonation (pinking) sensor
2 Sensor, coolant temperature
3 Sensor, intake air temperature
4 Sensor, crankshaft position
5 Sensor, camshaft position
6 Idle speed regulator
7 HFM control unit
8 Spark plug
9 HFM reference resistor
10 Ignition coil, Nos. 1 and 4
11 Ignition coil, Nos. 2 and 3
12 Diagnostic test socket

1.9.0. IGNITION COILS

To gain access to the ignition coil, the air cleaner housing must be removed on some of the engines (M272 engine for example). On other models (V6 and V8) unclip the cover at the front side of the engine. Remove the coils after removal of the bolt (1) in Fig, 1.133. On M112 and M113 engines first disconnect the spark plug connectors (3), on the M272 engine detach the ignition coil with the spark plug connector and then disconnect the connector.

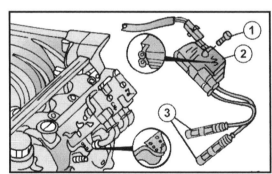

Fig. 1.133 – Location of the ignition coil of an M112 and M113 engine (V6 and V8) in model series 163. The circled details refer to the connector identification.

1   Bolt, 0.8 kgm
2   Ignition coil, No. 1 to 8
3   Spark plug connector

The ignition coils of an M111 engine are removed by referring to Fig. 1.134. Coil (1) supplies the current for cylinders No. 1 and

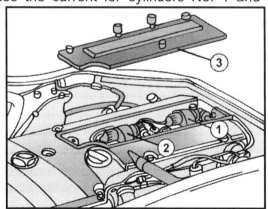

No. 4, coil (2) for cylinders No. 2 and 3. The cover (3) must be removed to gain access to the coils.

Fig. 1.134 – Location of the double spark ignition coils (1) and (2) in the case of an M111 engine fitted to model series 163 (ML 230). The cover (3) must be removed.

1.9.1. IGNITION TIMING

As already mentioned, there are no

provisions to adjust the ignition timing point, as the timing point is controlled automatically in conjunction with the fuel injection system. The timing point can be checked in a workshop, but electronic test instruments are required. Ignition timing point, idle speed and CO content are measured at the same time.

1.9.2. SPARK PLUGS

If spark plugs are removed, make sure that the surrounding area is clean to prevent foreign matter from falling into the plug holes as soon as the plugs are unscrewed. Suitably mark the plug leads to facilitate their re-connection. We must point out that a special plug spanner is used to remove the plugs in a workshop. Clean the plug face with a wire brush and check the electrodes for wear or burns. The removal of the plugs is fairly straight-forward.

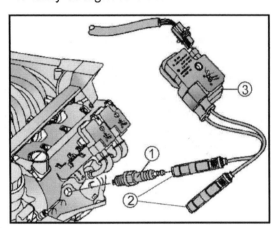

Fig. 1.135 – Remove the spark plug connectors (2) before removal of the plugs (1) – V6/V8 engines.

V6/V8 Engines (M112/M113/272)

Fig. 1.135 shows one side of the engine with the location of the plugs (1) and their connectors (2) and their connection to the ignition coil (3). In the case of the M272 engine the ignition coils must be removed before the spark plugs are unscrewed. If spark plugs are removed, make sure that the surrounding area is clean to prevent foreign matter from falling into the plug holes as soon as the plugs are unscrewed. We must point out that a special plug spanner (No. 112 589 01 09 00) is used to remove the plugs in a workshop. Clean the plug face with a wire brush and check the electrodes for wear or burns.

Remove the plugs as follows, referring to Fig. 1.135 for details of the installation.

- Disconnect the battery.
- Remove the top part of the air cleaner housing (if necessary).
- Remove the spark plug connectors (2). Mark their position if not sure.
- Unscrew the plugs with the special wrench specified above or another suitable plug spanner and an extension.

During installation fit the spark plug by hand as far as they will go and then tighten them to 2.8 kgm (20 ft.lb.) – 2.3 kgm (16.5 ft.lb.) specified for the M272 engine. Reconnect the connector plugs. All other operations are carried out in reverse order.

All Engines

Use a feeler gauge to check the electrode gap and close the gap if necessary, by tapping the outside electrode with the handle of a screwdriver. To open up a plug gap, insert the blade of a small screwdriver and bend up the side electrode. Never bend the centre electrode in order to correct plug gaps as this will damage the insulator. Either Beru, Bosch, NGK or Champion plugs are fitted during production. The electrode gap on Champion plugs is 1.1 mm, on the other plugs 1.0 mm.

Note: Spark plugs are sometimes changed. Always ask for the latest plugs if buying new ones. Tighten the spark plugs, if possible, with a torque wrench to a torque setting of 2.8 kgm (20 ft.lb.) in the case of a V6/V8 engine and the 271 engine or 2.3 kgm (16.5 ft.lb.) in the case of the 272 engine.

Note: Spark plugs are sometimes changed. The above types only shows typical spark plugs used in the engines.

Inspect the condition of the insulator tip and the electrodes. Following there are a few examples to interpret the condition of plugs removed from the engine.

Normal Plug Face: The colour of the of the insulator should appear greyish-brown or tan-coloured. The electrodes should be black or sooted. These are signs of a plug which has been used under normal conditions with alternative short and long driving periods. White or yellow deposits mean that the car has been used for long periods at high speeds and can be ignored.

Worn Plug Appearance: Insulator tip and electrodes are burnt off. All plugs which show this condition must be replaced. Always replace the whole set and make sure to fit the correct plug.

Oiled-up Appearance: Normally this condition is recognised by wet oil deposits which have been left by excessive ingress of oil into the combustion chamber (worn piston rings or pistons, inlet valves or valve guides, worn bearings, etc.). Hotter plugs are normally able to overcome the fault, but in serious cases an overhaul of the engine is necessary.

Burnt or Overheated Appearance: Burnt or overheated plugs can normally be recognised by their electrodes being coloured white or being burnt, or by the presence of blisters on the insulator or the electrodes. Electrodes may also be burnt off. Faults can be traced to the cooling system or improper ignition timing.

2   CLUTCH

2.0.   Introduction

Only the ML230 is fitted with a clutch and a manual transmission, but note that two different transmissions (type 716 and 717) can be fitted, each with a different clutch operating system. The clutch is operated by means of a hydraulic system. Pressure is generated by the depressing of the clutch pedal and transmitted via the clutch master cylinder to a so-called central clutch operator inside the clutch bell housing which takes the place of the clutch slave cylinder but incorporates the clutch release bearing, in the case of transmission type 716 or with a slave cylinder and a separate clutch release bearing in the case of type 717 (CDI models). We refer you to your MB parts department if the clutch must be replaced, quoting the engine type and engine number.

2.1.   Technical Data

Type:	Single plate, dry clutch with diaphragm spring.
Clutch operation:	By hydraulic system (see below)
Pedal adjustment:	Automatic take-up.
Clutch release bearing	Sealed ball-type bearing in constant contact with the clutch plate, incorporated in sealed clutch operator or as described above.

2.2   Clutch Unit

2.2.0.   CHECKING THE CLUTCH OPERATION

The clutch can be checked for proper operation when fitted to the vehicle. To do this, proceed as follows:

- Start the engine and allow to idle. Depress the clutch pedal and wait approx. 3 secs. Engage the reverse gear. If grating noises can be heard from the transmission, it can be assumed the clutch or driven plate needs replacement, as the driven plate no longer connects the clutch pressure plate with the flywheel.

- To check the clutch for signs of slipping, drive the vehicle until the clutch and transmission have reached operating temperature. Stop the vehicle, firmly apply the handbrake and engage the 3rd gear. Keep the clutch pedal fully depressed and accelerate the engine to approx. 3000 - 4000 rpm. Release the clutch pedal suddenly. The clutch operates satisfactorily if the engine stalls immediately.

2.2.0.   REMOVAL AND INSTALLATION

Important Note: Pressure plate and diaphragm spring cannot be dismantled and must be replaced together. Clutches and driven plates are sometimes modified to improve their operation. If a new clutch or driven plate is purchased always quote the model and the engine type and number.

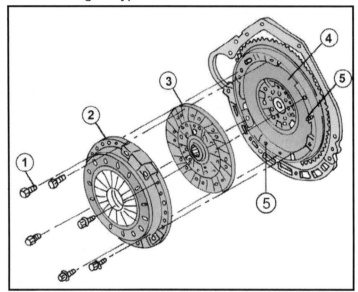

Fig. 2.1 – The component parts of the clutch. All clutches look similar.
1   Clutch securing bolts
2   Clutch pressure plate
3   Clutch driven plate
4   Flywheel
5   Dowel pins

The clutch cannot be removed without removing the transmission. Removal of the transmission is described in section "Manual Transmission". The operations are the same on all models. After the clutch has been removed you will have the parts shown in Fig. 2.1.

- Remove the engine and transmission or the transmission (Section 3.1).
- Mark the clutch in its fitted position on the flywheel if there is a possibility that the clutch unit is re-used. To remove the clutch, unscrew the six bolts (1) in Fig. 2.1, securing the pressure plate (2) to the flywheel (4) and lift off the clutch unit and then the driven plate (3), now free. Before removing the driven plate, note the position of the longer part of the driven plate hub, as the driven plate must be refitted in the same way. Note that the clutch plate is located in position by means of the dowel pins (5).
- Immediately check the friction face of the flywheel, as it is possible that the rivets of the driven plate have left their mark on the flywheel face if the linings have worn excessively.
- Check the separate clutch release bearing or the central clutch operator, depending which type is fitted and replace as necessary.

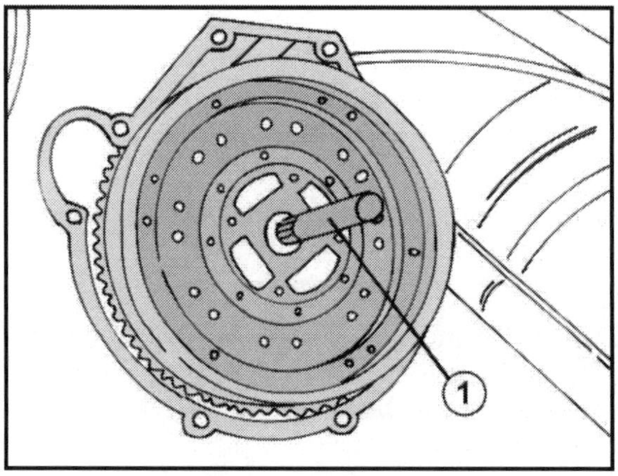

Fig. 2.2 – The clutch centring mandrel (1) is inserted into the driven plate.

Install in the reverse sequence to removal, noting the following points:

- If the old clutch unit is fitted, align the marks made before removal. A new clutch can be fitted in any position.
- Coat the splines of the clutch drive shaft with a little Molykote BR2 grease.
- A centring mandrel is required to centre the clutch driven plate inside the flywheel. Tool hire companies normally have sets of mandrels for this purpose. An old transmission (clutch) shaft for the transmission in question, which you may be able to obtain from a Mercedes workshop, can also be used. Experienced D.I.Y. mechanics will also be able to align the clutch plate without the help of a mandrel. Insert the mandrel as shown in Fig. 2.2. Fit the clutch pressure plate (2) over the dowel pins (5) in Fig. 2.1.
- Fit and tighten the six clutch to flywheel bolts (1) to a torque reading of 2.5 kgm (18 ft.lb.), in gradual steps. The flywheel must be locked against rotation when the clutch bolts are tightened.
- Refit the engine and transmission or the transmission and operate the clutch pedal at least 5 times before the engine is started.

Fig. 2.3. – To check the driven plate for run-out, clamp it between the centres of a lathe and check with a dial gauge.

2.3.　Servicing

The cover assembly – pressure plate and diaphragm spring – must not be dismantled. Replace, if necessary with a complete assembly from your dealer or distributor.

Inspect the driven plate and the linings, replacing the complete plate if the linings are worn down close to the rivets. A driven plate with the linings contaminated with grease or oil cannot be cleaned successfully and should also be replaced. All rivets should be tight and the torsion springs should be sound and unbroken.

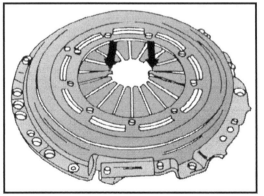

Fig. 2.4 – The "fingers" of the diaphragm spring can wear at the positions shown. All must be at the same height.

Check the condition of the driven plate splines. Clamp the driven plate between the centres of a lathe and apply a dial gauge to the outside of the plate as shown in Fig. 2.3, at a diameter of approx. 175.0 mm (6.4 in.). The max. run/out of the driven plate should be no more than 0.5 mm (0.02 in.).

Check the rivet fastening of the clutch pressure plate and replace the plate if loose rivets can be detected. The fingers of the diaphragm spring must all be at the same height. It may be possible to bend them slightly with a pair of pliers, but renewal is always the best remedy.

Check the inner ends of the clutch plate at the position shown in Fig. 2.4. If wear is detected (more than 0.3 mm) replace the clutch unit.

Place a straight edge (steel ruler) over the friction face of the pressure plate and insert feeler gauges between the ruler and the surface. If the gap at the innermost spot of the friction face is no more than 0.03 mm (0.012 in.), the plate can be re-used. Fig. 2.5 shows this check.

Clutch

Fig. 2.5 – Checking the clutch pressure plate for distortion. The gap should not be more than given below.

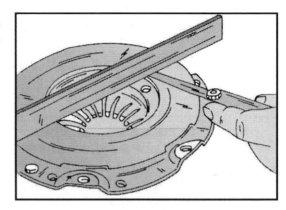

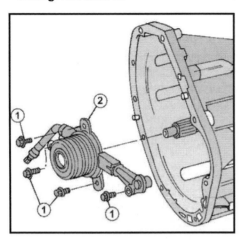

Fig. 2.6 – Attachment of the central clutch operator inside the gearbox housing. The numbers are referred to during the removal instructions.

2.4.   Clutch Release Mechanism

Engagement and disengagement of the clutch is by means of the central clutch operator inside the transmission housing with incorporated clutch release bearing if a transmission of type 716 is fitted. A separate clutch release bearing is fitted to the 717 transmission. The system is free of clearance and any wear of the driven plate is automatically compensated by the system.

2.4.0.   HYDRAULIC CLUTCH OPERATOR – REMOVAL AND INSTALLATION – 6 speed transmission

Precautions when working with Brake Fluid

As the hydraulic system is filled with brake fluid read the notes below before any operations are carried out on the hydraulic clutch system.

*   Only store brake fluid in a closed container, tin, etc. which must be marked accordingly. Brake fluid can damage your health if swallowed.
*   Protect your hands with gloves and if possible your eyes with goggles. If your hands come into contact with brake fluid immediately wash them with water and soap.
*   Take care not to drip brake fluid onto painted areas of the vehicle. Brake fluid will damage the paint. If it happens, wipe it off immediately.
*   Brake fluid is able to absorb moisture from the air. This is the reason that it must be kept in a closed container.
*   Even the smallest quantity of oil in the brake fluid can damage the rubber parts of the hydraulic system.
*   Brake fluid released from the system, as is the case during the bleeding operation, must not be re-used to top-up the fluid reservoir.

The transmission must be removed to gain access to the hydraulic clutch operator. Fig. 2.6 shows the attachment of the parts in question. With the transmission removed unscrew the four bolts (1) and take off the central clutch operator (2) from the gearbox (3).

Check the clutch release bearing for noises, rough operation, leakage or wear and replace the complete assembly if necessary.

The installation is carried out in reverse order. Use new micro-encapsulated bolts (1). Tighten the bolts to 1.0 kgm (7 ft.lb.). Mercedes-Benz recommends to use a suitable thread cutter to re-cut the bolt threads inside the gearbox housing before the clutch operator is fitted. After installation of the gearbox bleed the clutch system as described further on in the text.

2.4.1.   CLUTCH RELEASE BEARING

Fitted to transmission type 717.

On this arrangement the engagement and disengagement of the clutch is by means of the slave cylinder push rod, acting on the clutch release lever and sliding the ball bearing-type release bearing along a guide tube on the clutch shaft of the transmission. The release system is free of play, as the wear of the clutch linings is compensated automatically.

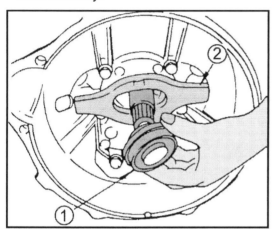

Fig. 2.7 – Removal of the clutch release bearing (1) from the release lever (2).

The transmission must be removed to replace the release bearing. Remove the bearing from the bearing sleeve on the front transmission housing cover, as shown in Fig. 2.7. To remove the release fork, refer to Fig. 2.8 and move it in direction of arrow (a) and then pull it from the ball pin in the clutch housing in direction of arrow (b).

Thoroughly grease the guide sleeve on the front transmission cover, the ball pin and all of the parts of the release mechanism in contact with the release bearing with long term grease. Push the release lever in reverse direction of arrow (b) over the ball pin until the spring clip of the release lever engages with the ball pin. Check for secure fitting. Then move the lever in reverse direction of arrow (a) until the slave cylinder push rod is engaged with the ball-shaped cut-out in the release lever.

Fig. 2.8 – Removal and installation of the clutch release lever (see text).
1 Ball pin   2 Release lever

Grease the release bearing on the inside and on both sides at the rear, where it rests against the release lever and slip the bearing over the guide sleeve. Rotate the bearing until it snaps in position into the release lever. Check that the bearing is properly fitted and refit the transmission.

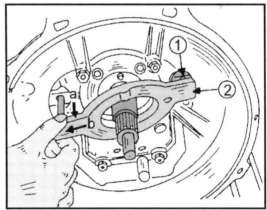

2.4.2.   CLUTCH SLAVE CYLINDER – 717 Transmission

The clutch slave cylinder is fitted to the side of the transmission. The cylinder can be removed as follows:

- Unscrew the fluid pipe from the slave cylinder, using an open-ended spanner. Close the end of the pipe in suitable manner to prevent fluid leakage (rubber cap for bleeder screw).

- Remove the two cylinder securing screws and take off the cylinder. Observe the fitted shim.
- When fitting, insert the shim with the grooved side against the clutch housing and hold in position. Fit the slave cylinder, engaging the push rod into the ball-shaped cut-out of the clutch release lever, and insert the two screws. Tighten the screws. Finally bleed the clutch system as described in the next section.

2.4.3. CLUTCH MASTER CYLINDER

As the removal and installation of the clutch master cylinder is a complicated operation and the cylinder will have a long service life, we suggest to have the cylinder replaced in a workshop.

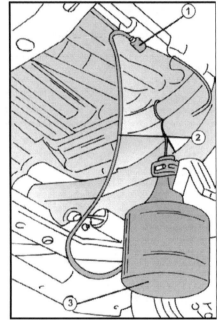

Fig. 2.9 – The bleeding screw (1) is located on the side of the gearbox if a central clutch operator is fitted. The attached bleeder hose (2) is inserted into a glass jar (3).

2.5. Bleeding the Clutch System

A pressure bleeder is used by Mercedes workshops. The following description involves the brake system and is therefore to be treated with caution.

Make absolutely sure that the brakes have correct operating pressure after the clutch has been bled. A transparent hose of approx. 1 metre (3 ft.) in length is required. Proceed as follows, noting that the bleed hose is connected:

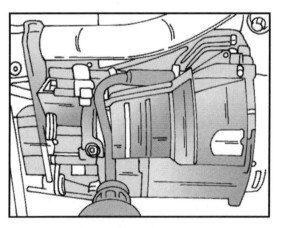

Fig. 2.10 –
The bleeding screw is located at the end of the clutch slave cylinder, if one is fitted.

- Fill the brake/clutch fluid reservoir.

Remove the dust cap of the bleeder screw in the side opening of the gearbox, shown in Fig. 2.9 or as shown in Fig. 2.10, if a slave cylinder is fitted, and push the hose over the bleeder screw and place the hose end into a glass container filled with some brake fluid. Open the bleeder screw.

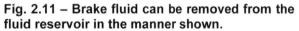

Fig. 2.11 – Brake fluid can be removed from the fluid reservoir in the manner shown.

- Ask a second person to operate the brake pedal until the hose is completely filled with brake fluid and no more air bubbles can be seen in the glass container. Place a finger over the hose end to prevent fluid from running out.
- Tighten the bleed screw and remove the hose from the end of the screw.

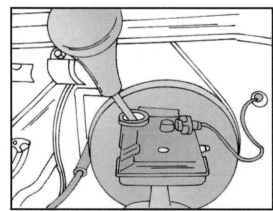

•   Check the fluid level in the reservoir and, If necessary, top it up to the "Max." mark. Do not overfill. If necessary extract some fluid in the manner shown in Fig. 2.11. Start the engine, depress the clutch pedal and engage reverse. No grating noises should be heard.

2.6.   Clutch Faults

Below we list some faults which may occur in connection with the clutch. The faults are not directed specifically to the models covered in this manual.

A Slipping Clutch
1 Clutch plate slipping   Replace driven plate
2 Clutch pressure too low   Replace clutch unit
3 Clutch plate linings full of oil   Replace driven plate, find oil leak
4 Clutch overheated   Replace driven plate, maybe clutch plate
5 Hydraulic operator leaking   Replace central clutch operator

B Clutch will not release
1 Air in the system   Bleed clutch system
2 Master cylinder or operator leaks   Replace cylinder in question
3 Distorted clutch driven plate   Replace driven plate
4 Driven plate linings broken   Replace driven plate
5 Driven plate jammed on shaft   Investigate and rectify
6 Clutch plate lining sticking on   Engage 1st gear and depress clutch
   flywheel (after long lay off)   pedal. Have the vehicle towed a short
                                         distance, with ignition switched off

C Clutch jerky
1 Refer to point A3
2 Wrong driven plate (after repair)   Check and rectify
3 Release bearing defect   Replace central clutch operator
4 Pressure plate has uneven pressure   Replace pressure plate
5 Engine/gearbox mountings defect   Check and if necessary replace

D Clutch does not release and slips
1 Clutch pressure plate damaged   Replace pressure plate

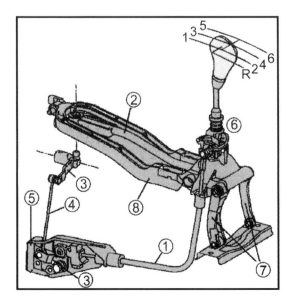

Fig. 3.1 – The component parts of the gear change mechanism of the six-speed transmission "716".
1   Selector cable
2   Shift rod
3   Transfer lever
4   Selector rod
5   Bracket
6   Floor shaft
7   Swivel lever
8   Coupling arm

3	Manual Transmission

Only the ML 230 model covered in this manual are either fitted with a five-speed transmission, with the technical designation type "717". The type is important when it is intended to fit a second-hand transmission during the life-span of your vehicle, mainly as other models in the ML range of vehicles can be fitted with a six-speed transmission of type "716". The transmission is also identified by different letters/numbers which can be identified details available from supplier. Fig. 3.1 shows the layout of the gear change mechanism.

The overhaul of the transmission is not described in this manual. The description in the overhaul section is limited to some minor repair operations, not involving the gear train or the gear shafts. If the transmission appears to be damaged or faulty, try to obtain an exchange unit. Transmission overhaul is now limited to specialised workshops which are equipped with the necessary special tools.

3.0.   Technical Data

Fitted transmission:.. 717- different end numbers

Transmission Ratios: **ML 230 (163)**
- First gear: 3.860 : 1
- Second speed: 2.183 : 1
- Third speed: 1.380 : 1
- Fourth speed: 1.000 : 1
- Fifth speed: 0.800 : 1
- Reverse speed: 4.222 : 1
- Axle ratio: 4.730: 1

Oil capacity: ....1.5 litres
Lubrication oil: As in automatic transmissions

3.1.   Removal and Installation

The following text describes the general removal and installation operations. The transmission is heavy and the necessary precautions must be taken when it is lifted out. We must point out that the transfer case must be removed before the actual transmission can be removed, irrespective of the type of transmission (five-speed, six speed or automatic). The battery must be disconnected.

Refer to Fig. 3.2 to remove the transfer case as follows:

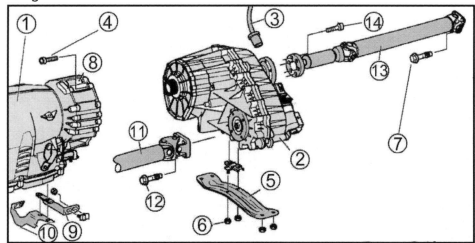

Fig. 3.2 – Details for the removal and installation of the transfer case (all transmissions). See text.

- Place the front end of the vehicle on chassis stands and remove the rear section of the sound-proofing panel underneath the vehicle.
- Unscrew the exhaust bracket (9) and the bracket (10) from the exhaust.

Fig. 3.3 – Removal and installation details for the transmission (716).
1 Transmission
2 Safety bolt
3 Shift rod
4 Shift rod
5 Gear change lever
6 Hydraulic pipe
7 Pipe securing lock (retainer)
8 Transmission bolts

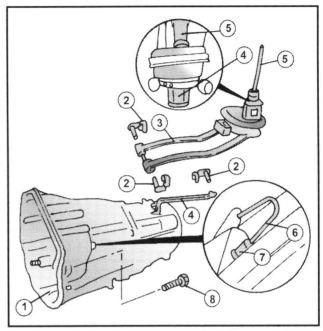

- Remove the bolts (14) and separate the propeller shaft (13) from the flange on the transfer case (2). The shaft can be removed after removal of bolts (7). Tighten the bolts to 4.0 kgm (29 ft.lb.) during installation when connecting to the case and rear axle. Then remove the bolts (12) and remove the propeller shaft (11) from the transfer case. Use a wire sling, push the shafts to one side and tie them up to the underbody. Take care not to damage the shaft universal joint and in the case of shaft (13) the joint and the centre bearing. Note that these bolts are tightened to 5.0 kgm (25 ft.lb.) when connecting to the front axle. In both cases new bolts must be fitted. Also remove the starter motor.
- Detach the plug connector (3) from the actuator motor (if fitted).
- Place a mobile jack or other lifting device underneath the transmission and remove the rear engine crossmember (5) with the engine mounting. The nuts (6) securing the rear crossmember to the body are tightened to 4.0 kgm (29 ft.lb.). The same torque applies when the engine mounting is fitted.
- Slightly lower the transmission unit and now support and lift the transfer case (2) on the jack. The workshop uses a plate to lift the case. Remove the bolts (4) and withdraw the case from the adapter housing (8) towards the rear (carefully).

The installation of the transfer case is carried out in reverse order. Tighten the bolts (4) to 2.0 kgm (14.5 ft.lb.), irrespective of the fitted transmission. Before installation check the oil level in the transfer case. The oil must be to the bottom edge of the filler plug opening. The plug is tightened to 3.0 kgm (22 ft.lb.).

Continue with the removal of the transmission as follows. Refer to Fig. 3.3. The instructions are based on a transmission of type "716":
- Unhook and pull out a so-called "safety bolt" (2) and unhook the shift rod (3) from shift (gear change) mechanism on the transmission (1).
- Remove the "safety bolt" (2) out of the shift rod (4) and separate the linkage. Separate the linkage (4) on the other side from the gear change lever (5).
- On one side of the transmission remove the pipe securing lock (7) and withdraw the hydraulic pipe (6) out of the transmission. Some fluid may run out. Seal off the end of the pipe in suitable manner.
- Disconnect the connector plug from the reversing light switch and other plugs at the rear end of the transmission.

- Disconnect the electrical leads from the starter motor, remove the starter motor mounting bolts and withdraw the starter motor from the engine and transmission.
- Place the jack underneath the transmission and lift it up slightly.
- Remove the transmission-to-crankcase bolts (8). The two upper bolts are removed last.
- Rotate the transmission towards the left and remove it horizontally towards the rear and away from the clutch housing before it is lowered. Make absolutely sure that the clutch shaft has disengaged from the clutch driven plate before the gearbox is lowered. Failing to observe this can lead to distortion of the clutch shaft or damage to the driven plate.

The installation of the gearbox is carried out as follows:
- Coat the dowel pin and the clutch shaft splines with long-term grease and lift the gearbox until it can be pushed in horizontal position against the engine.
- Engage a gear, slightly rotate the gearbox towards the left and rotate the drive flange at the end of the transmission to and fro until the splines of the clutch shaft have engaged with the splines of the clutch driven plate. Now push the gearbox fully against the engine until the gap is closed.
- Bolt the gearbox to the engine (4.0 kgm/29 ft.lb.).
- Fit the starter motor and re-connect the cable connections.
- Fit the gear change linkages to the gear change levers and secure them with the retaining clips.
- The remaining operations are carried out in reverse order. The clutch hydraulic system must be bled of air as described in section "Clutch". Finally check and if necessary correct the oil level. Tighten the oil filler plug to 3.5 kgm (25 ft.lb.). If the transmission oil has been drained tighten the oil drain plug to 5.0 kgm (36 ft.lb.).

3.2   Transmission Repairs

Complete dismantling of the transmission requires special tools. A damaged transmission should be replaced by an exchange unit. We recommend to contact a Mercedes-Benz dealer to enquire about the availability of exchange gearboxes. Make sure that the correct transmission for the model in question is obtained. In the case of the ML230 a transmission of type "716" will be required.

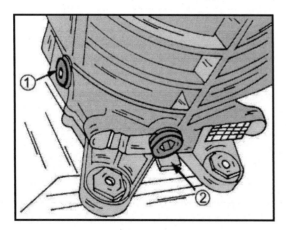

Fig. 3.4 – Location of the gearbox oil filler plug (1) and drain plug (2).

3.2.2.   GEARBOX OIL LEVEL

The gearbox oil is only changed after the first 6000 miles and is then filled for life. To check the oil level remove the plug (1) in Fig. 3.4 (Allen key) and insert the tip of the forefinger to reach for the oil. If necessary top-up with the recommended oil. You may have to clean an oil can of old oil to use for the topping-up operation.

4   Propeller Shafts

All vehicles are fitted two propeller shafts, one between the transfer case and the front axle, the other one between the transfer case and the rear axle. This is shaft (13) in Fig. 3.2. The attachment of the front shaft on model series 163 is shown in Fig. 4.1. The arrangement on models series 164 is more or less identical but different tightening torques apply to the propeller shaft bolts. Bolts and nuts and the lock plates (shims) must always be replace if removed.

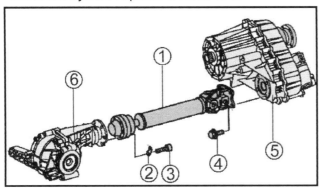

Fig. 4.1 – Propeller shaft between front axle drive and transfer case, shown in the case of a 163 model. See text.

4.1. Removal/Installation

The propeller shaft between the transfer case and the rear axle is removed as described during the removal of the transfer case in Section 3.2. Remove the front shaft, shown in Fig. 4.1 as follows:

- Place the vehicle on secure chassis stands.
- Remove the bolts (4) securing the shaft flange to the transfer case (5) and then remove the bolts (3) securing the shaft flange to the front axle drive. Take off the lock plates (shims).
- Remove the propeller shaft downwards.

During installation make sure that the flange faces are clean. If the universal joint or the double universal joint are worn replace the complete propeller shaft. The shaft flange is tightened to 5.0 kgm (36 ft.lb.) to the transfer case or 4.0 kgm (29 ft.lb.) to the front axle.

ML 280/320 CD Diesel Models only: All self-locking nuts and bolts must be replaced during installation. Removal and installation is carried out in a similar manner as described above, with the following differences:

- The exhaust heat protection plate must be removed from the propeller shaft intermediate bearing (remove the bolts) and from the propeller shaft (remove the bolts).
- Mark the propeller shaft flange and the rear axle drive flange at opposite points, using paint and the propeller shaft flange and the flexible coupling in the same manner.
- Remove the bolts securing the propeller shaft flanges at both ends and unscrew the propeller shaft intermediate bearing and remove the shaft. The flexible coupling remains on the shaft. The shaft must be supported by a helper before the last bolts are removed as it will drop down.

The installation is a reversal of the removal procedure. Make sure that the paint marks on the flanges are in line. The following tightening torques must be observed: Front propeller shaft on transfer case (rear axle end) = 5.4 kgm (37 ft.lb.), rear propeller shaft to rear axle centre = 6.4 kgm (46 ft.lb.), propeller shaft intermediate bearing bolts to frame floor = 4.0 kgm (29 ft.lb.).

5   Front Axle and Front Suspension

Different front suspensions are fitted to the models introduced during the beginning of January 2005, i.e. the model series 164. Model series 163 where fitted with upper and lower suspension arms and torsion bars. The later models retain the upper and lower suspension arms, but the torsion bars have been replaced by coil springs.

5.1.   Front Axle Half – Removal and Installation – 163 Models

Fig. 5.1 shows details for the removal and installation of the front axle half. The complete front axle half can be removed as follows:

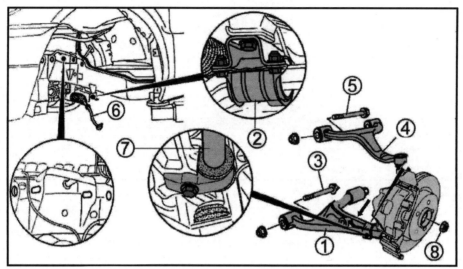

Fig. 5.1 – View of the assembled front suspension on one side. The numbers are referred to in the text.

- Jack up the front end of the vehicle and place chassis stands in position. Remove the front wheels. Make sure that the vehicle is adequately supported.
- Remove the collar nut (8) from the end of the drive shaft. The nut is tightened to a very high torque (49.0 kgm/353 ft.lb.).
- Remove the L.H. or R.H. front spring as described later on.
- Remove the panel inside the wing and remove the shock absorber as described later on.
- Locate the wheel speed sensor on the front suspension (follow the cable) and unplug the connector plug.
- Disconnect the brake hose from the brake pipe and remove the hose/pipe connection from the attachment. Close the open ends of hose and pipe in suitable manner to prevent entry of dirt. **Note the following during installation.** The union nut is tightened to 1.8 kgm (13 ft.lb.) without allowing the brake hose to twist. After installation have the steering wheel turned from left to right and the car bounced up and down whilst checking the brake hose to make sure it cannot come near other parts of the front suspension.
- Remove the nut securing the track rod ball joint (6) to the steering lever and separate the ball joint with a suitable puller. Immediately check the rubber dust cap and the ball joint for damage or excessive clearance. Fit new nuts during installation and tighten the nut to 5.5 kgm (40 ft.lb.).
- On vehicles with Xenon-type headlamps there is a link rod connected between the level controller and the lower suspension arm at the point shown by the arrow on the R.H. side. Disconnect it.
- Detach the upper transverse control arm (4), also referred to as suspension arm. Remove the bolt (5) and the nut on the other side. Note during installation: The nut is initially tightened hand-tight and must be tightened when the vehicle is back on its wheels, ready as used on the road. The nut/bolt attachment is tightened to 12.0 kgm (86.5 ft.lb.).

Fig. 5.2 – Removal of a front axle shaft.

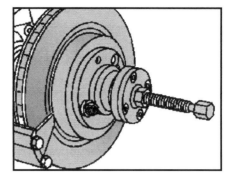

- Press the front axle out of the front axle shaft flange. You will need a puller, working on the principle shown in Fig. 5.2. The extractor is bolted to the flange.
- Place a mobile jack underneath the lower suspension arm, lift it up and detach the tension bar (7) from the lower suspension arm (1). The bolt is tightened to 6.8 kgm (49 ft.lb.) during installation.
- Detach the lower suspension arm (1) from the front axle carrier. During installation note the instructions given for the upper arm, but note that the front and rear attachment are tightened to different torque values. Tighten the bolt (3) at the front to 13.5 kgm (97 ft.lb.).
- Loosen the clamped joint at the rear of the lower suspension arm and fold down the bearing shell (2) at the position shown by the pointer. New nuts must be tightened as described above for the upper suspension arm. Tighten new nuts to only 3.0 kgm (22 ft.lb.).
- All parts can now be lifted out.

Installation is carried out in reverse order. Follow the instructions given during the removal. Bleed the brake system.

5.2. Front Springs (torsion bars) – Removal and Installation

A depth gauge is required to measure the spring pre-load of the torsion bar spring before removal, as the spring pre-load must be restored during installation. Not an easy operation.

- Place the front end of the vehicle on secure chassis stands.
- The initial operations are carried out by referring to Fig. 5.3. Measure the spring pre-load of the torsion bar (1) with the depth gauge as shown on the R.H, side, inserting the gauge into the hole of the counter plate (2). For the remaining operations we refer you to Fig. 5.4.

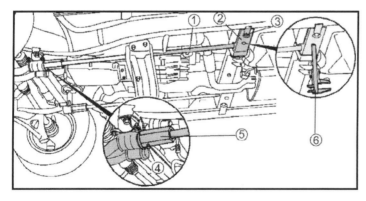

Fig. 5.3 – Details for the removal of a torsion bar spring. View from underneath the vehicle with location of some of the parts.

1   Torsion bar spring
2   Counter plate, 2 in Fig. 5.4
3   Bolt, 3 in Fig. 5.4
4   Bolt, 6 in Fig. 5.4
5   Sleeve, 5 in Fig. 5.4
6   Depth gauge

- Unscrew the bolt (3) and then release the tension of the torsion bar (1). Note that the bolt (3) must be greased during installation and the rubber bellows (9) in Fig. 5.4 must be filled with grease.

Fig. 5.4 – Installation details of a torsion bar spring. Refer to text.

- Remove the bolt (6) in Fig. 5.4 in the profile sleeve (5). In Fig. 5.3 you can see where the bolt is located,

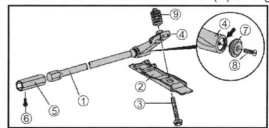

identified with (4). Slide back the sleeve (5) The bolt is tightened to 2.3 kgm (16.5 ft.lb.) during installation.

- Remove the torsion bar. To do this, remove the bolt (8) in Fig. 5.4 (tightened to 2.3 kgm/16.5 ft.lb.) and remove the end cover (7). Then remove the torsion bar (1) from the clamping lever (4). Note that the position of the torsion bar spring and the clamping lever (4) is indicated at the position shown by the arrow on the R.H. side in Fig. 5.4. Observe the marking during installation. The tooth profile must be greased.

The installation is a reversal of the removal procedure, noting the points given above.

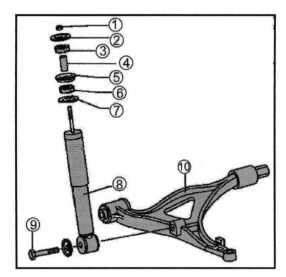

Fig. 5.5 – View of a shock absorber with the mounting details.

1	Nut
2	Mounting plate
3	Upper rubber mount
4	Spacer sleeve
5	Lower plate
6	Lower rubber mount
7	Lower mounting plate
8	Shock absorber
9	Mounting bolt
10	Lower suspension arm

5.3. Front Shock Absorbers – 163 Models

The shock absorbers are fitted between the body and the lower suspension arms. The attachment at the upper end is by means of a self-locking nut and other mounting parts, as shown in Fig. 5.5. Fig. 5.6 shows in detail the arrangement of the various items. The lower end is secured with a bolt, nut and a washer.

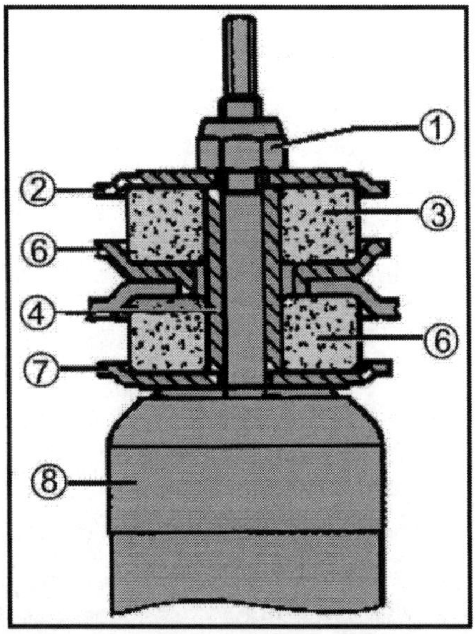

Fig. 5.6 – Arrangement of the various parts of the upper shock absorber mounting. The numbers refer to the parts shown in Fig. 5.5.

As the piston rod may rotate when the upper nut is slackened you can use an open-ended spanner to counterhold the end of the shock absorber. Also note that the vehicle must be on its wheels when the nut at the upper end is slackened and when the lower mounting bolt is tightened.

- Slacken the nut (1) in Fig. 5.5, counterholding the piston rod as described.
- Place the front end of the vehicle on chassis stands and remove the panel (liner) inside the front wing.
- Fully remove the nut and take off the parts shown in Fig. 5.5 one after the other, **but note:** If a black version of the upper mountings and the lower rubber mountings are fitted, mark their fitted position as they are different. If new rubber mountings are fitted, fit the white-coated rubber mounting (harder mounting) at the upper end and the yellow-coated mounting (softer) at the bottom.

- Detach the lower shock absorber mounting from the suspension arm and take out the unit.

The installation is a reversal of the removal procedure. The following points must be observed as you proceed:

- Place the parts over the upper end of the damper in the order shown in Fig. 5.6 and insert the shock absorber from below. Fit the bolt and washer to the lower end. Tighten the bolt to 13.5 kgm (97 ft.lb.) when the wheels are resting on the ground.
- Fit the rubber bush and the dished washer to the upper end and fit and tighten the nut to 3.0 kgm (22.lb.).

5.4. Front Axle – Removal and Installation – 163 Models

The complete front axle can be removed as described below, very unlikely, but possible. Fig. 5.7 shows a view of the complete front axle and will help you. The front end of the vehicle must be resting on secure chassis stands.

- Remove the front wheels after the upper shock absorber mounting nuts have been removed (see section 5.3). The shock absorber is now removed as described.
- Locate and unplug both connectors from both wheel speed sensors.
- Disconnect the brake hose from the brake pipe. Follow the instructions in section 5.1.
- Detach the propeller shaft from the flange on the front axle transmission. Bolts are tightened to 4.0 kgm (29 ft.lb.).
- Remove both front springs (section 5.2).
- Remove the lower engine compartment panelling and detach the torsion bar (8) from the vehicle frame. Tighten the retaining brackets to 10.0 kgm (72 ft.lb.).
- Remove the upper suspension arm (3) from the vehicle frame as described during the removal of the front axle half (section 5.1). Note the instructions during installation and the tightening torque.

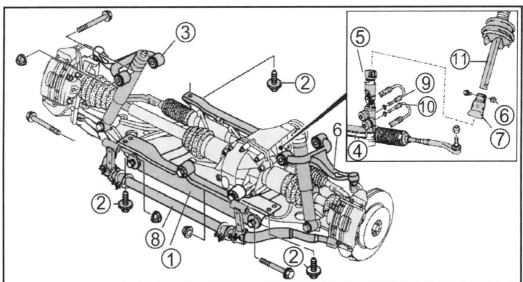

Fig. 5.7 – View of the front axle of a 163 model with details of the removal. See text.

- Detach the bracket securing the oil lines between the transmission and the oil cooler from the front axle carrier (1).
- Unclip the brake line at the rear of the front axle cross member.

- On vehicles with Xenon-type headlamps there is a link rod connected between the level controller and the lower suspension arm at the point shown in Fig. 5.1 by the arrow on the R.H. side. Disconnect it.
- Extract the fluid from the fluid reservoir for the power steering in a similar manner as shown in Fig. 2.11.
- Turn the steering wheel to the centre position and secure it in position by removing the ignition key and locking the steering.
- Detach the plug connector for the speed-sensitive power steering from the timing case (if fitted).
- Remove the nut (6) and the bolt from the steering coupling (5) and pull the lower steering shaft (11) up and out of the steering coupling. The clamping groove can be enlarged with a screwdriver to facilitate the removal. Do not damage the coupling shield (7). During installation the rack and pinion steering (4) must be set to the centre position before the steering coupling (5) is fitted. The self-locking nut (6) must be replaced and tightened to 2.6 kgm (19 ft.lb.).
- Disconnect the return pipe (10) and the high-pressure hose (9) from the steering. Close off the open ends. The connections are either by end fittings or banjo bolts. Replace the sealing rings. Banjo bolts are tightened to 3.0 kgm (22 ft.lb.), end fittings are tightened to 1.5 kgm (11 ft.lb.).
- Detach the bleeding and venting hose from the differential.
- Place a mobile jack underneath the front axle carrier (1) until under tension and remove the bolts (2) from the carrier. The bolts must be replaced. Make sure that the threads have engaged before the bolts are tightened to 20.0 kgm (144 ft.lb.).
- Slowly lower the front axle carrier on the jack, pushing all hoses away from the carrier during the removal. The front axle carrier has guide pins which must be inserted into holes in the side member during installation.

Installation is carried out in reverse. Steering and brake systems must be bled after installation.

5.5. Torsion Bar – Removal and Installation – 163 Models

The attachment of the torsion bar is shown in Fig. 5.8. The upper attachment is marked with (A) and (B). Version (B) is fitted from August 1998 onwards. The bar can be removed and installed as follows:

Fig. 5.8 – Details for the removal and installation of the torsion bar (163 models). See text.

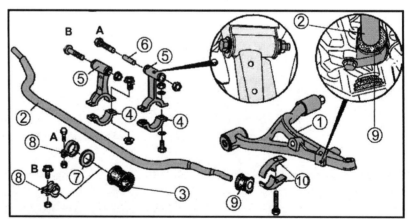

- Place the front end of the vehicle on secure chassis stands and re-move the bottom engine compart-ment panelling or the noise encapsulation.
- Remove the bracket (10) securing the torsion bar (2) from the lower suspension arm (1) and also remove the retaining bracket (4). The bolt for bracket (10) is tightened to 10.0 kgm (72 ft.lb.) during installation. The bolt or nut securing the bracket (4), depending on the version (A) or (B) are tightened to 5.0 kgm (36 ft.lb.).
- The torsion bar (2) can now be removed. Make a note of the installation position of the bar before you take it out.

- Pull the rubber mounts (9) and (3) off the torsion bar, again noting the fitted position.
- On models before August 1998 remove the washers (7)
- Undo and remove the bracket (8), referred to as anti-shift device. During installation centre the torsion bar before tightening the bolt and nut to 1.5 kgm (19 ft.lb.).
- Remove the retaining bracket (5) at the upper end. Note that the L.H. and R.H. bracket are not the same and must be marked accordingly. The bolt of each version (A or B) is tightened to 10.0 kgm (72 ft.lb.). The sleeve (6) must be pressed out of the retaining bracket, but note that a repair kit will contain the version fitted as of August 1998.

5.6. Upper Suspension Arms – 163 Models

A two-arm puller/extractor is required to remove the ball joint from the steering knuckle. Removal and installation are straight-forward. The front end of the vehicle must be on chassis stands, the shock absorber removed (see earlier on) and the brake line bracket removed from the steering knuckle. The suspension arm bolts/nuts must be tightened with the wheels resting on the ground.

Remove the ball joint nut and separate the ball joint from the steering knuckle. Remove the bolts and nuts securing the suspension arm to the vehicle frame and remove it. The steering knuckle should be tied to the shock absorber with a piece of wire to prevent it from tilting downwards.

Installation is carried out in reverse order. Fit the ball joint stud and tighten the nut to 5.0 kgm (36 ft.lb.). The suspension arm nuts/bolts are tightened finger-tight and tightened to 12.0 kgm (86 ft.lb.) when the wheels are resting on the ground, vehicle in "ready-to-drive" condition.

5.7. Lower Suspension Arms – 163 Models

Most of the operations have already been described in the earlier sections. To remove a suspension arm, remove the front springs and the steering knuckle (section 5.8) and detach the torsion bar from the lower control arm. Disconnect the linkage if Xenon headlamps are fitted. Then detach the lower control arm from the front subframe. At the rear of the arm remove the clamped joint and fold down the bearing shell.

Installation is a reversal of the removal procedure. Note during installation: The nut is initially tightened hand-tight and must be tightened when the vehicle is back on its wheels, ready as used on the road. The nut/bolt attachment is tightened to 13.5 kgm (97.5 ft.lb.), clamped joint 3.0 kgm (22 ft.lb.). The torsion bar to 6.8 kgm (49 ft.lb.).

5.8. Steering Knuckle – 163 Models

With the vehicle on secure chassis stands remove the front wheel. Slacken the collar nut securing the axle drive shaft to the steering knuckle.

Follow the cable connections and unclip the cables for the wheel speed sensor and the brake pad wear indicator from the guides. The speed sensor bracket must be removed from the steering knuckle. Then proceed as follows:

- Remove the brake disc as described in section "Brake System".
- Remove the nut securing the track rod ball joint to the steering lever and separate the ball joint with a suitable puller. The nut is tightened to 5.5 kgm (40 ft.lb.) during installation.
- Also with a suitable puller separate the upper ball joint from the steering knuckle after removal of the nut (5.0 kgm/36 ft.lb.) and the lower ball joint after removal of

the nut (8.5 kgm/61 ft.lb.). Note the difference in the tightening torques. Attention: The steering knuckle can fall down after removal of the ball joint.
- Remove the steering knuckle towards the front.

Installation is a reversal. Check the upper and lower ball joints for wear and the rubber caps for damaged before refitting the parts. The axle shaft nut is tightened to 49.0 kgm (353 ft.lb.).

5.9. Front Struts – Removal and Installation – 164 Models

The removal of any part of the front suspension of 164 models on models with all-round level control system is not possible under DIY conditions as the AIRmatic system must be drained and re-charged with special equipment. In general the removal and installation is a complicated operation but can be carried out on models without level control system. Some items mentioned in the description are only fitted to models with level control system – ignore them. Take care to follow the tightening torques for the specified nuts and bolts – can be confusing.

- Place the front end of the vehicle on secure chassis stands and remove the wheel on the side in question.
- At the upper end of the spring strut (damper) remove the three nuts securing the strut to the body. The nuts are tightened in three stages during installation. First tighten to 3.0 kgm (22 ft.lb.), then slacken them by half a turn and then tighten to 2.7 kgm (19.5 ft.lb.).
- Remove the front section of the wing panel (liner) on the inside of the front wing in question.
- Cut a cable tie on the steering knuckle. Must be replaced. Next to the cable tie you will find the brake hose bracket. Remove it to free the brake hose. Do not damage the brake hose. Near the lower end of the strut there is another cable tie (near the drive shaft connection) which must also be cut and removed (again replace).
- Locate and unscrew a nut from the tie rod from the steering knuckle and take off the rod. Tighten the nut to 4.5 kgm (32.5 ft.lb.) and then a further quarter of a turn.
- At the upper end of the spring strut remove a nut and disconnect the connecting link from the spring strut. The nut is tightened to 20.0 kgm (144 ft.lb.).
- At the lower end of the spring strut remove a nut and remove the spring strut from the suspension arm. This nut is tightened to 26.5 kgm (191 ft.lb.).
- Disconnect the connecting link from the spring strut. The nut is tightened to 20.0 kgm (144 ft.lb.).
- At the upper end of the spring strut remove the nut securing the upper control arm to the steering knuckle and separate the ball joint with a suitable puller. The ball joint nut is tightened to 2.0 kgm (14.5 ft.lb.) and from the final position a further quarter of a turn. Check the ball joint and rubber cap before installation.
- Pull the suspension arm downwards until the front suspension strut can be removed.

Installation is carried out in reverse order, but note the different tightening torques. If parts have been replaced have the front wheel alignment checked.

Replacing the Coil Spring and/or Spring Strut
A spring compressor is necessary to remove the front springs. As the special compressor used in a workshop may not be available you can use a standard compressor, the claws of which are placed over three to four of the coils. Make sure the compressor has adequate strength for the springs. Remove a spring as follows, noting that the spring strut must be removed.

- Clamp the suspension strut into a vice and place the spring compressor over the spring coils until the upper end lower ends are free of their spring seats.
- At the end of the spring strut upper end remove a cap and remove the nut below to remove the shock absorber. The piston rod will rotate and must be prevented from rotating.
- Remove the parts from the top end of the strut. These are the top spring retainer, the upper spring seat, the stop damper, the rubber bellows and the clamped coil spring. Make a note how each part is fitted. The spring clamp can remain in position if the same spring/strut is to be fitted.
- Replace any components with oil contamination, cracks or deformation.

Release the spring compressor slowly, checking that the spring is fitted properly at the upper end lower ends and that all parts are fitted in their original order before tightening the piston rod nut to 3.0 kgm (22 ft.lb.).

The front wheel alignment and the headlamp adjustment must be checked after the completed installation.

5.10. Suspension Arms – Removal and Installation – 164 Models

L.H. upper suspension arm

Bolts and nuts must only be tightened when the vehicle is resting on its wheels, ready to drive. Note that slightly different instructions apply to the L.H. and R.H. arms. First remove the engine cover in the centre of the engine.

- Remove the air filter housing.
- Remove the nut securing the ball joint to the upper suspension arm and separate the joint with a suitable ball joint puller. The nut is tightened to 2.0 kgm (14.5 ft.lb.) and from the final position a further quarter of a turn.
- Remove a bolt and detach the L.H. front level sensor bracket from the suspension arm (only with level control system).
- Locate and remove two nuts and two bolts from the front end and detach the suspension arm from the front end of the vehicle. Bolts and nuts are tightened to 6.1 kgm (44 ft.lb.).

Install in reverse order.

R.H. upper suspension arm

Removal is carried out as described above, but the air plenium chamber must be removed instead of the air cleaner housing. The same tightening torques apply.

Lower suspension arms

Bolts and nuts must only be tightened when the vehicle is resting on its wheels, ready to drive. Self-locking nuts and bolts must be replaced.

- Place the front end of the vehicle on secure chassis stands and remove the wheel.
- Detach the bottom engine compartment panelling or the sound proofing (CDI engine).
- Remove the two bolts securing the stabiliser bar (anti-roll bar) brackets on each side and move the bar downwards. Careful – the stabiliser bar is under tension. The bracket bolts are tightened to 5.0 kgm (26 ft.lb.).
- Mark the installation position of the rear bearing bracket of the lower suspension arm in relation to the front axle carrier and remove the mounting bolts at both sides to detach the suspension arm from the front axle carrier. If new parts are fitted transfer the marks to the new parts to ensure that the suspension arm is fitted to its original position. The bolts are tightened to 25 kgm (180 ft.lb.).

- Remove the bolt and nut securing the suspension arm to the front axle carrier. A spacer washer is fitted underneath the bolt head and must be fitted to the inside. Note the direction of fitting before removal. The bolt/nut is tightened to 2.7 kgm (199.5 ft.lb.).
- Remove the bolt securing the suspension strut to the suspension arm, located immediately next to the drive shaft bellow. Tighten this bolt to 26.5 kgm (191 ft.lb.).
- Remove the ball joint stud nut at the outside of the suspension arm and separate the ball joint and detach the suspension arm from the steering knuckle. The nut is tightened to 23.0 kgm (165.5 ft.lb.).

The installation is carried out in reverse order. Study the tightening torques given above to avoid mistakes. Insert the spacer washer the correct way round to the inside the suspension arm. The wheel alignment must be checked if parts have been replaced (workshop operation).

5.11. Stabiliser Bar – Removal and Installation – 164 Models

The stabiliser bar is fitted across the front of the vehicle, attached with clamps to the front axle carrier and connected with link rods to the suspension (shock absorber) struts. The front end of the vehicle must be supported on secure chassis stands. Nuts and bolts must be tightened when the vehicle is on its wheels.

- Detach the lower engine compartment panelling or the noise encapsulation (CDI models).
- Remove the nuts securing the link rods to the stabiliser bar. If the link rods must be removed detach them from the suspension struts. Nuts are tightened to 20 kgm (144 ft.lb.) in both cases.
- On each side of the bar remove the mounting clamp bolts and remove the clamps. The stabiliser bar is pre-loaded. Take care when the clamps are removed. The bolts are tightened to 11 kgm (79 ft.lb.).
- The stabiliser is also fitted with a so-called torsional bearing on each end, also retained with mountings clamps. If the stabiliser bar is to be replaced remove the clamp bolts and take out the bearing after marking its fitted position. The bolts are tightened in this case to 3.5 kgm (25 ft.lb.).

The installation is carried out in reverse order, noting the following points and order of tightening:

- If the torsional bearing has been replaced transfer the previously made marks to the new stabiliser bar. Do not tighten the nuts securing the mounting clamps.
- Position the stabiliser bar on the front axle carrier, fit the retaining clamps and insert the bolts at both ends. The angled ends of the bar must face downwards, the bar must be centred. Do not tighten the mounting clamp bolts at this stage.
- Fit the link rods to the stabiliser bar and the front struts. Again do not tighten the nuts.

Fig. 5.9 – Removal of a front drive shaft. 163 model shown.

- Check the correct position of the bar and the torsional bearing (if removed) and tighten all bolts and nuts to the torques given during the removal, in the order: torsional bearing clamps, stabiliser bar retaining clamps, link rod nuts.

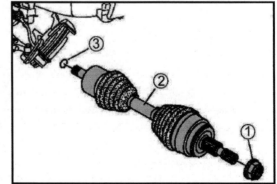

5.12. Front Axle Shafts/Front Axle Drive – Removal and Installation

163 Models

- Place the front end of the vehicle on secure chassis stands and remove the front wheel. Remove the collared nut (1) in Fig. 5.9. A helper should apply the brake pedal.
- Remove the front brake caliper without disconnecting the brake hose. Suspend the caliper with a piece of wire to the front suspension.
- Disconnect the track rod ball joint from the steering knuckle, using a suitable puller. In the same manner disconnect the upper suspension arm from the steering knuckle.
- Press the front axle shaft (2) out of the front axle shaft flange as already shown in Fig. 5.2. Push the steering knuckle to one side and attach it with wire.
- Lever the axle shaft out of the front axle drive gear without damaging the protective shield and withdraw the shaft.

Installation is carried out in reverse order. The slot in the retaining circlip (3) must face downwards when the shaft is inserted. Tighten the upper suspension arm ball joint nut to 5.0 kgm (36 ft.lb.), the track rod ball joint nut to 5.5 kgm (40 ft.lb.) and the axle shaft nut to 49 kgm (353 ft.lb.).

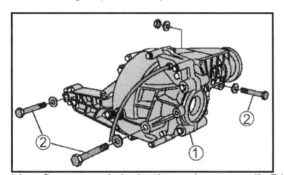

Fig. 5.10 – Front axle drive – 163 models.

Removal of front axle drive – 163 models

Fig. 5.10 shows the attachment of the front axle drive case on these models. Remove the two axle shafts as described above, disconnect the propeller shaft from the axle drive flange and drain the axle case oil. Disconnect a vent hose and remove the bolts, nuts and washers (2), as applicable and remove the axle case (1). Support the assembly on a mobile jack to lower it.

Installation is carried out in reverse order. Tighten the axle bolts to 13.5 kgm (97 ft.lb.) and the propeller shaft connection to 4.0 kgm (29 ft.lb.).

164 Models

The instructions apply to the R.H. axle shaft as the L.H. shaft remains attached to the L.H. front axle shaft flange. The front axle drive gear is removed to free the L.H. shaft. Proceed as follows:

- Place the front end of the vehicle on secure chassis stands and remove the front wheel. Remove the collared nut (1) in Fig. 5.9. A helper should apply the brake pedal.
- Remove the bottom engine compartment panelling or the sound-proofing (CDI models).
- Locate the electrical cables on the spring strut and free them from their brackets. Near the brake hose bracket cut a cable tie (replace) and remove the brake hose from the brake hose bracket.
- Press the front axle shaft out of the front axle shaft flange as already shown in Fig. 5.2. Push the steering knuckle to one side and attach it with wire.
- Disconnect the R.H. track rod ball joint from the steering knuckle, using a suitable puller. In the same manner disconnect the R.H. upper suspension arm from the steering knuckle. Move the steering knuckle to one side to create more space. Track rod ball joint nut = 4.5 kgm (32.5 ft.lb.) + 90°, upper suspension arm ball joint nut = 2.0 kgm (14.5 ft.lb.) + 90°.

- Pull the R.H. shaft out of the front axle drive gear and remove. Some oil may run out.

Remove the L.H. drive shaft as follows:

- Remove the brake hose from the brake hose bracket on the L.H. side and near the brake hose cut a cable tie.
- Disconnect the L.H. track rod ball joint from the steering knuckle, using a suitable puller. In the same manner disconnect the L.H. upper suspension arm from the steering knuckle. Move the steering knuckle to one side to create more space. Tightening torques are the same as given for the R.H. assemblies given above.
- Pull the L.H. axle shaft out of the front axle drive gear. The shaft remains attached to the axle shaft flange.
- Mark the installation position of the propeller shaft flange and the front axle drive flange in suitable manner and detach the propeller shaft flange from the axle case.
- Detach the hose from the front axle case (protect the hose end against entry of dirt).
- Place a mobile jack with a suitable support plate underneath the front axle case and remove the mounting bolts securing the case to the L.H. front axle carrier and the R.H. front axle carrier. The axle case can now be lowered on the jack. Note the tightening torques of the front axle bolts: Bolts on the L.H. side = 9.3 kgm (67 ft.lb.), bolts on the R.H. side = 5.0 kgm (36 ft.lb.).
- Remove the L.H. shaft from the axle shaft flange.

Installation is a reversal of the removal procedure, noting the points given above. The axle shaft nuts are tightened to 52 kgm (374 ft.lb.) on these models.

5.13.   Oil Change in Front Axle

The front axle has a capacity of 1.2 litres. To remove the oil drain plug and the oil level/oil filler plug an Allen key of 14 mm A/F is required. Hypoid oil SAE 90 is used to fill the axle. Fig. 5.11 shows the location of the filler and oil drain plugs (163 model shown). Change the oil as follows:

- Drive the vehicle a short distance to warm up the oil.

Fig. 5.11 – Location of the oil filler plug (1) and the drain plug (2).

- Place a suitable container underneath the axle and remove the oil drain plug at the bottom of the axle. The oil level/filler plug can be removed from the axle cover to speed up the draining of the oil.
- Wait until the oil has drained, clean the drain plug and refit the plug to the axle and tighten it.

• Fill the axle housing with the oil and amount given above until the oil level can be seen at the lower edge of the filler hole. Clean the plug, fit it and tighten it. Both plugs are tightened to 5.0 kgm (36 ft.lb.).

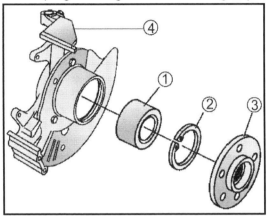

Fig. 5.12 – Wheel bearing components on one side.
1   Wheel bearing
2   Bearing circlip
3   Axle drive flange
4   Steering knuckle

5.14.   Wheel Bearings

We strongly recommend to have the wheel bearings replaced in a workshop. The steering knuckle can be removed as described earlier on and taken to the dealer to have the bearings replaced. If you want to attempt the replacement, with the steering knuckle removed, remove the circlip on the outside of the knuckle and replace the double-row angular wheel bearing under a press. The workshop has, however, a special tool set to replace the bearing. Fig. 5.12 shows the fitting of a bearing.

5.15   Front Suspension/Axle – Tightening Torques

The main tightening torques are given for the 163 models in kgm. Multiply by "7.2" to obtain "ft.lb.". The values in brackets apply to the 164 models, if applicable. Most tightening torques are given during removal/installation of the component parts. Note the differences, avoid mistakes.

Nuts/bolts, upper suspension arms to front axle carrier (163) ....12.0 kgm
Nuts/bolts, upper suspension arms to front axle carrier (164) ....6.1 kgm
Nuts/bolts, lower suspension arms at front to front axle carrier ....13.5 kgm
Nut, upper suspension arm ball joints to steering knuckle (163) ....5.0 kgm
Nut, upper suspension arm ball joints to steering knuckle (163) .... 2.0 kgm + 90°
Bolts, lower suspension arms at front to front axle carrier ....3.0 kgm
Nuts, lower suspension arms at front to steering knuckle (164): ....23.0 kgm
Nut, lower suspension arms at front to front axle carrier (164): ....27.0 kgm
Nut, lower suspension arms at rear to front axle carrier (164): ....25.0 kgm
Bolt, torsion bar to control arm: ....6.8 kgm
Nut, front axle shaft to axle shaft flange (163): .... 49.0 kgm (164 = 52.0 kgm)
Nut, track rod ball joint to steering knuckle (163): ....5.5 kgm (4.5 kgm + 90° - 164)
Brake hose to brake pipe: ....1.8 kgm
Bolt, front axle case to front axle carrier: ....13.5 kgm
Oil filler plug/oil drain plug, front axle case: ....5.0 kgm
Propeller shaft flange to front axle case flange: ....4.0 kgm
Stabiliser bar clamp bracket to front axle carrier (163): ....10.0 kgm
Stabiliser bar to suspension arm (163): ....6.8 kgm
Stabiliser bar retaining bracket to bar (163): ....5.0 kgm
Stabiliser bar clamp (bolt) to bar (163): ....1.8 kgm
Stabiliser bar clamp bracket to front axle carrier (164): ....11.0 kgm
Torsion bearing clamp bracket (164): ....3.5 kgm
Connecting rods to shock absorber and torsion bar (164): ....20.0 kgm
Shock absorber to suspension arm (164) ....26.5 kgm
Shock absorber to front end (164) ....3.0 kgm, slacken, ½ a turn and tighten to 27.0 kgm

6   Rear Axle and Rear Suspension

The rear suspension is fitted with coil springs, upper and lower suspension (control) arms, a stabiliser bar and telescopic shock absorbers. Although not identical, the suspensions in series 163 and 164 are in general of similar construction. The following information are in general based on the earlier 163 models. 6.1 shows a view of the assembled rear suspension on one side. A similar arrangement is used on the 164 vehicles.

6.0.   Spring Struts – Removal and Installation

The shock absorbers act as rebound stop for the rear wheels. The operations can be carried out with the help of Figs. 6.1 and 6.2. The rear end of the vehicle must be on secure chassis stands and the wheels removed. Proceed as follows:

Fig. 6.1 – View of the assembled rear suspension on one side with details of the removal. See text. See also Fig. 6.2.

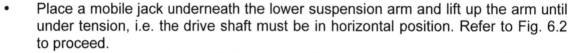

* Pull off the cover (1) in Fig. 6.1. During installation make sure it is fitted in correct position.
* Remove the nuts (2) from the upper spring strut mounting (nuts 13 in Fig. 6.2). Tighten the nuts equally to 2.0 kgm (14.5 ft.lb.) during installation.
* Remove the lower spring strut mounting nut (5) from the lower suspension arm. Fig. 6.2 shows details of the attachment. This is nut (14) in Fig. 6.2. The threaded end of the strut must be prevented from rotating by inserting an Allen key is shown in the circle of Fig. 6.1. The nut is tightened to 8.5 kgm (61 ft.lb.).
* Place a mobile jack underneath the lower suspension arm and lift up the arm until under tension, i.e. the drive shaft must be in horizontal position. Refer to Fig. 6.2 to proceed.
* Remove the connecting rod (1) between the lower suspension arm (2) and the torsion bar, i.e. stabiliser bar (3) by removing the bearing with the nut (8). The bearing (4), the bearing (5), the distance sleeve (6) and the bearing (7) can be removed. Tighten the nut (8) to 2.8 kgm (20 ft.lb.).

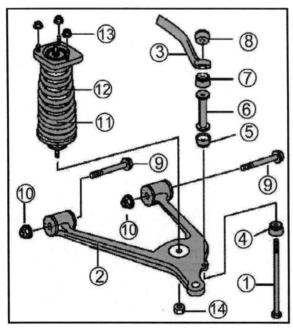

Fig. 6.2 – Removal of a rear spring strut. See text.

* Detach the lower control arm (2) from the rear axle carrier. Bolts (9) and nuts (10) must be removed. Tighten to 13.5 kgm (97 ft.lb.).
* Lower the control arm on the jack, pull it out of the guide and swing it downwards. The suspension strut is now pulled upwards until free of the suspension arm. If necessary use a plastic or rubber mallet and knock the strut (12) out the suspension arm. The strut is removed together with the coil spring (11).

Installation is a reversal of the removal procedure, noting the tightening torques given above. The headlamp adjustment must be checked.

Note: The removal of the rear springs of a 164 models is described in Section 6.2. It is not combined with the spring strut.

6.1.   Shock Absorbers – Removal and Installation

The shock absorbers of a 163 model is removed after the spring strut has been taken out as described in the last section. The shock absorber of a 164 model is not a part of the spring strut, i.e. the removal is easier, but access is more difficult (see below) and it may be better to have the removal and installation carried out in a workshop.

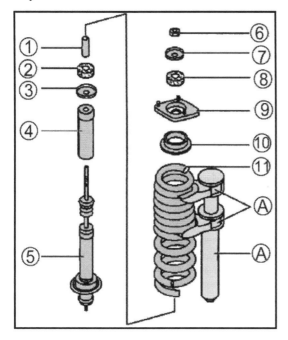

Fig. 6.3 – Details for the removal and installation of a shock absorber together with the coil spring (163). The spring compressor is identified with (A).

1   Sleeve
2   Upper spring mount
3   Metal plate
4   Spacer sleeve
5   Shock absorber
6   Nut, 3.0 kgm
7   Metal plate
8   Rubber mounting
9   Support bearing
10   Spring seat
11   Coil spring

To remove the shock absorber compress the coil spring as described for the front coil springs (refer to page 125) and remove the nut (6) in Fig. 6.3. Remove the parts shown in the illustration and remove the spring together with the compression tool, if the same coil spring is fitted.

The installation is a reversal of the removal procedure. Tighten the self-locking nut at the upper end to 3.0 kgm (22 ft.lb.).

164 Models

Although the removal and installation of the shock absorber is fairly easy, the preliminary operations are not. The trim panel inside the rear compartment must be removed. Underneath there is a sound-deadening mat which must be cut in the area of the upper shock absorber mounting, i.e. you will have to know where to cut. The wing liner inside the rear wing must also be removed. Therefore a workshop operation. Otherwise the shock absorber is attached at the upper end by a self-locking nut (2.1 kgm/15 ft.lb.) and at the lower end with a nut to the suspension arm (26.5 kgm (19 ft.lb.). The suspension arm must be lifted until the nuts are removed and then lowered until the shock absorber can be compressed and taken out.

6.2.   Rear Springs – Removal and Installation

A rear spring of a 163 model is removed together with the spring strut as described above, i.e. the spring must be compressed. As described on page 125. Fig. 6.3 shows details of the items to be removed. If a new spring is fitted, quote the model, engine, model year, etc. to make sure the correct spring is fitted.

A rear spring of a 164 model can be removed with the wheel removed and the rear end of the vehicle on secure chassis stands. Each spring is fitted with various parts, i.e. a rubber insert, the upper spring plate, two spacers, a plastic ring and a rubber boot and all parts should be marked to ensure correct installation.

Rear Axle and Rear Suspension

The removal of a spring requires, as for the front springs, a spring compressor or suitable compressor hooks. Compress the spring in a suitable manner until it is free of the upper and lower spring seats and remove it.

Rear springs must always be replaced in pairs. Note during installation: The lower cup has been modified. If the spring has been removed always fit a new cup, which will, however, have a different shape. The one you receive will have a tap which must engage into the groove of the lower suspension arm. The upper spring cup and the rubber insert must be checked for signs of damage and replaced if necessary.

Installation is carried out in reverse order. When releasing the spring compressor, observe the correct engagement of the spring into its upper and lower seats.

6.3. Stabiliser Bar – Removal and Installation

The stabiliser bar (1) in Fig. 6.4, shown on a 163 model, is fitted by means of a connecting link (5) between the lower suspension arm (11) and the frame floor. Removal and installation can be carried out by referring to the illustration.

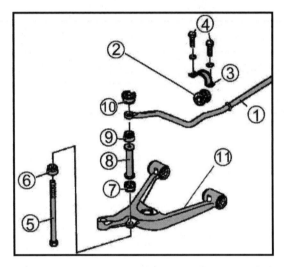

Fig. 6.4 – Details of the stabiliser bar installation.
1   Torsion bar
2   Rubber mount
3   Retaining clamp
4   Mounting bolts, 2.8 kgm
5   Link rod
6   Bearing
7   Bearing
8   Spacer sleeve
9   Bearing
10 Bearing with nut, 2.1 kgm
11 Suspension arm

All types have a similar arrangement. During removal (rear end of vehicle on secure chassis stands) make a note of the order of part installation. The securing nut (10) is at the same time a rubber bearing and it tightened to 2.1 kgm (15 ft.lb.). The two bolts (4), on each side of the bar, are tightened to 2.8 kgm (20 ft.lb.) when tightened to the rear axle carrier.

The removal of the stabiliser (torsion) bar of a 164 model is carried out in a similar manner, but different tightening torques apply. The torsion bar retaining clamp bolts are tightened to 11.0 kgm (79 ft.lb.), and the nuts securing the link rods to the suspension arms (track control arms) and to the ends of the torsion bar are tightened to 18.0 kgm (130 ft.lb.).

6.4. Rear Suspension Struts/Arms

6.4.0. UPPER WISHBONES – REMOVAL AND INSTALLATION

The operations described apply to the model series 163. The rear end of the vehicle must be resting on secure chassis stands and the wheels removed. Fig. 6.5 shows some details of the removal operations. (5) indicates where the lower wishbone is connected.

*   Remove the L.H. or R.H. wheel speed sensor (7).
*   Remove the brake caliper (6) and suspend it with a piece of wire to the rear suspension. Must not hang down on the brake hose.
*   Remove the spring strut (1) from the longitudinal frame member after unscrewing the nuts (9) – 2.0 kgm (14.5 ft.lb.).

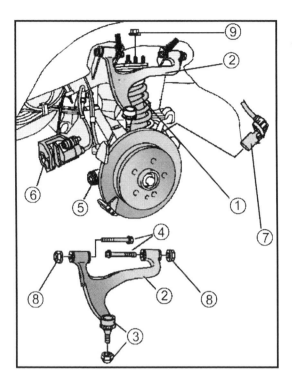

Fig. 6.5 – Details for the removal of an upper wishbone, shown on a 163 model. See text.

- Remove the nut securing the ball joint (3) to the wheel carrier and separate the joint with a suitable ball joint puller. The nut is tightened to 5.0 kgm (36 ft.lb.) during installation.

- Jack up the rear axle until the rear axle shaft is in horizontal position and remove the nuts (8) securing the upper suspension arm (2) to the frame member. The heads of the mounting bolts (4) must be marked in relation to the frame member (arrows in Fig. 6.5).

- Remove the mounting bolts (4). When removing the bolt you will have to press down the mounting of the lower wishbone to guide the bolts passed the top of the spring strut. Bolts/nuts are tightened to 12.0 kgm (86.5 ft.lb.) with the axle shaft in horizontal position.

Installation is carried out in reverse order. The rubber mounts of the suspension arm (wishbone) can be replaced, but we recommend to consult a workshop (dealer). Note the tightening torques.

6.4.1. LOWER WISHBONES – REMOVAL AND INSTALLATION

The operations described apply to the model series 163. The rear end of the vehicle must be resting on secure chassis stands and the wheels removed. Fig. 6.6 shows some details of the removal operations. The illustration shows two versions, i.e. the earlier version, marked (A) and the later version, marked (B). Note that washers (10) are fitted to the early version. If a new arm is fitted, quote the vehicle type, the engine type and the model year when purchasing the arm.

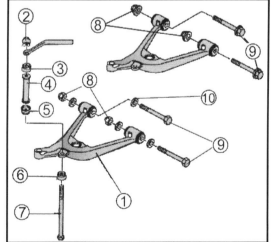

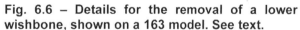

Fig. 6.6 – Details for the removal of a lower wishbone, shown on a 163 model. See text.

- Remove the spring strut from the lower wishbone (1). The nut is tightened to 8.5 kgm (61 ft.lb.) during installation.

- Remove the bearing with the nut (2) and the bolt (7), i.e. the connecting link, from the lower wishbone (1) after the axle assembly has been jacked up to bring the axle shaft to a horizontal position. Otherwise the torsion bar bearings will be damaged. Remove the rubber bearing (3) and (5).

- Detach the lower wishbone (1) from the rear axle carrier by removing the nuts (8) and bolts (9), axle shaft still in horizontal position.

- Swivel the lower wishbone on the rear axle carrier downwards.

- Remove the nut securing the ball joint to the lower wishbone. The ball joint stud can be held with a Tory-head insert of suitable size. The nut is tightened to 12.5 kgm (90 ft.lb.) during installation. The wishbone can now be removed.

Installation is carried out in reverse order. The rubber mounts of the suspension arm (wishbone) can be replaced, but we recommend to consult a workshop (dealer). Note the tightening torques.

6.5. Rear Suspension – 164 Models

The rear suspension of these models consists of the upper and lower suspension arms, the spring struts, coil springs, torsion (stabiliser) bar and various rods and struts. Removal and installation of some of the items is described below. The terminology is based on the manufacturer.

Radius Rod

This is the strut (1) in Fig. 6.7 in the L.H. view, also referred to as "tension arm". The strut is fitted between the rear axle carrier and the wheel carrier and is secured with a nut and a bolt on each end. The rear of the vehicle must be on secure chassis stands or a garage lift and the wheel removed. A mobile jack must be placed underneath the suspension ball joint of the lower suspension arm to retain the suspension in position when the rod is removed.

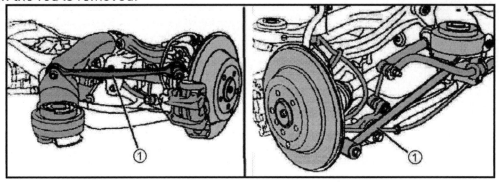

Fig. 6.7 – The radius rod (1), also tension arm and the track rod (1) on the R.H. side (164 model).

Remove the bolt and self-locking nut on one end and the self-locking nut, bolt and a washer on the opposite end and take out the rod. The rubber mountings can be replaced (workshop).

During installation insert the bolt and screw on a new nut and with the washer on one side. On the side without the washer the bolt head must face into the direction of travel, on the side with washer into the direction opposite the direction of travel. Both nuts must be tightened hand-tight. Lift the rear suspension on the jack until it is in its normal position and tighten both bolt/nut combinations to 11.0 kgm (77 ft.lb.). Refit the wheel and lower the vehicle to the ground.

Track Rod

This is the strut (1) in Fig. 6.7 in the R.H. view. The track rod, also referred to as tie rod, is fitted between the rear axle carrier and the wheel carrier. The rod is attached with a bolt and nut on each end. To remove the rod, first remove the torsion bar clamp from the rear axle carrier (11.0 kgm/77 ft.lb.). The head of the bolt on the inside must be marked with a coloured pencil in relation to an eccentric disc to ensure installation in the original position.

Remove the bolt and nut on the other end (a washer is used) and remove the rod. The rubber mountings can be replaced (workshop).

Removal and installation of the bolts is identical as described for the radius rod, but the tightening torques are different. The self-locking nut (new) on the rear axle carrier is tightened to 9.3 kgm (67 ft.lb.), the nut of the wheel carrier to 11.0 kgm (77 ft.lb.). Make sure that the marks made in bolt head and eccentric disc on one side are aligned before bolt and nut are tightened.

Camber Strut

The camber strut is inserted between the rear axle carrier and the wheel carrier. The removal is carried out in the same manner as described for the radius rod, but a wiring harness bracket must be removed from the strut and pulled slightly forward. Again the strut is attached on one side with an eccentric disc and disc and bolt head must be marked before removal.

Note the different tightening torques. The self-locking nut (new) on the rear axle carrier is tightened to 9.3 kgm (67 ft.lb.), the nut of the wheel carrier to 11.0 kgm (77 ft.lb.). Make sure that the marks made in bolt head and eccentric disc on one side are aligned before bolt and nut are tightened.

6.6.   Rear Axle Drive Shafts

Remove as follows, noting the different operations on the two versions:

163 Models
- Slacken the wheel bolts, jack up the rear end of the vehicle and remove the large axle shaft nut. A helper must depress the brake pedal. A new nut must always be fitted and is tightened to 49 kgm (353 ft.lb.) after installation of the shaft.
- Locate the wheel speed sensor on the wheel carrier (upper end) and remove the bracket securing bolt from the sensor and remove the sensor. The bolt is tightened to 1.0 kgm (7.2 ft.lb.).
- Remove the upper suspension arm ball joint nut from the wheel carrier and separate the ball joint, using a suitable puller. The nut is tightened to 5.0 kgm (36 ft.lb.) during installation. In the same manner disconnect the ball joint of the track rod joint (at the lower end, below the stabiliser bar) out of the wheel carrier. This nut is tightened to 5.5 kgm (40 ft.lb.) during installation.
- Using a puller, of the type shown in Fig. 5.2 and press the rear axle shaft out of the axle shaft flange. The rear axle shaft must be pressed as far as it will go towards the rear axle centre and swing the wheel carrier towards the outside.
- The axle shaft must now be pressed out of the rear axle centre assembly. A tyre lever is required. Apply the lever behind the axle shaft joint and press it away from the rear axle centre. Take care not to damage the rubber boot. The retaining snap ring at the end of the shaft must be removed and replaced.

The installation is a reversal of the removal procedure. Arrange the new retaining snap ring with the opening at the bottom. Note the tightening torques given above.

164 Models

The removal and installation is carried out in a similar manner as described above, with the difference that the tie rod (track rod), the camber strut and the torque strut must be detached from the wheel carrier. Removal and installation details are given earlier on in section 6.5 together with the tightening torques. The brake cable must be unclipped from the bracket on the rear axle carrier and another brake cable bracket from the camber strut. Different is the tightening torque of the collar nut at the end of the drive shaft (must be replaced), as in this case it is tightened to 52 kgm (375 ft.lb.).

6.7.   Wheel Bearings

We strongly recommend to have the wheel bearings replaced in a workshop. The wheel carrier can be removed as described earlier on and taken to the dealer to have the bearings replaced. If you want to attempt the replacement, remove the circlip on the outside of the wheel carrier and replace the double-row angular wheel bearing under a press. The workshop has, however, a special tool set to replace the bearing.

Fig. 5.12 shows the fitting of a bearing in the case of a front axle shaft. The same arrangement will be found on the rear axle shafts. The brake disc must be removed.

6.8.   Oil Change in Rear Axle

The rear axle has a capacity of 1.65 litres in the case of a 163 model. The capacity in the case of a 164 model is 1.1 litres if no differential lock is fitted or 1.8 litres if a differential lock is fitted. To remove the oil drain plug and the oil level/oil filler plug an Allen key of 14 mm A/F is required. Hypoid oil SAE 90 is used to fill the axle. Fig. 6.8 shows the location of the filler and oil drain plugs (163 model shown). To check the oil level unscrew the oil filler plug and check that the oil reaches the bottom edge of the filler hole. Change the oil as follows:

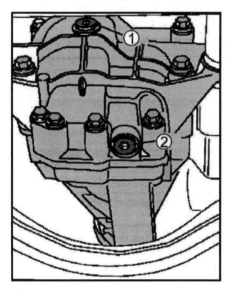

Fig. 6.8 – Location of the oil filler plug (1) and the drain plug (2) in the rear axle (163 shown).

- Drive the vehicle a short distance to warm up the oil.
- Place a suitable container underneath the axle and remove the oil drain plug (2) at the bottom of the axle. The oil level/filler plug (1) can be removed from the axle cover to speed up the draining of the oil.
- Wait until the oil has drained, clean the drain plug and refit the plug to the axle and tighten it.
- Fill the axle housing with the oil and amount given above until the oil level can be seen at the lower edge of the filler hole. Clean the plug, fit it and tighten it. Both plugs are tightened to 5.0 kgm (36 ft.lb.).

6.9.   Rear Wheel Alignment

The checking and adjusting of the rear wheel alignment requires the use of special equipment and special wrenches and we recommend to have the alignment checked in a workshop. If you have removed parts of the suspension which will alter the alignment and have followed the advise to mark the eccentric bolts and washers there will be no problems to drive the vehicle to the wheel alignment centre to have the settings checked.

6.10.   Rear Axle/Suspension – Tightening Torques

The main tightening torques are given in kgm. Multiply by "7.2" to obtain "ft.lb.". Most tightening torques are given during removal/installation of the component parts. Note the differences, avoid mistakes.

163 Models

Nut, link rods to torsion bar: ....2.2. kgm
Bolt, torsion bar rubber mounts/mounting clamps to rear axle carrier: ....2.8. kgm
Nut, shock absorber to lower suspension: ....8.5 kgm
Nut, shock absorber to frame side member: ....2.0 kgm
Nut, shock absorber to rear spring (piston rod): ....3.0 kgm
Nut, lower suspension arm to front axle carrier: ....13.5 kgm
Nut, lower suspension arm ball joint stud to suspension arm: ....12.5 kgm
Nut, upper suspension arm to frame: ....12.0 kgm
Nut, upper suspension arm ball joints to wheel carrier: ....5.0 kgm
Nut, track rod ball joint to wheel carrier: ....5.5 kgm
Nut, wheel speed sensor to wheel carrier: ....1.0 kgm
Collar nut, axle shaft to axle shaft flange: ....49.0 kgm
Oil filler and drain plugs: ....5.0 kgm

164 Models

Nut, shock absorber to spring control arm: ....26.5 kgm
Nut, shock absorber to frame floor: ....2.1 kgm
Bolt, torsion bar rubber mounts/mounting clamps to rear axle carrier: ....11.0. kgm
Nut, tie rod to rear axle carrier: ....9.3 kgm
Nut, linkage rod to rear axle carrier and torsion bar: ....18.0 kgm
Nut, tie rod (tension arm) to rear axle carrier and wheel carrier: ....11.0 kgm
Nut, camber strut to rear axle carrier: ....9.3 kgm
Nut, camber strut to wheel carrier: ....11.0 kgm
Collar nut, axle shaft to axle shaft flange: ....52.0 kgm
Oil filler and drain plugs: ....5.0 kgm

7   Steering

7.0.   Technical Data

Type: .... Rack and pinion with power assistance
Filling capacity of steering system: .... 1.2 litre (all models)
Fluid type: .... As for automatic transmissions

7.1.   Checks on the Steering

Checking the Steering Play

Excessive play in the steering can be adjusted, but this should be left to a Mercedes dealer who has the necessary special tools. The steering can, however, checked as follows:

• Place the front wheels in the straight-ahead position and reach through the open window and turn the steering wheel slowly to and fro.

• The front wheels must move immediately as soon as you move the steering wheel.

• If there is no play in the straight-ahead position but the steering wheel is more difficult to move as you rotate the steering wheel further you can assume that the steering gear is worn and must be replaced.

Checking the track rod ball joints for excessive play

With the wheel fitted grip the track rod ball joint and move it up and down with a considerable force.

A worn track rod ball joint can be recognised by excessive "up and down" movement. If this exceeds 2 mm, replace the ball joint.

Checking the steering rubber gaiters

Check the rubber gaiter over its entire length and circumference for cuts or similar damage. Also check that the gaiters are securely fastened at both ends. Track rods with worn ball joints or damaged rubber gaiters must be replaced as described earlier on.

7.2.   Steering Repairs

7.2.0.   REMOVAL AND INSTALATION

The removal and installation of the steering is a complicated operation, as amongst other operations the front axle drive gear must be removed (all models). As it will be

Steering

very rare to remove the steering, we recommend that the work is carried out in a workshop. A brief description of the removal follows below.

The following precautions must be followed if any work on the steering system is necessary:

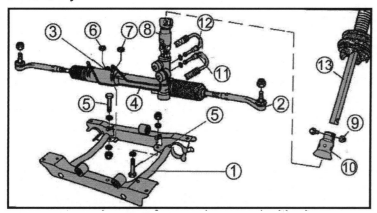

Fig. 7.1 – Details for the removal and installation of the power steering (163).

• All operations must be carried out under the cleanest of conditions.

• After disconnecting any pipes or hoses from the steering system clean the connecting points immediately. All removed parts must be placed onto a clean surface and covered with clean paper or rags.

• Never use fluffy rags to clean any parts of the steering system.

• If fitting new parts take them out of the packing just before they are fitted. Only fit original parts.

• Never re-use fluid drained from the steering system.

The steering can be removed as follows, applicable to all 163 model. Front of vehicle on secure chassis stands, front wheels removed. Fig. 7.1 shows details of a 163 model. Remove the front axle gear as described earlier on and then proceed:

• On a 163 model with speed-sensitive power steering unplug a connector for the power steering from the timing case. Some 164 models have a so-called memory package (driver seat, steering column, mirrors) which must be deactivated. Your Owners Manual will give you the instructions.

• Extract the fluid from the steering fluid reservoir as shown in Fig. 2.11 in the case of the brake fluid reservoir.

• Detach the lower engine compartment panelling or the bottom section of the sound-proofing capsule (on some 164 models).

• Disconnect the track rod ball joints (2) in Fig. 6.1 from the lever on the steering knuckle, using a suitable ball joint puller after removal of the stud nut. A new nut must be fitted, 5.5 kgm (40 ft.lb.) in the case of a 163 model or 5.0 kgm (36 ft.lb.) +60° in the case of a 164 model.

• Position the steering wheel in the centre position, i.e. front wheels in straight-ahead position and remove the ignition key (steering locked).

• In the case of a 164 model there is a connector near the steering pinion. Disconnect it.

• Detach the fluid return pipe (11) and the high pressure expansion hose (10). Either fittings or banjo bolts are used. Protect the disconnected pipe/hose to prevent entry of dirt. The sealing rings must be replaced during installation, but note the tightening torques: If a screw joint fitting is used, tighten the return pipe and high pressure hose to 1.5 kgm (10 ft.lb.), if a banjo (hollow) bolt is fitted tighten both fluid lines to 3.0 kgm (22 ft.lb.).

• Remove the nut (9) from the steering coupling (8) and pull the lower steering shaft (13) upwards and out of the coupling. Do not damage the coupling shield (10) during removal. The nut (9) must be replaced. Tightened to 2.8 kgm (20 ft.lb.). Remember that the steering must be in the centre position during installation.

• Detach the rack-and-pinion steering (4) from the front axle carrier (1) by removing the bolts (5). Note the position of the shims (6) and (7) on the R.H. side, inserted between the rubber mount and the front axle carrier as they are different in thickness. The bolts are tightened to 5.0 kgm (36 ft.lb.) during installation in the case of a 163 model. The bolts of a 164 model are tightened in four stages: First tighten to 5.0 kgm (36 ft.lb.), then slackened by half a turn, then tightened to 5.0 kgm once more and from the final position a further quarter of a turn (90°).

• After removal of the steering check the rubber mount (3) for damage and replace if necessary.

Installation is a reversal of the removal procedure, adhering to the torque values given above. The steering must be filled and bled of air after installation. The front wheel alignment should be checked in a workshop if any of the parts have been replaced.

7.2.1. TRACK RODS – REPLACEMENT

Before you decide to have a track rod ball joint or a track rod replaced, you can carry out the following checks:

• Check the track rod ball joints rubber dust caps for cuts or other damage.

• Have the steering wheel turned into one lock (helper required), grip the track rod ball joint with one hand and ask the helper to move the steering wheel to and fro. The engine should be started to facilitate the steering wheel movements. Excessive play requires the fitting of a new track rod ball joint.

• Place the front end of the vehicle on chassis stands and grip the track rod with one hand. Move the track rod up and down. Excessive play in the ball joints requires the replacement of the joint.

• Similar checks can be carried out on the inner ball joint. In this case the rubber gaiter must be detached from the steering rack. Excessive clearance at the inner joints requires the replacement of the track rod. As the steering must be removed to replace a track rod we recommend a dealer as the only solution.

7.2.2. TRACK ROD BALL JOINTS - REPLACEMENT

The ball joints at the ends of the track rods can be replaced with the steering fitted. The operations are similar on all models but the tightening torques are not the same. After disconnecting the ball joint from the steering lever undo the locknut securing the ball joint end to the track rod and unscrew the end piece from the track rod, at the same time counting the number of turns necessary.

When fitting the new ball joint screw it onto the track rod by the same number of turns (also half-turns) and provisionally tighten the locknut. If the operations have been carried out properly there should be no need to check the toe-in setting.

Tighten the locknut to 5.0 kgm (36 ft.lb.) in the case of model series 163 or 6.0 kgm (43 ft.lb.) in the case of model series 164. Also different is the torque for the ball joint stud nut. Either 5.5 kgm/40 ft.lb. (163) or 4.5 kgm +90°/32.5 ft.lb. +90° (164).

Have the front wheel alignment checked if possible or if not sure.

7.3. The hydraulic System

7.3.1. FILLING THE SYSTEM

If the steering system has been drained for any reason it must be refilled and bled of air. Fluid drained from the system must not be re-used to fill the reservoir. The filter must be replaced if the system has been completely drained or the fluid is changed for any reason. The following sequence must be adhered to:

• Remove the screw cap from the fluid reservoir. There is a seal inside the cap which could drop out.

• Fill the reservoir to the upper edge.

- Start the engine a few times and immediately switch it off again. This will fill the complete steering system. During this operation the fluid level in the reservoir will drop and must be corrected immediately. Never allow the reservoir to drain as otherwise fresh air will be drawn into the system. A helper is obviously required to start and switch off the engine.
- When the fluid level in the reservoir remains the same the system is filled and the fluid level must be within the markings on the fluid dipstick. As already shown the dipstick has an upper and a lower mark. The total capacity of the system is given as 1.2 litre.
- Push the seal into the screw cap and refit the cap to the reservoir.

We recommend to check the fluid level during each check of the engine oil level. This will assure you not to overlook the check. During the level check or topping-up of the reservoir make sure that no foreign bodies or dirt can enter the system.

7.3.2. BLEEDING THE HYDRAULIC SYSTEM

After the fluid level remains the same after the engine has been started and switched off a few times bleed the system as described below. A helper is required to turn the steering wheel:

- Have the steering wheel moved from one lock to the other and back again to eject the air out of the steering cylinder. The steering wheel must be moved slowly, just enough for the piston inside the steering cylinder to contact its stop.
- Observe the fluid level in the reservoir during this operation. If the level drops, fill in additional fluid, as it must remain on the MAX mark. No air bubbles must be visible during the bleeding operation.

7.3.3. CHECKING THE SYSTEM FOR LEAKS

Sometimes it is possible that fluid is lost for some unknown reason. A quick check may establish where the fluid is lost:

- Ask a helper to turn the steering wheel from one lock to the other, each time holding the wheel in the maximum lock.

This will create the max. pressure in the system and any obvious leaks will be shown by fluid dripping on the floor.

- From below the vehicle (on chassis stands) check the area around the steering pinion. Slacken the rubber gaiters on the steering rack and check the ends of the rack. The rack seals could be leaking.
- Check the hose and pipe connections. These must be dry.

8	**Brake System**

8.0. Technical Data

Type of system   See description below

Front Brakes
All possible versions listed. Differences will apply between 163 and 164 models. Also covers petrol models. Data given as available:

Caliper piston diameter, front brakes:	60.00 mm
Thickness of brake pads, incl. back plate:	Inner pad – 163 models 16.5 mm
	Outer pad – 163 models 15.5 mm
	Both pads – 164 models 19.75 mm
Min. thickness of linings:	2.0 mm (without metal plate)

Brake disc thickness:	26.0 mm (163), 32.0 mm (164)
Brake disc diameter:	303, 330 or 345 mm, depending on model
Min. thickness of brake disc:	24.0 mm (163). 30,0 mm (164)
Max. run-out of brake discs:	0.10 mm
Wear limit of brake discs, per side:	max. 0.05 mm

Rear Disc Brakes

Caliper piston diameter:	Depending on fitted version 38.0 or 40.0 or 42.0 mm
Brake disc diameter:	285 or 331 300 mm
Brake disc thickness:	Between 10 and 22 mm (depending on version)
Min. brake disc thickness:	8.0 mm or 20.0 mm
Min. thickness of brake pads, incl. metal plate:	16.0 mm (163), 19.8 mm (164)
Min. thickness of pad linings:	2.0 mm

Handbrake

Min. width of brake linings:	1.00 mm (0.04 in.)
Number of notches required for fully engaging handbrake, using average force:	5 – 8
Number of notches until handbrake becomes effective:	1

8.1. Short Description

All models covered in this manual are fitted with a hydraulic dual-circuit brake with vacuum-operated brake servo unit. The brake servo unit is supplied with vacuum from the inlet manifold (petrol models) or a separate vacuum pump (diesel models). Sliding (floating) calipers or fixed calipers are fitted to the front wheels. Disc brakes, working on the same principle as the fixed front brake calipers are used on the rear wheels. The brake calipers are not the same on all models and again you can consult the technical data section for details. Otherwise enquire at your parts supplier, quoting the exact model identification number, model year, etc. if new parts are required.

The brake system is diagonally split, i.e. one circuit serves one of the front brake calipers and the diagonally opposed rear brake caliper. The other circuit operates the other two brake assemblies accordingly. If one brake circuits fails, the brakes will operate as normal, but more brake force will be required. The information and instructions in the following description will try to cover all possible versions.

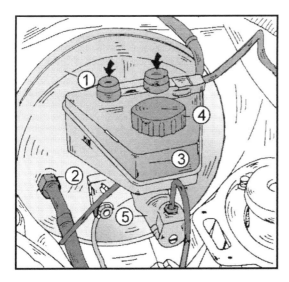

Fig. 8.1 – The brake fluid reservoir is fitted to the master brake cylinder. Note the "min" and "max" marks on the outside of the cylinder. The two buttons shown with the arrows can be depressed to check the brake fluid level.

1. Brake servo unit
2. Vacuum hose
3. Fluid reservoir
4. Screw cap
5. Master brake cylinder

Checking the Brake Fluid Level

The brake fluid reservoir is fitted above the master brake cylinder in the position shown in Fig. 8.1. At all times make sure that the brake fluid is between the "Min" and "Max" marks on the outside of the cylinder. If the brake fluid level sinks below the "Min" mark there are other reasons which must be investigated.

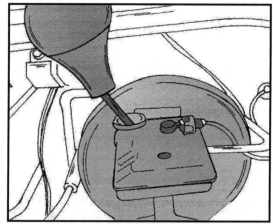

Fig. 8.2 – Brake fluid can be removed from the fluid reservoir as shown, when it is necessary to drain the brake system.

Brake fluid must sometimes be removed from the reservoir. If this is necessary we recommend the method shown in Fig. 8.2.

8.2.   Front Disc Brakes

As already mentioned, sliding brake calipers with one piston are fitted to the front wheels. The assemblies consist of a caliper mounting bracket bolted rigidly to the front axle steering knuckle and a separate caliper cylinder. When the brake is operated, the piston pressed first with its brake pad against the brake disc. The caliper cylinder then slides on glide bolts and moves against the direction of the pressure, until the other brake pad is pressed against the brake disc on the other side. Only the caliper cylinder must be removed to replace the brake pads, the mounting bracket remains on the steering knuckle.

8.2.0.   FLOATING CALIPERS

Floating calipers are fitted to model series 164 and models in the 163 range. Fig. 8.3 shows this type of caliper. Note that floating calipers on the rear axle are fitted in a similar manner.

Checking and Replacing the Brake Pads – 163 Models

To check the pad thickness without removing the pads, the wheels must be removed (front or rear). Use a torch and shine through the opening in the caliper. You will have a view as shown in Fig. 8.4. If the thickness of the pad material appears to be less than 3.5 mm (0.14 in.), replace the brake pads on both sides. The min. permissible thickness is 2.0 mm (0.08 in.).

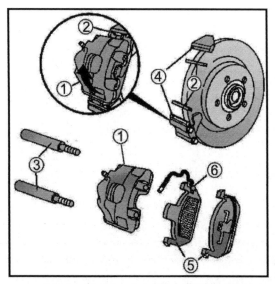

Fig. 8.3 – Fitted brake caliper with the location of some of the parts. Refer to text.

Important: If it is possible that the brake pads can be re-used, mark them in relation to the side of the car and to the inside or outside position of the caliper. Never interchange brake pads from left to right or visa versa, as this could lead to unequal braking.

To remove the brake pads, either for examination or replacement, first jack up the front end of the vehicle and remove the wheel. Then proceed as follows:

- Unplug the contact sensor connector from the L.H. caliper. Fig. 8.6 shows where the connector can be found.
- Remove the guide bolts (3) on the wheel carrier (4). Always use new bolts.

Fig. 8.4 – The thickness of the pad material (1) can be checked through the opening in the caliper.

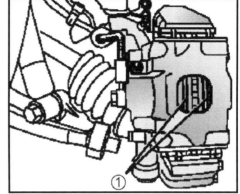

- Remove the floating caliper (1) from the wheel carrier and with a piece of wire or cord suspend the caliper from some part of the front suspension. Do not allow to let it hang down on the brake hose. Do not disconnect the hose. Remove the caliper (1) upwards in direction of the arrow together with the brake pads. The slide rails (2) must be removed (replace).

- Remove the brake pads (5) from the sides of the caliper. The pads are not the same on both sides. Press out the L.H. brake pad contact sensor (6) out of the metal plate of the brake pad (5). The sensor for the brake pad wear indicator is fitted to the inner brake pad as shown. The connector tab of the sensor can be withdrawn from the pad if new pads are fitted.

Measure the thickness of the pad material. If the thickness is around 3.5 mm, fit new pads. Although the pad material can be worn down to 2.0 mm, you will find that the pad wear indicator lights up when a thickness of 3.5 mm is reached. Never replace one pad only even if the remaining pads look in good order.

The sensors for the brake pad wear indicator should be replaced if the insulation shows signs of chafing or other damage.

- Check the thickness of the brake disc and compare the dimensions given in Section 8.0. Replace the discs if the thickness is below the minimum permissible. Although different thicknesses apply you will be able to determine from the thickness given which value applies to your particular model.

Before fitting the new pads clean the caliper opening with a brush and clean brake fluid or methylated spirit. Wipe off any spirit remaining and lubricate the exposed part of the piston with rubber grease. Fit the pads as follows:

- Open the fluid reservoir and draw off some of the fluid as shown in Fig. 8.2.

Fig. 8.5 – Using the special tool (clamp) to push the piston back into its bore.
1   Brake caliper
2   Piston
3   Cylinder housing
4   Special tool

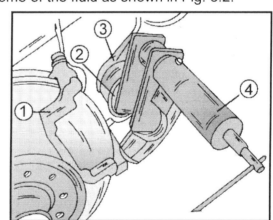

- Push the piston back into its bore. Either use the special pliers available for this purpose (see Fig. 8.5) or place a wooden block in position and lever back the piston carefully with a large screwdriver blade.

- Insert both brake pads into the caliper carrier slide rails and carefully lower the caliper housing carefully over the pads. First insert the inner brake pad into the caliper piston and then insert the outer brake pad. Use new self-locking bolts and tighten the bolts to 3.0 kgm (22 ft.lb.)

- Coil the brake pad wear indicator cable and connect to the terminal on the brake caliper. Fit the connector protective cover.

- Apply the foot brake several times after installation of the brake pads. This is an essential requirement to allow the new pads to take up their position. Bleed the brake system if necessary and check and if necessary correct the fluid level in the master cylinder reservoir.

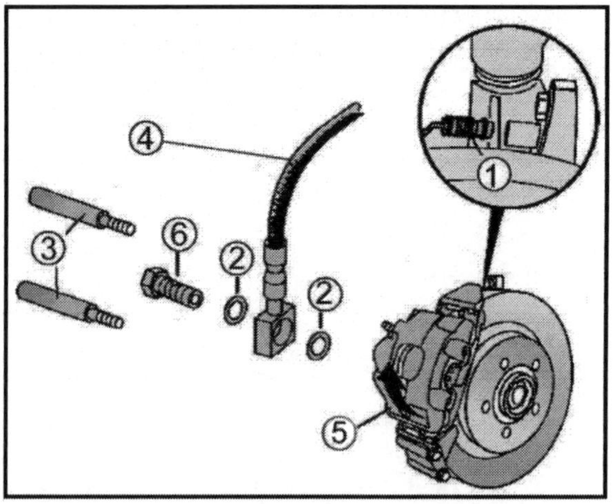

Fig. 8.6 – Details for the removal of a brake caliper. See text.

Removal and Installation of a Brake Caliper

The front end of the vehicle must be resting on chassis stands and the wheel removed. Removal details are shown in Fig. 8.6.

- Place a bleeder hose over the bleeder screw (remove the rubber cap first) and insert the other end of the hose into a container (glass jar). Open the bleeder screw and pump the brake pedal until all fluid has been drained from the system.
- Unplug the contact sensor connector (1) at the position shown.
- Unscrew the banjo bolt (6) for the brake hose (4) from the caliper (5). The sealing rings (2) must be replaced during installation. The bolt is tightened to 3.0 kgm (22 ft.lb.).
- Unscrew the two guide bolts (3) from the brake caliper. Always replace the bolts.
- Swivel the caliper upwards in the direction of the arrow and remove it together with the brake pads.

The installation of the caliper is a reversal of the removal procedure. First insert the inner brake pad into the caliper piston and then insert the outer brake pad. Tighten the new caliper guide bolts to the torque given above. Finally bleed the brake system as described later on.

Brake calipers - Overhaul

Remove the caliper from the steering knuckle and have it overhauled at a dealer or a workshop dealing with brake system.

Checking and Replacing the Brake Pads – 164 Models

The instructions given for the 163 models also apply to the 164 models, but the attachment of the brake caliper is different. A retaining spring, as shown in Fig. 8.7 is fitted and must be removed by inserting a screwdriver into the retaining spring as shown and disengage it from the brake caliper housing.

On the inside of the caliper you will find two protective rubber caps (one at the upper end, one at the lower end). Remove the caps and unscrew the guide bolts (replace them).

The remaining operations follow the description for the 163 models. After the guide bolts have been fitted push the rubber caps in position. Fit the retaining spring to the anchoring points.

Fig. 8.7 – Removal of the retaining (tensioning) spring from the caliper.

Removal and Installation of a Brake Caliper – 164 models

The front end of the vehicle must be resting on chassis stands and the wheel removed.

- Place a bleeder hose over the bleeder screw (remove the rubber cap first) and insert the other end of the hose into a container (glass jar). Open the bleeder hose and pump the brake pedal until all fluid has been drained from the system.

- Disconnect the brake pipe from the brake hose at the inside of the wheel arch housing by unscrewing the union nut. Knock out the spring plate to free the hose. Suitably close the hose and pipe ends to prevent entry of dirt. The brake line connection is tightened to 1.8 kgm (13 ft.lb.).
- Lift the two lugs for the cover of the brake pad wear connector with a small screwdriver and pull off the plug. The brake hose can be unscrewed from the brake caliper, if desired, whilst the caliper is still fitted.
- Unscrew the brake caliper mounting bolts and lift off the unit. Discard the bolts as new bolts must be used during installation. The brake pads can now be removed from the caliper.

The installation of the caliper is a reversal of the removal procedure. Tighten the new caliper mounting bolts to 20 kgm (144 ft.lb.). Finally bleed the brake system as described later on.

8.2.1. FRONT BRAKE CALIPERS – Fixed Calipers

Checking and Replacing the Brake Pads – 163 Models

When the thickness of the brake pad linings has reached 3.5 mm, a warning light in the dashboard will light up, signalling that new brake pads must be fitted.

- Place the front end of the vehicle on chassis stands and remove the front wheels. The caliper will now have the appearance shown in Fig. 8.8. First withdraw the contact sensor connectors (7).
- Using a drift of suitable diameter drive the retaining pins out of the caliper from the outside towards the inside in the manner shown in Fig. 8.9. Remove the retaining spring in the centre.
- Remove the brake pads. The workshop used a special tool to withdraw the pads.
- Otherwise hook a piece of wire through the two brake pad holes and withdraw the pads one after the other with a short, sharp pull.

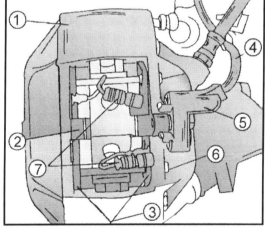

Fig. 8.8 – View of a brake caliper after removal of the wheel.

1 Brake caliper
2 Cross spring
3 Brake pads
4 Cable
5 Cable connector plug
6 Retaining pins
7 Contact sensor, brake pad
  wear indicator

- Push the pistons back into their bores, using a re-setting pliers as shown in Fig. 8.10. Otherwise use a piece of wood and carefully push the piston into the bore. It may be that the fluid reservoir overflows during this operation. Keep an eye on it. If necessary remove the fluid (Fig. 8.2).
- Withdraw the contact sensor out of the metal plate of the brake pad. The sensor must be replaced if the insulating layer on the contact plate is worn or any other part of the sensor or its cable is damaged.
- Measure the thickness of the pad material. If the thickness is around 3.5 mm, fit new pads. Although the pad material can be worn down to 2.0 mm, you will find that the pad wear indicator lights up when a thickness of 3.5 mm is reached. Never replace one pad only even if the remaining pads look in good order.

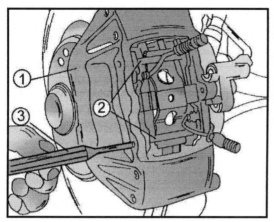

Fig. 8.9 – The retaining pins are removed from the outside towards the inside when the pads are removed.
1 Brake caliper
2 Retaining pins
3 Drift

- Check the thickness of the brake disc and compare the dimensions given in Section 8.0. Replace the discs if the thickness is below the minimum permissible. Although different thicknesses apply you will be able from the thickness given which value applies to your particular model.

Fig. 8.10 – Piston can be pushed into their bores using a pair of re-setting pliers. Brake fluid could overflow from the fluid reservoir.

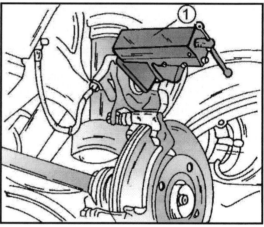

Before fitting the new pads clean the caliper opening with a brush and clean brake fluid or methylated spirit. Wipe off any spirit remaining and lubricate the exposed part of the piston with rubber grease. Fit the pads as follows:

- Coat the brake pad metal plates and their sides with Molycote paste and insert the pads into the brake caliper mounting brackets.
- Place the tensioning spring over the brake pads and insert the two retaining pins from the inside towards the outside into the caliper and through the brake pads. The pins have a clamping shape on one side which will keep them in position. Carefully drive them in position to their stop.
- Operate the brake pedal a few times to set the brake pads against the brake disc.
- Check the fluid level in the fluid reservoir and correct if necessary. Treat the new brake pads with feeling at the beginning before they are fully bedded in.

Removal and Installation of a Brake Caliper – 163 Models
The removal and installation of the caliper is carried out as described for the other type. One fitted bolt and a normal bolt are used to secure the caliper. Both are tightened to 18 kgm (130 ft.lb.) during installation.

Brake calipers - Overhaul
Refer to the points to be observed for the other caliper type. Additionally note that the two halves of a caliper must not be separated. A caliper should be overhauled by a specialist.

8.3.   Rear Disc Brakes

8.3.0.   BRAKE PADS - REPLACEMENT

Floating calipers with four pistons or fixed calipers are fitted (see below). The rear wheels must be removed to check the pad thickness. The remaining pad material can be checked by inspecting the thickness as shown in Fig. 8.4. If the thickness is less than 2.0 mm (0.8 in.), replace the brake pads of both rear calipers.
A view of a rear floating caliper and its attachment is shown in Fig. 8.11. Two bolts are used to attach the caliper. The instructions refer to the illustration.

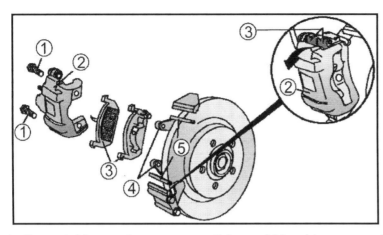

Fig. 8.11 – View of the rear brake caliper of a 163 model. Similar on a 164 model. See text.

ATTENTION: If it is possible that the brake pads can be re-used, mark them in relation to the side of the car and to the inside or outside position of the caliper. Never interchange brake pads from the inside to the outside, or visa versa, as this could lead to uneven braking.

- Place the rear of the vehicle on chassis stands and remove the rear wheels.
- Remove the bolts (1) and tilt the caliper in the direction of the arrow to remove it together with the brake pads (3). Remove the brake pads. The pads are different, make a note of the installation position.

Before fitting clean the caliper opening with a brush and clean brake fluid or methylated spirit. Wipe off any remaining spirit and lubricate the exposed parts of the piston with rubber grease. Push the pistons back into their bores. Either use the method described above (re-insert one of the old brake pads) or use a wooden block in position and lever back the piston carefully with a screwdriver blade. Note that one pad must be placed into the caliper as the other piston is pushed into the bore, otherwise the opposite piston will be pushed out when one of the pistons is pushed in. As this is done the level in the master cylinder reservoir will rise so either empty some of the fluid or alternatively release the bleeder screw to allow some fluid to escape as the piston is pushed in. The bleeder screw is only opened a little, and only whilst the piston is moved. It should not be necessary to bleed the brake system.

- Push the piston back into its bore. Either use the special pliers available for this purpose (see Fig. 8.5) or place a wooden block in position and lever back the piston carefully with a large screwdriver blade.
- Replace the two slide rails (5) for the brake pads (3) in the wheel carrier (4).
- Insert both brake pads into the caliper carrier slide rails (5) and carefully lower the caliper housing carefully over the pads. First insert the inner brake pad into the caliper piston and then insert the outer brake pad. Use new self-locking bolts and tighten the bolts to 2.3 kgm (16.5 ft.lb.).
- Apply the foot brake several times after installation of the brake pads. This is an essential requirement to allow the new pads to take up their position. Bleed the brake system if necessary and check and if necessary correct the fluid level in the master cylinder reservoir.

164 Models – with Fixed Calipers

The brake pads can be replaced after the calipers have been removed as described below. The fixed calipers are, however, fitted to petrol models and after a certain vehicle number to 163 models with CDI engine.

8.3.1.   BRAKE CALIPERS – REMOVAL AND INSTALLATION

The removal of a brake caliper is a simple operation. The following operations are valid for all models, but note that a different tightening torque must be observed when the caliper is fitted. Figs. 8.12 and 8.13 show the attachment of a caliper.

Brake System

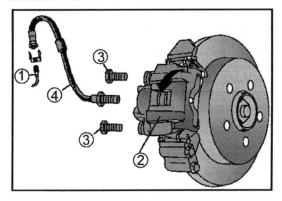

Fig. 8.12 – Rear brake caliper in fitted position (163 shown). Refer to text.

• Jack up the rear end of the vehicle, place chassis stands in position and remove the wheel on the side in question.

• Place a bleeder hose over the bleeding screw in the caliper (remove the rubber dust cap first) and insert the other end of the hose into a container (glass jar). Open the bleeder screw and pump the brake pedal (helper) until the fluid has been drained from the system.

Fig. 8.13 – Fitted floating caliper to a 164 model.

1   Caliper mounting bracket
2   Brake hose
3   Guide bolt
4   Floating caliper
5   Spring clip

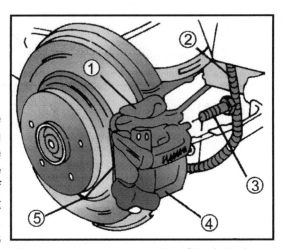

• Refer to Fig. 8.12 and disconnect the brake pipe from the brake hose (4) from the brake pipe (1) and free the brake hose from its bracket. Suitably close the hose and pipe ends to prevent entry of dirt. Slacken the brake hose connection at the caliper whilst the caliper is still fitted. Then unscrew the caliper mounting bolts (3) and lift off the caliper (2). Discard the bolts as new ones must be fitted during installation. The brake pads can now be removed from the caliper.

The installation is a reversal of the removal procedure. Use new bolts (3) and tighten them to 2.3 kgm (16.5 ft.lb.). In the case of a 164 model the bolts to 15.0 kgm (108 ft.lb.). Tighten the brake hose-to-brake pipe union nut with 1.8 kgm (13 ft.lb.), if it has been disconnected from the caliper. The brake system must be bled of air after installation of the caliper.

163 and 164 Models – with Fixed Calipers

Removal and installation is carried out in a similar manner as described above, but the connector plug must be disconnected from the wheel speed sensor und the sensor securing bolt removed (if fitted). The bolt is tightened to 0.9 kgm (7 ft.lb.). The items shown in Fig. 8.12 also apply to the 164 models, but the bolts (3) securing the brake caliper(s) to the wheel carrier are tightened to 11.5 kgm (83 ft.lb.).

8.4.   Brake Discs

Brake discs can be re-machined, but not below the thickness given in Section 8.0. As discs are sometimes changed we advise you to obtain the latest information from your dealer, quoting the model, engine, etc. Remove a brake disc as follows (in general for all models):

• Place the front or rear end of the vehicle on chassis stands and remove the wheel. If the rear disc is removed release the handbrake.

• Remove the two bolts securing the brake caliper (bolts must be replaced) and lift off the caliper. Attach the caliper with a piece of wire to the chassis. Do not allow the caliper to hang down on the brake hose.

Fig. 8.14 – Details for the removal and installation of a front brake disc.

1   Caliper bracket bolt
2   Splash guard
3   Brake disc
4   Screw
5   Clamping sleeve
6   Front drive shaft flange
7   Cylinder housing
8   Brake caliper bracket
9   Brake hose

The brake disc can now be removed after unscrewing the small securing screw. Use a rubber or plastic mandrel to knock off a sticking disc. Figs. 8.14 and 8.15 show general views how the discs are fitted.

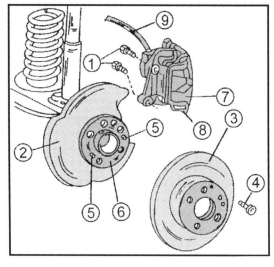

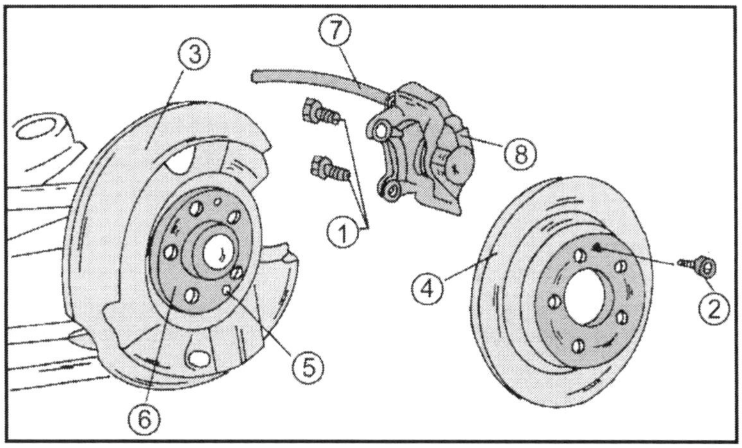

Fig. 8.15 – Details for the removal and installation of a rear disc brake (general view).

1   Brake caliper bolts
2   Disc securing screw
3   Splash guard
4   Brake disc
5   Dowel pin (not fitted)
6   Axle flange
7   Brake hose
8   Brake caliper

•

New discs are coated for protection and a suitable solvent must be used to clean them. Refit the disc as follows:

•   In the case of the front discs, fit the disc and tighten the securing screw to 2.3 kgm (16.5 ft.lb.) in the case of a 163 model, but only to 1.0 kgm (7.2 ft.lb.) in the case of a 164 model. Tighten the caliper mounting bolts as described during the installation of the brake calipers, again noting the difference in the tightening torques.

•   In the case of the rear discs, fit the disc and tighten the securing screw to 2.3 kgm (16.5 ft.lb.) in the case of a 163 model, but only to 1.0 kgm (7.2 ft.lb.) in the case of a 164 model. Tighten the caliper mounting bolts as described during the installation of the brake calipers, again noting the difference in the tightening torques, mainly as there are differences between floating calipers and fixed calipers which must not be overlooked.

Fig. 8.16 – Checking a brake disc for run-out.

1   Brake disc
2   Dial gauge bracket
3   Dial gauge

•   After installation of the disc, place a dial gauge against the brake disc as shown in Fig. 8.16. Slowly rotate the disc and observe the reading of the dial gauge. If the run-out of the disc is more than specified in section 8.0, there could be two reasons:

Brake System

- The brake disc is not fitted correctly to the hub. In this case remove the disc, move it around to the next fitting position and refit the disc.
- The brake disc is distorted (overheated for example).

Before driving off operate the brake pedal several times to establish the correct clearance between the brake pads and the brake disc. Check the fluid level in the reservoir and top-up if necessary.

8.5. Master Brake Cylinder

All vehicles use a tandem master cylinder with a twin reservoir, enabling the supply of brake fluid to the two circuits to the dual-line brake system. The brake pipes are split between the front and rear brakes. The piston nearest to the push rod operates the front brakes, the intermediate piston operates the rear brakes. The master cylinder should not be overhauled. Fit a new unit if the original one is worm beyond use.

The fluid level in the reservoir is monitored by means of a warning light in the instrument panel. The operation of the light must be checked when the reservoir is topped-up. To do this, switch on the ignition, release the handbrake and, using the thumb, press down the two rubber caps, shown by the arrows in Fig. 8.1.

The following information are given for the master cylinder fitted to 163 models, but one of two different versions can be fitted. Fig. 8.17 shows the later version. The two ESP brake pressure sensors 1 and 2 (12 and 13) are not fitted to earlier versions. Also not fitted is the heat shield (3).

The removal and installation of 164 models is more complicated and cannot be recommended. Amongst the difficult operations is the detachment of the left partition wall from the bulkhead inside the engine compartment. Only one ESP brake pressure sensor is fitted to the bottom the cylinder instead of the two shown in Fig. 8.17.

To remove the cylinder of a 163 model proceed as follows. The engine cover must be removed on certain engines:

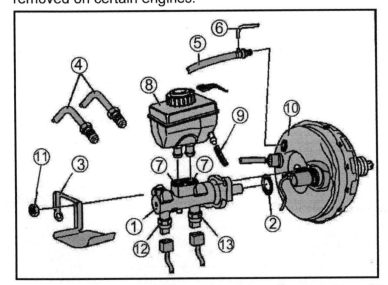

Fig. 8.17 – Details for the removal and installation of the master cylinder.

1	Brake master cylinder
2	Sealing ring
3	Heat shield
4	Brake pipe, 2.0 kgm
5	Vacuum pipes
6	Vacuum pipe (diesel only)
7	Rubber grommets
8	Fluid reservoir
9	Hose, with M/T
10	Brake servo unit
11	Cylinder securing nut
12	ESP pressure sensor 1
13	ESP pressure sensor 2

- Place a bleeder hose over one of the bleeder screws of one of the front calipers and another one over a bleeder screw of one of the rear calipers (remove the rubber dust cap first). Insert the other end of the hoses into a container (glass jar). Open both bleeder screws and operate the brake pedal until the system is empty.
- Remove the fuse and relay module covers. There are 2 covers, 5 bolts on the rear cover.
- Unplug the connector from the fluid reservoir (8).

- Disconnect the vacuum pipe (5) from the brake servo unit (10) and in the case of a diesel engine the vacuum pipe (6) from the splash wall. In the latter case also remove a vacuum hose from the vacuum pump and separate two hoses from a bracket.

- Detach hoses from the side of the fuse and relay module and place them to one side.

- Unscrew the brake pipe (4) from the master cylinder. Make a note where the pipes are connected, if not sure. The union nuts are tightened to 2.0 kgm (14.5 ft.lb.) during installation. Plug up the open brake pipes to avoid entry of dirt.

- If fitted, unplug the connectors of the two ESP brake sensors (12) and (13). A release catch at the underside of the plugs must be pressed to release them.

- Remove the nuts (11) securing the cylinder. New nuts must be used during installation and tightened to 2.0 kgm (14.5 ft.lb.). If fitted, remove the heat shield (3).

- Remove the cylinder by pulling it out straight towards the front. The sealing ring (2) must be replaced during installation. Note that the reservoir of a 164 model is attached with a screw.

- If a manual transmission is fitted remove the hose (9) from the fluid reservoir and plug up the opening.

- To remove the reservoir (8) place it on a bench, make sure it is empty and withdraw the reservoir. Install new rubber grommets (7) if necessary.

The installation is a reversal of the removal procedure. The "O" sealing ring must always be replaced as the connection must be vacuum-tight. Insert the sealing ring into the groove of the cylinder. Tighten the cylinder securing nuts to 2.0 kgm (14.5 ft.lb.). There is no need to adjust the master cylinder push rod. Fill the brake system and bleed the complete system as described later on.

Note: If the cylinder of a 164 model is removed, note different tightening torques: Brake pipes to master cylinder = 1.8 kgm (13 ft.lb.), master cylinder to brake servo unit = 1.0 kgm (7.2 ft.lb.), screw for fluid reservoir = 0.4 kgm.

8.6. Parking Brake

The parking brake (handbrake) is a "duo-servo-type" brake shoe system. "Duo" indicates that the brake is effective in both directions of brake disc rotation, "servo" indicates the transmission of the brake shoe movement from one shoe to the other.

8.6.0. PARKING BRAKE SHOES – REMOVAL AND INSTALLATION

Although similar in operation, the arrangement of the individual parts is not the same on 163 and 164 models. The main difference is, however, the location of the thrust piece with the adjusting wheel. On 163 models it is fitted as shown in Fig. 8.18, on the 164 models it is located at the upper end of the brake shoe assembly.

The special installation tool 116 589 01 62 00 is required to remove the brake shoes with the rear wheel hub fitted. Otherwise the rear hub must be removed to gain access to the hold-down springs. Fig. 8.19 shows a sectional view of the brake system and should be referred to locate the individual parts. 163 vehicles are fitted with an automatic handbrake cable compensating mechanism which must be tensioned before the following operations can be carried out and must de-tensioned after the operations are completed. The operation is described later on. Remove the brake shoes as follows. The description is valid for 163 models. Similar operations are carried out on 164 models with the difference that the items mentioned are arranged differently:

Brake System

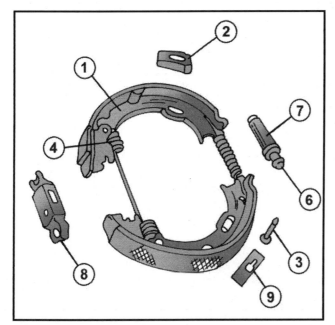

Fig. 8.18 – Component parts of the handbrake brake shoes as fitted to 163 models.
1 Brake shoes
2 Retaining spring
3 Adjuster
4 Retracting spring
5 Retracting spring
6 Thrust piece
7 Thrust pin
8 Expanding lock
9 Retaining spring

- Place the rear end of the vehicle on secure chassis stands and remove the wheels.
- Tension the automatic handbrake cable compensator (Section 8.6.2).

- Remove the brake caliper and the brake disc as already described. You will now have the view shown in Fig. 8.20. The special tool mentioned above is now necessary. The shape of the tool is shown in Fig. 8.21. It may be necessary to make up a similar handle with a hook at the end. Insert the tool into the retracting spring (4) in Fig. 8.18 and disconnect it. During installation make sure that the spring is correctly engaged.

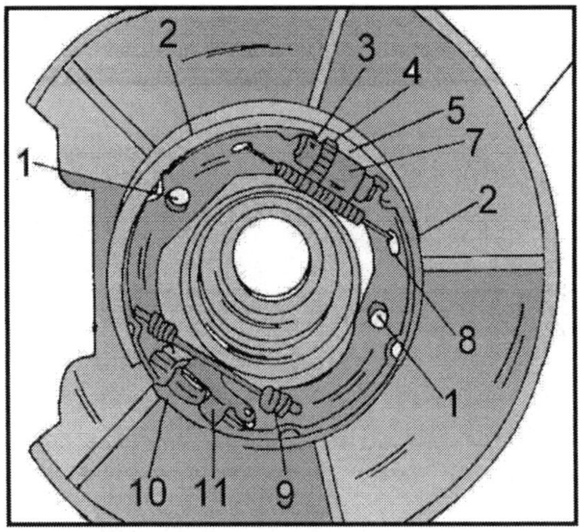

Fig. 8.19 – Removal and installation of brake shoes.
1 Hold-down spring
2 Brake shoes
3 Thrust piece
4 Adjuster wheel
5 Brake back plate
6 Cover plate
7 Thrust sleeve
8 Upper shoe return spring
9 Lower shoe return spring
10 Brake carrier
11 Expanding lock

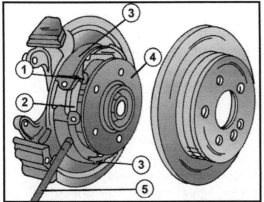

Fig. 8.20 – Using the special spring removal tool.
1 Retracting spring
2 Expanding lock
3 Brake shoes
4 Rear axle drive flange
5 Spring removal tool

- Remove the retracting spring (2) and the pin (7). Again make sure that the spring is correctly seated during installation.
- Remove the brake shoes. To do this, pull the two brake shoes apart until they can be lifted over the axle shaft flange towards the top. Disconnect the upper return spring (5) and remove the expanding lock (8)

The installation of the new brake shoes is carried out as follows:

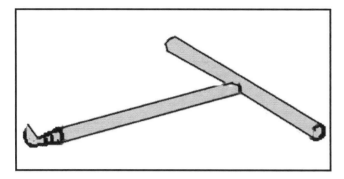

Fig. 8.21 – The special spring removal tool.

- Coat all bearing and sliding faces on the expanding lock with Molykote paste and fit the expanding lock. Then push the expanding lock against the cover plate.

- Coat the threads of the thrust piece and the cylindrical portion of the adjuster wheel (6) with long-term grease and assemble the adjusting device. Turn the adjuster completely back.

- Insert the adjuster between the two brake shoes, with the adjuster wheel pointing in the direction shown in Fig. 8.18. Fit the upper return spring (5) to the two brake shoes.

- Pull the brake shoes apart at the bottom, lift them over the drive shaft and attach them to the expanding lock.

- Fit the retracting spring (4) to one of the brake shoes, insert the installation tool, compress the spring slightly and then turn it by 90° to attach it to the cover plate. Check that the spring is correctly fitted and fit the other hold-down spring in the same manner.

- Fit the lower return spring with the smaller hook to one of the brake shoes and expand the spring until it can be engaged into the other brake shoe. This can be accomplished by means of a wire hook and a screwdriver to guide the spring into the anchor hole.

- Finally fit the brake disc and the caliper as described earlier on and adjust the braking brake as described in the next section.

8.6.1. PARKING BRAKE - ADJUSTMENT

The parking brake must be adjusted if it can be operated by more than 5 "clicks" of a total of 6 without locking the rear wheels. To adjust the handbrake proceed as follows, noting the difference between 163 and 164 models:

Fig. 8.22 – Adjusting the parking brake. The location of the adjusting wheel (1) of a 163 model. The threaded hole must be opposite. The arrow shows the direction of adjustment.

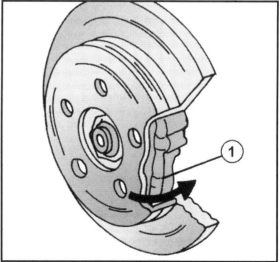

- Operate the parking brake pedal and check the pedal travel. Adjust if outside the limit given above.

- Place the rear end of the vehicle on chassis stands. **In the case of a 164 model** remove the rear wheels and on the outside of the brake discs locate the rubber plugs and remove it.

- **In the case of a 163 model** remove one of the wheel bolts on each wheel and turn one of the wheels until the threaded hole (where the wheel bolt was fitted) is in the approximate position shown in Fig. 8.22. The wheels can, however, be removed to facilitate the adjustment.

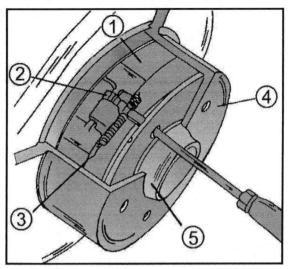

Fig. 8.23 – Adjusting the parking brake.
1   Brake shoe
2   Adjuster wheel
3   Upper return spring
4   Brake disc/drum
5   Wheel shaft flange

163 Models

• Insert a screwdriver blade of suitable diameter into the hole. The screwdriver will pass through the brake disc/drum and the drive shaft flange and engages with the adjuster wheel inside the brake drum. Fig. 8.23 shows where the engagement takes place. The drum has been cut-away to give a better view and the screwdriver is of course, inserted on the other side.

• Operate the screwdriver in the correct direction, referring to the arrow in Fig. 8.22 until the wheel is locked. The adjusting wheel must be moved from left to right in the case of both wheels.

• With the wheel locked, turn back the screwdriver by 5 to 6 "clicks" of the adjuster wheel until the wheel once more is free to rotate. Refit the rear wheels (if removed) and re-check the adjustment. De-tension the brake compensator.

164 Models

• Insert a screwdriver blade of suitable diameter into the hole where the rubber insert was located. The screwdriver will pass through the brake disc/drum and the drive shaft flange and engages with the adjuster wheel inside upper end of the brake drum.

• Operate the screwdriver in the correct direction until the wheel is locked. In the case of the L.H. adjusting wheel turn it from the top to the bottom, in the case of the R.H. adjusting wheel turn it from the bottom to the top.

• With the wheel locked, turn back both adjusting wheels by the same number of turns. It must be possible to rotate the rear wheels or the brake disc completely freely using the hands only. Refit the rear wheels and push the rubber inserts into the brake discs.

8.6.2.   THE AUTOMATIC PARKING BRAKE COMPENSATOR

As already mentioned the compensator must be pre-tensioned bore the removal of the parking brake shoes and de-tensioned after installation. Fig. 8.24 shows the compensator. Read the instructions carefully as it is rather complicated.

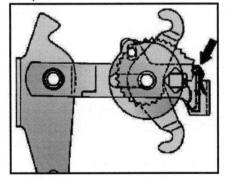

Fig. 8.24 – View of the handbrake compensating mechanism.

To de-tension the compensator after completing the work on the brake shoes use a screwdriver and lift the spring clip shown by the arrow. The compensator will then be de-tensioned and the length of the handbrake cable will be automatically compensated. Operate the handbrake a few times to set the mechanism into operation.

8.6.3.   PARKING BRAKE CABLES – REPLACEMENT

The replacement of the front handbrake cable and the rear handbrake cables is a very complicated operation, which we cannot recommend to carry out under DIY conditions. If the front cable or the rear cables require replacement you will have to seek the help of a Mercedes dealer.

8.7.   Brake Servo Unit

Brake servo units should not be dismantled, as special tools are required to dismantle, assemble and test the unit. Different servo units are fitted to Mercedes-Benz models, manufactured by either Teves, Bendix or Girling. Always make sure to fit the correct part if the servo unit is replaced. Remember that a failure of the servo unit to act will not affect the efficiency of the braking system but, of course, additional effort will be required for the same braking distance to be maintained.

ATTENTION! If you coast downhill, for whatever reason, with a vehicle equipped with a brake servo unit, remember that the vacuum In the unit will be used up after a few applications of the brake pedal and the brake system will from then onwards operate without power-assistance. Be prepared for this.

8.8.   Bleeding the Brakes

Bleeding of the brake system should be carried out at any time that any part of the system has been disconnected, for whatever reason. Bleeding must take place in the order left-hand rear side, right-hand rear, left-hand front and right-hand front. If only one of the brake circuits has been opened, either bleed the front or the rear circuit. The procedure given below should be followed and it should be noted that an assistant will be required, unless a so-called "one-man" bleeding kit is available.

Always use clean fresh brake fluid of the recommended specification and never re- use fluid bled from the system. Be ready to top up the reservoir with fluid (a brake bleeding kit will do this automatically) as the operations proceed. If the level is allowed to fall below the minimum the operations will have to be re-started.

Obtain a length of plastic tube, preferably clear, and a clean container (glass jar). Put in an inch or two of brake fluid into the container and then go to the first bleed point. Take off the dust cap and attach the tube to the screw, immersing the other end of the tube into the fluid in the container.

Open the bleed screw about three quarters of a turn and have your assistant depress the brake pedal firmly to its full extent while you keep the end of the tube well below the fluid level in the container. Watch the bubbles emerging from the tube and repeat the operation until no more are seen. Depress the brake pedal once more, hold it down and tighten the bleed screw firmly.

Check the fluid level, go to the next point and repeat the operations in the same way. Install all dust caps, depress the brake pedal several times and finally top up the reservoirs.

8.9.   Tightening Torques – Brakes

The tightening torques for the individual items for 163 and 164 models are given in the individual sections, dealing with the parts in question. When referring to the torque values, make sure to read for values (kgm or ft.lb.) applicable to the model in question. All data are given to the best of our knowledge. We would like to point out that torque values are sometimes changed without prior publications. Therefore latest values, if changed, are only available immediately to Mercedes-Benz dealers.

9   Electrical System

9.0.   Battery

Voltage: .... 12 volts
Polarity: .... Negative earth (ground)
Condition of Charge:
   Well charged: 1.28
   Half charged : 1.20
   Discharged: 1.12

To check the voltage of the battery, use an ordinary voltmeter and apply between the two battery terminals. A voltage of 12.5 volts or more should be obtained.

If a hydrometer is available, the specific gravity of the electrolyte can be checked. The readings of all cells must be approximate by the same. A cell with a low reading indicates a short circuit in that particular cell. Two adjacent cells with a low reading indicates a leak between these two cells.

A battery can be re-charged, but the charging rate must not exceed 10% of the battery capacity, i.e. 7.2 amps. The battery must be disconnected from the electrical system. Charge the battery until the specific gravity and the charging/voltage are no longer increasing within 2 hours. Add distilled water only. Never add acid to the battery.

The level of the battery electrolyte should always be kept above the top of the plates.

9.1.   Alternator

9.1.0.   ROUTINE PRECAUTIONS

The vehicle covered in this manual employs an alternator and control unit. This equipment contains polarity-sensitive components and the precautions below must be observed to avoid damage:

- Check the battery polarity before connecting the terminals. Immediate damage will result to the silicon diodes from a wrong connection—even if only momentarily.
- Never disconnect the battery or alternator terminals whilst the engine Is running.
- Never allow the alternator to be rotated by the engine unless ALL connections are made.
- Disconnect the alternator multi-pin connector before using electric welding equipment anywhere on the vehicle.
- Disconnect the battery leads if a rapid battery charger is to be used.
- If an auxiliary battery is used to start the engine. take care that the polarity is correct. Do not disconnect the cables from the vehicle battery.

9.1.1.   DRIVE BELT TENSION

Always tension the drive belt whenever the alternator, water pump or drive belt have been removed or slackened for any reason. The single drive belt is properly tensioned when the operations described in Section "Cooling System" are followed. The alternator runs at higher speed than the older D.C. dynamo generators and the belt tension should be maintained accurately for the best results. When a new belt has been fitted, it is as well to re-check the tension after a few hundred miles have been covered.

9.1.2.   ALTERNATOR – REMOVAL AND INSTALLATION

The alternator is rigidly attached to the engine. Remove as follows, noting that some differences will be found within the engine range.

Series 163 with M111, M112 and M113 Engine

The removal of the alternator is rather complicated as the parts to be removed and/or disconnected must be located. Fig. 9.1 shows the attachment of the alternator, in this case shown for the M112 engine. Removal and installation is a complicated operation as various parts must be removed as specified. The difficult part is to locate the individual items. If you attempt the removal (not recommended) proceed as follows:

- Disconnect the battery earth cable.
- In the case of all engines remove the air cleaner housing.
- If an M112 or M113 engine is dealt with remove the engine trim cover after pulling it upwards and separating it from the cylinder head covers.
- Remove or slacken the Poly V-belt. Slackening the belt will be sufficient in most cases (section "Cooling System").
- Refer to Fig. 9.1 and disconnect the cables (1) from the terminal "30" (B+) and the cable (2) from the terminal "61" (D+) after removal of the nuts. In the case of an M112 and M113 engine the cap (4) must first be withdrawn. Note the tightening torques when tightening the nuts. Terminal "B+" is tightened to 1.5 kgm in the case of the M111 engine and to 1.8 kgm in the case of the other engines. The nut of terminal "D+" is tightened to 0.4 kgm in the case of the M111 engine or 0.5 kgm in the case of the other engines.

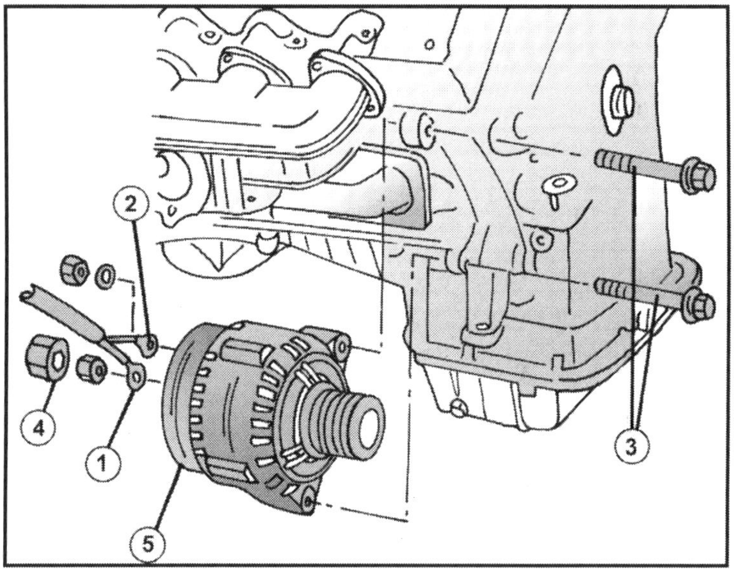

Fig. 9.1. – Details for the removal and installation of the alternator (M111, M112 and M113 engine).
1 Cable to terminal 30 (B+)
2 Cable to terminal 61 (D+)
3 Mounting bolts
4 Cap (if fitted)
5 Alternator

- The alternator can now be removed by referring to Fig. 9.1. Remove the bolts (3) at the upper and lower end of the alternator (5) and lift out the unit. The bolts are tightened to 4.2 kgm (30 ft.lb.) in the case of all engines.

The installation is a reversal of the removal procedure noting the tightening torques given above.

Fig. 9.2 – Alternator fitted to the M272 engine.
1 Protective cap
2 Nut
3 Cable to terminal 30 (B+)
4 Cable plug to terminal 61 (D+)
5 Lower mounting bolts, 2.0 kgm
6 Upper mounting bolts, 2.0 kgm
7 Alternator

M272 engine in model 164 (ML 350)

Fig. 9.2. shows the fitted alternator. Four bolts are used to secure the alternator to the

engine. Remove as follows:
- Disconnect the battery and remove the engine trim cover.
- Remove the R.H. air intake hose.
- Completely remove the Poly V-belt.
- Remove the protective (1) in Fig. 9.2. remove the nut (2) and withdraw the cable connector plug (3) from the terminal 30 (B+) from the alternator (7). The nut is tightened to 1.5 kgm.
- Withdraw the connector plug from the terminal 61 (D+) from the alternator (shown with (4).
- Remove the bolts (5) and (6) at the positions shown and remove the alternator towards the bottom. The bolts are tightened to 2.0 kgm (14.5 ft.lb.).

The installation is a reversal of the removal procedure. Note the tightening torque values given above when fitting the bolts and the terminal connections. After installation start the engine and check that the alternator is operating properly.

Fig. 9.3 – The dimension "a" gives the remaining brush length.

9.1.3.   SERVICING

A Bosch alternator is used on the engines dealt with in this manual, having a different output, depending on the engine. Remember that alternators are sometimes changed. Always check the applicable part number when a new alternator is fitted.

We do not recommend that the alternator or control unit should be adjusted or serviced by the owner. Special equipment is required in the way of test instruments and the incorrect application of meters could result in damage to the circuits.

The alternator is fitted with sealed-for-life bearings and no routine attention is required for lubrication. Keep the outside of the alternator clean and do not allow it to be sprayed with water or any solvent.

The alternator brush gear runs in plain slip rings and the brushes have a long life, requiring inspection only after a high mileage has been covered. To inspect the brushes, we recommend the removal of the alternator. Take out the two screws from the brush holder assembly and withdraw for inspection.

Measure the length of the brushes, shown by "a" in Fig. 9.3. If the protruding length is less than 5.0 mm (0.2 in.) or approaching this length, replace the brushes. New brushes will have to be soldered in position. We would like to point out that it is not an easy operation to guide the brushes over the slip rings when the slip ring cover is being fitted.

9.2.   Starter Motor

9.2.0.   REMOVAL AND INSTALLATION

Disconnect the battery earth (ground) cable. Again we try to separate the different models. Read the instructions before you commence with the job – Complicated on some of the models:

M111 engine in series 163
The front of the vehicle must be resting on secure chassis stands as the starter motor must be removed from below.

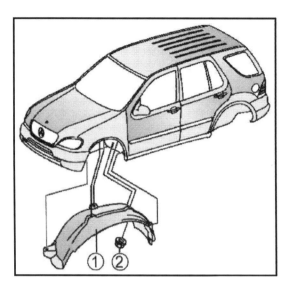

Fig. 9.4 – Removal of the wing liner (1) inside the front wing. Secured by means of nuts (2).

- Disconnect the battery earth cable.
- Remove the wing liner (see Fig. 9.4) inside the wing on the side of the starter motor.
- Disconnect the cable connections at the rear of the starter motor. Tighten the upper nut to 1.4 kgm (10 ft.lb.) and the lower nut to 0.6 kgm during installation.
- Remove the starter motor mounting bolts and remove the unit from below.

The installation is a reversal of the removal procedure. The bolts are tightened to 4.2 kgm (30 ft.lb.). Make sure that the mating faces are clean before bolting up. Re-connect the wires and the battery terminal.

M112 and M113 Engines

Fig. 9.5 shows the fitting of the starter motor on these engines. Remove as follows:

Fig. 9.5 – Removal and installation of the starter motor in the case of M112 and M113 engines (shown on model series 163).

1 Cable to terminal 30
2 Cable to terminal 50
3 Starter motor bolts, 4.2 kgm
4 Nuts, cable connections
5 Engine mounting cover
6 Nut
7 Washer
8 Starter motor

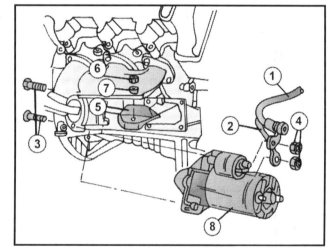

- Disconnect the battery.
- Remove the wing liner (see Fig. 9.4) inside the wing on the side of the starter motor.
- In the case of the M112 engine remove the nut (6) securing the protective cover (5) from the L.H. engine mounting and remove the cover (shield). The nut (6) is tightened to 6.5 kgm (47 ft.lb.) during installation.
- Disconnect the cables from the rear of the starter motor. The cables are connected to terminal 30 (1) and terminal 50 (2). Tighten the nut of terminal (1) to 1.4 kgm (10 ft.lb.) and the nut of terminal (2) to 0.6 kgm.
- Remove the starter motor bolts (3) and take out the unit towards the side. Turn the starter motor in order to guide past any obstructing parts. The two bolts (3) are tightened to 4.2 kgm (30 ft.lb.).

Installation is a reversal of the removal procedure.

9.2.1.   SERVICING

It may be of advantage to fit an exchange starter motor if the old one has shown fault. Exchange starter motors carry the same warranty as a new unit.

9.3. Headlamps - Replacement

As the replacement of a headlamp requires the adjustment of the headlamp beams, which should be carried out at a Mercedes dealer or a workshop dealing with headlamp adjustments we will not describe the operations for the removal and installation of the units. Fig. 9.6 shows the individual parts of a headlamp as fitted to a 163 model, which can be referred to when you intend to remove a lamp unit. The location of the bulbs on the same model range can be seen in Fig. 9.7. Removal of the headlamps on a 164 model is similar, but under no circumstances do we recommend to carry out any work if Xenon headlamps are fitted. On these models it will be necessary to remove the front bumper. Remember, always have the headlamp alignment checked after a headlamp is replaced.

With some knowledge it will be possible to replace a headlamp unit as follows, but remember that the information is given for the 163 model:

*   With the bonnet open, unlock the cover (1) in Fig. 9.6 at the clip (arrow A) under the lamp unit and unhook it. During installation of the headlamp make sure that the clip is locked correctly.
*   Unscrew the bolt (2) at the upper end of the headlamp unit.
*   Remove the three nuts (3) at the lower end of the headlamp unit. Again note during installation. The distance of the cover to the bumper must be even. Check before the nuts are tightened.
*   Unhook the L.H. or R.H. headlamp unit (5) from the hole (arrow B) using a drift (4) and pull the headlamp unit forward.
*   Disconnect the headlamp harness connector (6) and remove the headlamp towards the front.

Installation is carried out in reverse order.

9.4. Bulb Table

Main and dipped beam:	Halogen H4, 60 & 55 watts, ECE H4
Fog lamps:	Halogen H3, 55 watts, ECE H3
Indicator lamps, front end rear:	ECE P, 21 watts
Reversing light, rear fog lamp:	ECE P, 21 watts
Parking lamps:	ECE T, 4 watts
Tail lights:	ECE R, 10 watts
Number plate lights:	5 watts
Luggage compartment, interior lamps:	10 watts

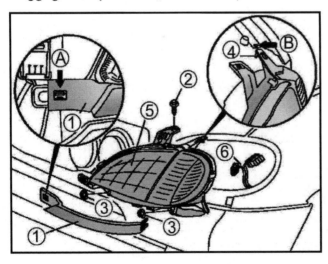

Fig. 9.6 – The component parts of a headlamp unit (163 model). The arrow (A) shows where a clip under the lamp unit must be unhooked. (B) shows where the lamp unit must be unhooked.
1   Cover
2   Securing bolts
3   Securing nuts
4   Retaining pin
5   Lamp unit
6   Headlamp wiring harness

Fig. 9.7 – The location of the bulbs at the rear of the headlamps (163 model).

1   Lamp cover
2   Bulb cover
3   Catch lever
4   Electrical connector plug
5   Retaining clip
6   High beam bulb
7   Low beam bulb
8   Fog lamp bulb
9   Headlamp unit

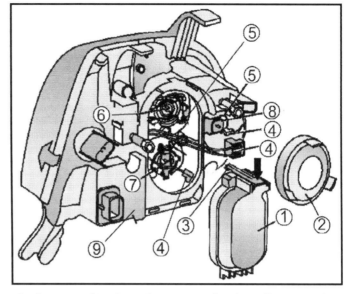

9. 5   Headlamp Bulb Replacement

Fig. 9.7 shows where the headlamp bulbs are fitted to the rear of a headlamp unit. Bulbs can be replaced as follows:

*   Remove the cover (1) by pressing on the catch lever (3) in the direction of the arrow and remove.
*   Remove the cover (2).
*   Disconnect the electrical connections (4) for the bulbs.
*   Open the retaining clip (5) for the bulbs and remove the bulbs as given in Fig. 9.7. Do not touch the bulbs with the fingers only. Use a paper towel or similar.

During installation make sure that the bulbs are correctly installed.

Make sure that the correct bulb for the light in question is used.

10	Automatic Transmission

Different types of automatic transmissions are fitted to the model range, however, all transmissions are of type "722" with different end numbers. All models in series 163 are fitted with a five-speed transmission, model series 164 with a 7-speed transmission.

10.0.   Technical Data

Fitted transmission:
– ML 230 (163):..722.660
– ML 320 (163):..722.662
– ML 350 (163):..722.674
– ML 430 (163):..722.663
– ML 500 (163):..722.663
– ML 350 (164):..722.906
– ML 500 (164):..722.901

Transmission Ratios - 163:	**ML 320**	**ML 430**
- First gear:	3.93 : 1	3.59 : 1
- Second speed	2.41 : 1	2.19 : 1
- Third speed	1.49 : 1	1.41 : 1
- Fourth speed	1.00 : 1	1.00 : 1
- Fifth speed	0.83 : 1	0.83 : 1

Automatic Transmission

- Reverse speed	3.16 : 1	3.16 : 1
- Axle ratio	3.16 : 1	3.16 : 1

Transmission Ratios - 163:	**ML 500**	**ML 350**
- First gear:	3.59 : 1	4.60 : 1
- Second speed	2.19 : 1	2.19 : 1
- Third speed	1.41 : 1	1.41 : 1
- Fourth speed	1.00 : 1	1.00 : 1
- Fifth speed	0.83 : 1	0.83 : 1
- Sixth speed	0.82 : 1	0.82 : 1
- Reverse speed	3.16 : 1	3.17 : 1
- Axle ratio	3.70 : 1	3.70 : 1

Series 164:	**ML 350**	**ML 500**
- First gear:	4.38 : 1	3.38 : 1
- Second speed	2.56 : 1	2.56 : 1
- Third speed	1.92 : 1	1.92 : 1
- Fourth speed	1.37 : 1	1.37 : 1
- Fifth speed	1.00 : 1	1.00 : 1
- Sixth speed	0.82 : 1	0.82 : 1
- Seventh speed	0.73 : 1	0.73 : 1
- Reverse speed	3.42 : 1	3.42 : 1
- Axle ratio	3.90 : 1	3.90 : 1

Filling Capacity:
–163 series – Initial filling: ....7.5 litres
– Other models – Initial filling: ....9.0 litres

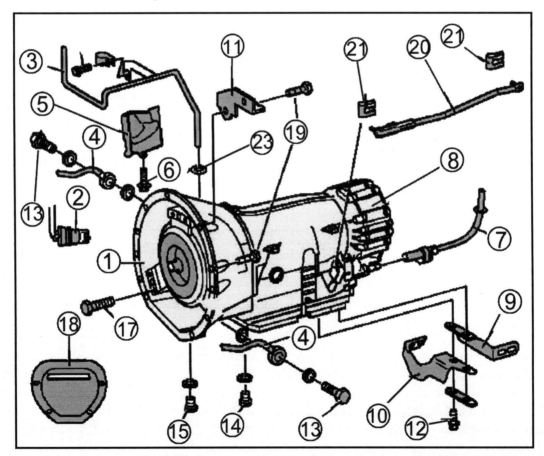

Fig. 10.1 – Details for the removal of the automatic transmission in the case of a 163 model (270 and 400 CDI). Refer to text.

10.1. Removal and Installation

As the engine can be removed without the transmission there may be no need to remove the transmission except when an exchange transmission is to be fitted. The following operations describe the removal and installation of the transmission as fitted to 163 models, followed by a summary of the operations in the case of a 164 model. Fig. 10.1 shows details of the location of the various parts to be disconnected or removed. The following numbered items refer to the illustration. A mobile jack will be required to lower the transmission.

- Disconnect the battery and place the vehicle on secure chassis stands.
- Remove the transfer case as described in section 3.1 commencing on page 115 from the adapter end (8) of the transmission.
- Detach the oil filler pipe (3) from the crankcase. Secured by bolts (22). Note the "O" sealing rings (23) on the pipe ends.
- Remove the heat shield (5) after removal of the bolt (6) and disconnect the 13-pin connector (2). The bolt (6) is tightened to 0.8 kgm (6 ft.lb.).
- Remove the shift rod (20). The securing clip (21) must be removed with a pair of pliers.
- From the rear end of the transmission remove the L.H. exhaust bracket (9) and the R.H. exhaust bracket (10) after removal of he bolt (12).
- Place a suitable container underneath the transmission and remove the fluid drain plug (14) from the transmission oil sump. Allow the fluid to drain and immediately refit the plug. Tighten the plug to 2.0 kgm (14.5 ft.lb.). Also remove the oil drain plug (15), this time from the torque converter. Note that this plug is tightened to 1.6 kgm (11.5 ft.lb.).
- Detach the cable for the so-called park lock interlock (7) at the transmission. The cable is only fitted to some models. If fitted, position the selector lever or the range selector lever into position "P" and leave it in this position when the cable and transmission are removed.
- Detach the fluid cooling lines (4). The area around the connecting points must be thoroughly cleaned to prevent entry of foreign matter. The banjo bolts (13) must be removed.
- Remove the cover (18) and detach the torque converter from the driven plate. The bolts (17) are tightened to 4.2 kgm (30 ft.lb.) during installation.
- Place a mobile jack with a suitable lifting plate underneath the transmission and unscrew the bolts (19). The retainer (11) is secured with one of the bolts and must be pushed upwards. All transmission to engine bolts are tightened evenly all round to 4.0 kgm (29 ft.lb.). Remember to fit the retainer (11) underneath one of the bolts.
- Remove the transmission from the engine and lower it at an angle on the lifting device. The torque converter can drop out and must be secured in position.

The torque converter can be removed, but the workshop uses special grab handles to pull it out. We would also like to point out that the installed height of the torque converter, i.e. the distance from the transmission housing, is not the same on all transmissions. For example the dimension is 7 mm in the case of a transmission for some transmissions and 19.5 mm for others – we would say a job for a workshop.

Installation is a reversal of the removal procedure. Fill the transmission with oil (approx. 5 litres) and then check the oil level as described below. The workshop carries out a transmission check and we advise you to seek the assistance of a dealer if not satisfied with the operation of the unit.

Automatic Transmission

164 Models

The following instructions are given in general. The removal is more complicated as in the case of 163 models. Read through the information below before commencing the removal.

- Disconnect the battery earth cable and place the vehicle on secure chassis stands.
- Remove the complete exhaust system.
- Underneath the propeller shaft you will find some protective shields, secured by four nuts and 10 bolts. Remove them and take off the three-part shields.
- Detach the rear propeller shaft from the flange on the transfer case. Before separating the two flanges mark the outside edges with a coloured pen to refit them in the same position. All bolts must be replaced and are tightened to 5.4 kgm (39 ft.lb.).
- On one side of the transmission remove a heat shield and in the same area unplug a connector. The heat shield bolts are tightened to 0.9 kgm.
- On the torque converter side of the transmission remove a cover and detach the torque converter from the drive plate. The drive plate must be rotated to reach all bolts. The bolts are tightened to 4.2 kgm.
- Remove a bolt securing the oil cooler line from the bracket on the oil sump.
- On the alternator bracket there is a bolt securing a double clamp. Remove it. Tighten to 0.8 kgm (6 ft.lb.).
- On the side of the transmission locate the two oil cooler lines. Remove them from the transmission and the engine oil sump and place them to one side without bending them. Close the open ends in suitable manner. The "O" seals must be replaced during installation. The union nuts are tightened to 0.9 kgm.
- Place a mobile jack with a suitable lifting plate underneath the transmission and lift the unit. The workshop uses, of course, a special lifting device.
- Remove the engine crossmember. Bolts are used at the outer edges and in the centre. The rear engine mounting remains on the crossmember. The bolts must be replaced. The bolts are tightened to 5.5 kgm (40 ft.lb.).
- Detach the front propeller shaft from the transfer case. Before separating the two flanges mark the outside edges with a coloured pen to refit them in the same position. Push the shaft to one side and tie it up with wire or similar. All bolts must be replaced and are tightened to 5.4 kgm (39 ft.lb.).
- Detach the transmission from the engine and the engine oil sump. First the bolt on the vent line bracket and the vent line is removed on one side of the transmission. The starter motor will be free and must be moved to one side and secured with wire to prevent it from falling down (cables connected). All bolts are tightened to 4.0 kgm (29 ft.lb.), including the starter motor bolts.
- Remove the transmission from below. The torque converter must be secured to prevent it from falling out.

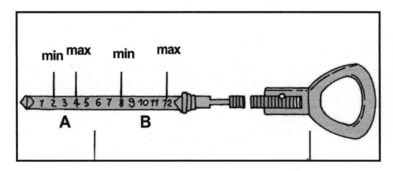

Fig. 10.2 – View of the fluid dipstick as fitted to an automatic transmission. The fluid must be within the area "A" when the fluid is cold or the area "B" when the fluid is hot.

Fig. 10.3 – Break off the lug on the plate (1) and push the pin downwards in the direction of the arrow. The cap (2) can then be removed.

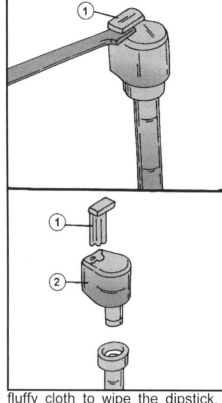

The installation is a reversal of the removal procedure, noting the tightening torques given above.

10.2. Fluid Level and Fluid Change

The fluid level in the transmission changes with the temperature of the transmission fluid. The fluid dipstick is marked with two levels, one for a temperature of around 30° C (cold) and one for around 80° C (hot). These are shown in Fig. 10.2 with "A" and "B". On the other side of the dipstick you will find the temperatures in Fahrenheit (F). If the fluid level is correct you will find the fluid between the "Min" and "Max" marks. The transmission is filled with automatic transmission fluid (ATF). Dexron II fluid is recommended. The total capacity is as given in section 10.0, but less fluid will be used during a fluid change.

Absolute cleanliness is to be observed during a fluid level check that even small particles entering the transmission can lead to malfunctions. Do not use fluffy cloth to wipe the dipstick. Tissue paper is best.

Filling in additional fluid is not straight forward. As you can see in Fig. 10.3, the upper end of the filler tube is fitted with a locking pin, which must be removed. To do this brake off the plate (1) of the pin with a screwdriver as shown and press out the remaining pin in the cap downwards. Remove the cap (2). The pin must, of course, be replaced.

The engine must be running at idle speed when fluid is filled in through the filler tube (a funnel is required). Apply the handbrake and depress the brake pedal and change through all gears. Finally leave the gear selector lever in position "P" and re-check the fluid level.

Finally refit the cap to the filler tube and press in a new locking pin until it locks in position.

The fluid can only be changed at a dealer as a diagnostic system is used to carry out the operation.

11 Exhaust System

11.1. Removal and Installation of the Exhaust System

ML 230 with M111 Engine

The exhaust system is shown in Fig. 11.1. It consists of the front and rear section with a three-way catalytic converter fitted as standard. The front exhaust pipe is connected to the rear silencer by means of an exhaust pipe clamp. A sealing ring is fitted between the end of the front pipe and the exhaust manifold.

- Lift up the vehicle and place secure chassis stands in position.
- Remove the heat shield (2) after removal of the bolts (3) at the positions shown.

Exhaust System

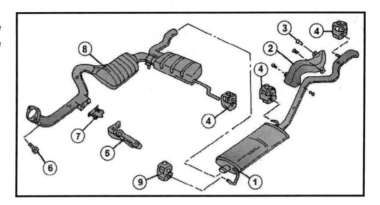

Fig. 11.1 – Details for the removal and installation of the exhaust system when an M111 engine is fitted (ML 230).

1 Location of pipe clamp
2 Protective head shield
3 Securing bolts
4 Rubber mountings
5 Bracket on transmission
6 Securing bolts to manifold
7 Nuts (bracket)
8 Catalytic converter
9 Rubber mounting

Remove in accordance with Fig. 11.1:

- Slacken the exhaust pipe clamp (1). Note that the clamp is welded to the pipe.
- Unhook the rear section of the exhaust system out of the two rubber mountings (4). Both mountings are withdrawn from the pins on the exhaust parts. The rubber mountings must be replaced if no longer in good condition.
- Separate the front section from the rear section. Take care that none of the shields on the underside of the vehicle are damaged when the system is separated. The rear exhaust section can now be removed.
- Place a mobile jack or other suitable lifting device underneath the transmission and remove the rear engine mounting.
- Remove the nuts (7) securing the bracket (5) to the transmission and remove the bracket. New nuts must always be used during the installation of the bracket.
- Unhook the front section of the exhaust from the rubber mounting (9). Again check the mounting and replace it if necessary.
- Remove the bolts (6) at the exhaust pipe/exhaust manifold connection and separate the joint. The bolts are tightened to 2.0 kgm (14.5 ft.lb.).
- Remove the three-way catalytic converter (8) together with the front section of the exhaust system. Again take care not to damage any of the protective shields.

Note the following points during installation:

- Check the mounting rubbers and replace them if no longer in perfect condition. Also check the connecting faces of the pipes for corrosion. Slight corrosion can be removed with emery paper.
- All other operations are carried out in reverse order to the removal procedure, noting the tightening torques given during the removal instructions.

Replacement of Rubber Suspension Rings

Three rubber suspension mountings are used in total. To replace the rubber mountings, jack up the rear end of the vehicle, place chassis stands under the sides of the body and unhook the mountings from the pins on exhaust and vehicle underbody. Check that the new rubber mountings are fully engaged when refitting them.

ML 320 and ML 350 with M112 Engine and ML 430 and ML 500 with M113 engine (Series 163) – Removal and Installation of a catalytic converter or the front exhaust section

As you will know, two catalytic converters are fitted. Fig. 11.2 shows a view of the fitted parts in the case of the M112 engine. The catalytic converters are fitted with Lambda probes and the electrical cables must be disconnected and the Lambda probes (O2 sensors) must be removed. The location of the cable connector plugs and sensors can be seen in the illustration.

As it is also necessary to remove the front springs and we recommend to have parts of the exhaust replaced in an exhaust centre. Below we give you, however, applicable operations and tightening torques, if you intend to remove one of the converters or the front section of the exhaust system. The vehicle must be resting on secure chassis stands. Ideally a garage pit should be used.

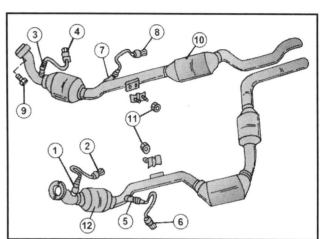

Fig. 11.2 – View of the front section of the exhaust system as fitted to an M112 and M113 engine (163 models).
1 L.H. Lambda probe upstream of CAT
2 Plug for L.H. sensor (1)
3 R.H. Lambda probe upstream of CAT
4 Plug for R.H. sensor (3)
5 L.H. Lambda probe downstream
6 Plug for L.H. sensor (5)
7 R.H. Lambda probe downstream
8 Plug for R.H. sensor (7)
9 Bolts, pipe to manifold
10 Rear catalytic converter
11 Nuts for retaining bracket
12 Front catalytic converter

- Slacken the exhaust clamps from the rear section of the exhaust system. The clamps are welded to the pipes.
- Remove the nuts (11) from the retaining bracket. The nuts must be replaced.
- In the case of the ML 430 and ML 500 with M113 engine remove the panel inside the front wing as already shown in Fig. 9.4.
- Remove the bolts (9) securing the pipe flanges to the exhaust manifold.
- Remove the three-way converters (10) and (12) together with the front section of the exhaust system. Take care not to damage any protective panels at the bottom of the vehicle underfloor.

The installation is a reversal of the removal procedure. The threads of the Lambda O2 sensors must be coated with heat resistant grease. Tighten them to 4.5 kgm/32.5 ft.lb) in the case of the M112 engine or 5.5 kgm/40 ft.lb. in the case of the M113 engine, avoid mistakes.

ML 320 and ML 350 with M112 Engine and ML 430 and ML 500 with M113 engine (Series 163) – Removal and Installation of complete Exhaust System

The removal is carried out by referring to Fig. 11.2. The rear section of the exhaust system is shown in Fig. 11.3.

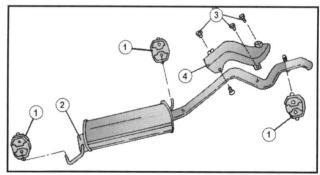

Fig. 11.3 – The parts of the rear section of the exhaust system (M112 and M113 engines, series 163).
1 Rubber mounting
2 Exhaust pipe clamp
3 Nuts for heat protection panel
4 Heat-protection panel (shield)

- Carry out the operations described in the last section, with the difference that there is no need to remove the remove the oxygen sensors (Lambda probes). Only disconnect the connector plugs at the positions shown in Fig. 11.2.
- Remove the bolts (3) and take off the heat shield (4) in Fig. 11.3.
- Slacken the exhaust pipe clamp (2) at the position shown from the rear section of the exhaust system.

- Unhook the exhaust system section from the rubber mountings (1). Replace the mountings if no longer in good condition.
- Separate the front section of the exhaust system from the rear section. Take care not to damage any protective panels at the bottom of the vehicle underfloor.
- All remaining operations are as described for the removal of a catalytic converter until the system is free and can be removed. The nuts (11) in Fig. 11.2 must always be replaced. The bolts securing the exhaust tube flanges to the manifolds are tightened to 2.0 kgm (14.5 ft.lb.).

The installation is a reversal of the removal procedure, noting the tightening torques already given during the removal instructions. Make sure that the system is free of stress.

ML 350 and ML 500 with M113 and M272 Engine (series 164) – Removal and Installation of complete Exhaust System

As you will know, two catalytic converters are fitted. The complete exhaust system is removed as a single unit.

Removal and installation requires the use of a garage-type lift, if possible. Otherwise place the front and rear end of the vehicle on secure chassis stands. After the vehicle is on the chassis stands place a mobile jack with suitable supports (for example a wooden plank) underneath the exhaust system. We strongly recommend to have the exhaust system replaced at an exhaust centre, as the operations are not straight forward as you will see from the description. The system can be removed as follows, but a helper must be available to lower the exhaust system. In the case of both engines remove the engine trim panel (cover) and the air cleaner housing.

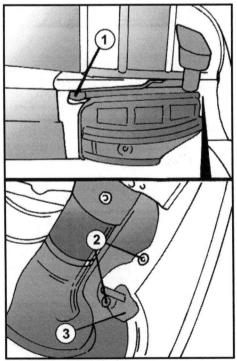

Fig. 11.4 – Attachment of the exhaust when an M113 or M272 engine is fitted to series 164.
1 Inner rubber mounting
2 Bolts
3 Outer rubber mounting

In general the removal and installation is carried out as already described for the other engines, but we would like to refer to the two rubber bearings on the inside and outside of the exhaust, shown in Fig. 11.4. in each case on both sides. The crossmember above the exhaust pipe must also be removed (4 in total). They are tightened to 4.5 kgm (32.5 ft.lb.) during installation (both engines). Other tightening torques to be observed are: Converter bracket to converter = 2.0 kgm (14.5 ft.lb.), exhaust pipe flanges to pipe or exhaust manifold = 2.0 kgm, exhaust rubber bearing to bracket = 1.2 kgm (9 ft.lb.). As mentioned above, have the complete exhaust replaced at an exhaust centre.

---

12.   SERVICING AND MAINTENANCE

Most of the maintenance operations can be carried out without much difficulties. In many cases it is, however, better to have certain maintenance operations carried out in a workshop as experience and special equipment, for example test instruments, are required to carry out a certain job. Most important are the regular inspections and checks which are described below. Operations to be carried out after a certain mileage are described later on in this section and the text will advise when specific jobs should be left to a Mercedes Dealer.

12.0. Regular Maintenance

Oil Level Check: Check the engine oil level every 500 miles. With the vehicle standing on level ground, remove the oil dipstick and wipe it clean with a clean rag or a piece of tissue paper. Re-insert the oil dipstick and remove once more. The oil level must be visible between the upper and the lower mark on the dipstick. If the oil level is below the lower mark, top-up with engine oil of the correct viscosity. The oil quantity between the two marks is approx. between 5.0 and 3.5 litre and from the actual level indicated you will be able to tell how much oil is missing. Never overfill the engine - the level must never be above the upper dipstick mark.

Checking the Brake Fluid Level: - The brake fluid reservoir is in the engine compartment on the drivers side. The reservoir is transparent and it is easy to check whether the fluid level is between the "Min" and "Max" mark. If necessary, top-up to the "Max" mark with the correct brake fluid.

Checking the Brake Lights: The operation of the brake lights can either be checked with the help of another person or you can check it by yourself by driving the vehicle backwards near the garage door. Operate the brake pedal and check if the reflection of the brake lights can be seen on the garage door by looking through the rear view mirror.

Checking the Vehicle Lights: In turn check every vehicle light, including the horn and the hazard warning light system. Rear lights and reversing lights can be checked in the dark in front of a garage door, without leaving the vehicle.

Checking the Tyre Pressures: Check the tyre pressures at a petrol station. Pressures are different for the various models. Either your Operators Manual or tyre charts will give you the correct pressures.

If continuous speeds of more than 100 mph are anticipated, increase the tyre pressure by 0.2 kg/sq.cm. (3 psi.).

Checking the Coolant Level: See Section "Cooling System". Never open the radiator filler cap when the engine is hot.

Checking the Fluid Level in the Automatic Transmission: The fluid level should be checked at regular intervals to ensure the correct operation of the transmission:

- Apply the handbrake and place the gear selector lever into the "P" position. Start the engine and allow to idle for 1 to 2 minutes.
- Remove the oil dipstick from the transmission and read off the fluid level. The level must be between the "Min" and "Max" mark when the transmission is at operating temperature, the level may be up to 10 mm (0.4 in.) below the "Min" mark if the transmission is cold.
- If necessary top-up the transmission with ATF fluid through the fluid dipstick tube. A funnel is required. Only use the fluid recommended for the transmission.

12.1. Service every 6,000 Miles

Changing the Engine Oil and Oil Filter: Some petrol stations will carry out an oil change free of charge – You only pay for the oil. The same applies to the oil filter (there may be a small extra charge), but not every petrol station will be able to obtain a Mercedes filter. To change the filter yourself, refer to the relevant page.

Lubrication Jobs: Apart from the engine lubrication there are further lubrication points which should be attended to. These include the throttle linkage and shafts (only grease the swivel points), the engine bonnet catch and the hinges (use a drop of engine oil) and perhaps the door mechanism.

12.2. Additional Service Every 12,000 Miles

Checking the Idle Speed: If the engine no longer idles as expected, have the idle speed checked and if necessary adjusted at your Dealer.

Air Filter Service: Remove the air filter element for cleaning.

Checking the Brake System: If no trouble has been experienced with the brake system, there is little need to carry out extensive checks. To safeguard for the next 6,000 miles, however, follow the brake pipes underneath the vehicle. No rust or corrosion must be visible. Dark deposits near the pipe ends point to leaking joints. Brake hoses must show no signs of chafing or breaks. All rubber dust caps must be in position on the bleeder valves of the calipers. Insert a finger underneath the master cylinder, where it is fitted to the brake servo unit. Moisture indicates a slightly leaking cylinder.
The brake pads must be checked for the remaining material thickness as has been described in Section "Brakes" for the front and rear brakes.

Adjusting the Parking Brake: Adjust the parking brake as described in Section "Brakes" under the relevant heading.

Brake Test: A brake test is recommended at this interval. Your will decide yourself if the brakes perform as you expect them to. Otherwise have the brakes tested on a dynamometer. The read-out of the meter will show you the efficiency of the brake system on all four wheels.

Checking the Wheel Suspension and Steering: In the case of the front suspension remove both wheels and check the shock absorbers for signs of moisture, indicating fluid leaks.
Check the free play of the steering wheel. If the steering wheel can be moved by more than 25 mm (1 in.) before the front wheels respond, have the steering checked professionally.
Check the rubber dust boots of the track rod and suspension ball joints. Although rubber boots can be replaced individually, dirt may have entered the joints already. In this case replace the ball joint end piece or the suspension ball joint.
Check the fluid level in the reservoir for the power-assisted steering. Refer to the "Steering" section for details. If steering fluid is always missing after the 12,000 miles check, suspect a leak somewhere in the system - See your dealer.

Tyre Check: Jack up the vehicle and check all tyres for uneven wear. Tyres should be evenly worn on the entire surface. Uneven wear at the inner or outer edge of front tyres points to misalignment of the front wheel geometry. Have the geometry measured at your dealer. Make sure that a tread depth of 1.6 mm is still visible to remain within the legal requirements. Make sure to fit tyres suitable for your model, mainly if you buy them from an independent tyre company.

Re-tighten Wheel Bolts: Re-tighten the wheel bolts to 9.0 – 11.0 kgm (65 – 80 ft.lb.). Tighten every second bolt in turn until all bolts have been re-tightened.

Checking the Cooling System: Check all coolant hoses for cuts, chafing and other damage. Check the radiator for leaks, normally indicated by a deposit, left by the leaking anti-freeze. Slight radiator leaks can be stopped with one of the proprietary sealants available for this purpose.

Checking the Clutch: Check the clutch operation. The fluid reservoir should be full. If it is suspected that the clutch linings are worn near their limit, take the vehicle to a dealer.

Checking the Anti-freeze: The strength of the anti-freeze should be checked every 12,000 miles. Petrol stations normally have a hydrometer to carry out this check. Make sure that only anti-freeze suitable for Mercedes engines is used.

Checking the Manual Transmission Fluid Level: Refer to Section "Manual Transmission".

Checking the Rear Axle Oil Level: Remove the filler plug at the side of the rear axle centre piece, just above one of the drive shafts (L.H. side). The oil level should be to the lower edge of the filler hole. If necessary top-up with differential oil. Refit the plug.

12.3.   Additional Service every 36,000 Miles

Automatic Transmission Oil and Filter Change: These operations should be carried out by a Dealer.

Air Cleaner Element Change: Refer to Section "Diesel Fuel Injection" for details.

Clutch: The wear of the clutch driven plate should be checked by a dealer with the special gauge available.

Propeller Shaft: Check the two shaft couplings for cuts or other damage. The sleeves must not be loose in the couplings. Check the intermediate bearing for wear by moving the shaft up and down in the bearing.

12.4.   Once every Year

Brake Fluid Change: We recommend to have the brake fluid changed at your dealer. Road safety is involved and the job should be carried out professionally. If you are experienced with brake systems, follow the instructions in the "Brakes" section to drain, fill and bleed the brake system.

12.5.   Once every 3 Years

Cooling System: The anti-freeze must be changed. Refer to Section "Cooling System" to drain and refill the cooling system.

FAULT FINDING SECTION

The following section lists some of the more common faults that can develop in a motor car, both for petrol and diesel engines. For the purpose of this manual, references to petrol engines are of course, first and foremost, as the detection of faults in a petrol engine is a job for a special workshop, dealing with fuel injection systems. The section is divided into various categories and it should be possible to locale faults or damage by referring to the assembly group of the vehicle in question. The faults are listed in no particular order and their causes are given a number. By referring to this number it is possible to read off the possible cause and to carry out the necessary remedies, if this is within the scope of your facilities.

Fault Finding Section

ENGINE FAULTS

Engine will not crank:	1, 2, 3, 4
Engine cranks, but will not start:	5, 6, 7, 8
Engine cranks very slowly:	1, 2, 3
Engine starts, but cuts out:	5, 6, 9, 10
Engine misfires in the lower speed ranges:	5, 6, 9, 11
Engine misfires in the higher speed ranges:	5, 6, 11, 12
Continuous misfiring:	5, 6, 7, 10 to 15, 21, 22
Max. revs not obtained:	5, 6, 12, 22
Faulty idling:	5, 6, 8 to 11, 13, 15, 16, 21 and 22
Lack of power:	3, 5 to 11, 13 to 15, 22
Lack of acceleration:	5 to 8, 12, 14 to 16
Lack of max. speed:	5 to 8, 10, 12, 13 to 15, 22
Excessive fuel consumption:	3, 5, 6, 15, 16
Excessive oil consumption:	16 to 19
Low compression:	7, 11 to 13, 16, 20 to 22

Causes and Remedies

1. Fault in the starter motor or its connection. Refer to "Electrical Faults".
2. Engine oil too thick. This can be caused by using the wrong oil, low temperatures or using oil not suitable for the prevailing climates. Depress the clutch whilst starting (models with manual transmission). Otherwise refill the engine with the correct oil grade, suitable for diesel engines.
3. Moveable parts of the engine not run-in. This fault may be noticed when the engine has been overhauled. It may be possible to free the engine by adding oil to the fuel for a while.
4. Mechanical fault. This may be due to seizure of the piston(s), broken crankshaft, connecting rods, clutch or other moveable parts of the engine. The engine must be stripped for inspection.
5. Faults in the glow plug system (diesel only).
6. Faults in the fuel system.
7. Incorrect valve timing. This will only be noticed after the engine has been re-assembled after overhaul and the timing belt has been replaced incorrectly. Re-dismantle the engine and check the timing marks on the timing gear wheels.
8. Compression leak due to faulty closing of valves. See also under (7) or leakage past worn piston rings or pistons. Cylinder head gasket blown.
9. Entry of air at inlet manifold, due to split manifold or damaged gasket.
10. Restriction in exhaust system, due to damaged exhaust pipes, dirt in end of exhaust pipe(s), kinked pipe(s), or collapsed silencer. Repair as necessary.
11. Worn valves or valve seats, no longer closing the valves properly. Top overhaul of engine is asked for.
12. Sticking valves due to excessive carbon deposits or weak valve springs. Top overhaul is asked for.
13. Cylinder head gasket blown. Replace gasket and check block and head surfaces for distortion.
14. Camshaft worn, not opening or closing one of the valves properly, preventing proper combustion. Check and if necessary fit new camshaft (s).
15. Incorrect valve (tappet) clearance. There could be a fault in the hydraulic tappets.
16. Cylinder bores, pistons or piston rings worn. Overhaul is the only cure. Fault may be corrected for a while by adding "Piston Seal Liquid" into the cylinders, but will re-develop.
17. Worn valve guides and/or valve stems. Top overhaul is asked for.
18. Damaged valve stem seals. Top overhaul is asked for.
19. Leaking crankshaft oil seal, worn piston rings or pistons, worn cylinders. Correct

as necessary.

20. Loose glow plugs, gas escaping past thread or plug sealing washer damaged. Correct.
21. Cracked cylinder or cylinder block. Dismantle, investigate and replace block, if necessary.
22. Broken, weak or collapsed valve spring(s). Top overhaul is asked for.

LUBRICATION SYSTEM FAULTS

The only problem the lubrication system should give is excessive oil consumption or low oil pressure, or the oil warning light not going off.

Excessive oil consumption can be caused by worn cylinder bores, pistons and/or piston rings, worn valve guides, worn valves stem seals or a damaged crankshaft oil seal or leaking gasket on any of the engine parts. In most cases the engine must be dismantled to locate the fault.

Low oil pressure can be caused by a faulty oil pressure gauge, sender unit or wiring, a defective relief valve, low oil level, blocked oil pick-up pipe for the oil pump, worn oil pump or damaged main or big end bearings, In most cases it is logical to check the oil level first. All other causes require the dismantling and repair of the engine. If the oil warning light stays on, switch off the engine IMMEDIATELY, as delay could cause complete seizure within minutes.

COOLING SYSTEM FAULTS

Common faults are: Overheating, loss of coolant and slow warming-up of the engine:

Overheating:
1. *Lack of coolant:* Open the radiator cap with care to avoid injuries. Never pour cold water in to an overheated engine. Wait until engine cools down and pour in coolant whilst engine is running.
2. *Radiator core obstructed by leaves, insects, etc.*: Blow with air line from the back of the radiator or with a water hose to clean.
3. *Cooling fan not operating:* Check fan for proper cut-in and cut-out temperature. If necessary change the temperature switch or see your Dealer.
4. *Thermostat sticking:* If sticking in the closed position, coolant can only circulate within the cylinder head or block. Remove thermostat and check as described in section "Cooling".
5. *Water hose split:* Identified by rising steam from the engine compartment or the front of the vehicle. Slight splits can be repaired with insulation tape. Drive without expansion tank cap to keep the pressure in the system down, to the nearest service station.
6. *Water pump belt torn:* Replace and tension belt.
7. *Water pump inoperative:* Replace water pump.
8. *Cylinder head gasket blown:* Replace the cylinder head gasket.

Loss of Coolant:
1. *Radiator leaks:* Slight leaks may be stopped by using radiator sealing compound (follow the instructions of the manufacturer. In emergency a egg can be cracked open and poured into the radiator filler neck.
2. Hose leaks: See under 5, "Overheating".
3. Water pump leaks: Check the gasket for proper sealing or replace the pump.

Long Warming-up periods:
1. Thermostat sticking in the open position: Remove thermostat, check and if necessary replace.

CLUTCH FAULTS

Clutch slipping: 1, 2, 3, 4, 5

Fault Finding Section

Clutch will not disengage fully:	4, 6 to 12, 14
Whining from clutch when pedal is depressed:	13
Clutch judder:	1, 2, 7, 10 to 13
Clutch noise when idling:	2, 3
Clutch noise during engagement:	2

Causes and Remedies

1. Insufficient clutch free play at pedal.
2. Clutch disc linings worn, hardened, oiled-up, loose or broken. Disc distorted or hub loose. Clutch disc must be replaced.
3. Pressure plate faulty. Replace clutch.
4. Air in hydraulic system. Low fluid level in clutch cylinder reservoir.
5. Insufficient play at clutch pedal and clutch release linkage. Rectify as described.
6. Excessive free play in release linkage (only for cable operated clutch, not applicable). Adjust or replace worn parts.
7. Misalignment of clutch housing. Very rare fault, but possible on transmissions with separate clutch housings. Re-align to correct.
8. Clutch disc hub binding on splines of main drive shaft (clutch shaft) due to dirt or burrs on splines. Remove clutch and clean and check splines.
9. Clutch disc linings loose or broken. Replace disc.
10. Pressure plate distorted. Replace clutch.
11. Clutch cover distorted. Replace clutch.
12. Fault in transmission or loose engine mountings.
13. Release bearing defective. Remove clutch and replace bearing.
14. A bent clutch release lever. Check lever and replace or straighten, if possible.
• The above faults and remedies are for hydraulic and mechanical clutch operation and should be read as applicable to the model in question, as the clutch fault finding section is written for all types of clutch operation.

STEERING FAULTS

Steering very heavy:	1 to 6
Steering very loose:	5, 7 to 9, 11 to 13
Steering wheel wobbles:	4, 5, 7 to 9, 11 to 16
Vehicle pulls to one side:	1, 4, 8, 10, 14 to 18
Steering wheel does not return to centre position:	1 to 6, 18
Abnormal tyre wear:	1, 4, 7 to 9, 14 to 19
Knocking noise in column:	6, 7, 11, 12

Causes and Remedies

1. Tyre pressures not correct or uneven. Correct.
2. Lack of lubricant in steering.
3. Stiff steering linkage ball joints. Replace ball joints in question.
4. Incorrect steering wheel alignment. Correct as necessary.
5. Steering needs adjustment. See your dealer for advice.
6. Steering column bearings too tight or seized or steering column bent. Correct as necessary.
7. Steering linkage joints loose or worn. Check and replace joints as necessary.
8. Front wheel bearings worn, damaged or loose. Replace bearing.
9. Front suspension parts loose. Check and correct.
10. Wheel nuts loose. Re-tighten.
11. Steering wheel loose. Re-tighten nut.
12. Steering gear mounting loose. Check and tighten.
13. Steering gear worn. Replace the steering gear.
14. Steering track rods defective or loose.
15. Wheels not properly balanced or tyre pressures uneven. Correct pressures or balance wheels.

16. Suspension springs weak or broken. Replace spring in question or both.
17. Brakes are pulling to one side. See under "Brake Faults".
18. Suspension out of alignment. Have the complete suspension checked by a dealer.
19. Improper driving. We don't intend to tell you how to drive and are quite sure that this is not the cause of the fault.

BRAKE FAULTS

Brake Failure: Brake shoe linings or pads excessively worn, incorrect brake fluid (after overhaul), insufficient brake fluid, fluid leak, master cylinder defective, wheel cylinder or caliper failure. Remedies are obvious in each instance.

Brakes Ineffective: Shoe linings or pads worn, incorrect lining material or brake fluid, linings contaminated, fluid level low, air in brake system (bleed brakes), leak in pipes or cylinders, master cylinder defective. Remedies are obvious in each instance.

Brakes pull to one side: Shoes or linings worn, incorrect linings or pads, contaminated linings, drums or discs scored, fluid pipe blocked, unequal tyre pressures, brake back plate or caliper mounting loose, wheel bearings not properly adjusted, wheel cylinder seized. Rectify as necessary.

Brake pedal spongy: Air in hydraulic system. System must be bled of air.

Pedal travel too far: Linings or pads worn, drums or discs scored, master cylinder or wheel cylinders defective, system needs bleeding. Rectify as necessary.

Loss of brake pressure: Fluid leak, air in system, leak in master or wheel cylinders, brake servo not operating (vacuum hose disconnected or exhauster pump not operating). Place vehicle on dry ground and depress brake pedal. Check where fluid runs out and rectify as necessary.

Brakes binding: Incorrect brake fluid (boiling), weak shoe return springs, basic brake adjustment incorrect (after fitting new rear shoes), piston in caliper of wheel cylinder seized, push rod play on master cylinder insufficient (compensation port obstructed), handbrake adjusted too tightly. Rectify as necessary. Swelling of cylinder cups through use of incorrect brake fluid could be another reason.

Handbrake ineffective: Brake shoe linings worn, linings contaminated, operating lever on brake shoe seized, brake shoes or handbrake need adjustment. Rectify as necessary.

Excessive pedal pressure required: Brake shoe linings or pads worn, linings or pads contaminated, brake servo vacuum hose (for brake servo) disconnected or wheel cylinders seized. Exhauster pump not operating (diesel). Rectify as necessary.

Brakes squealing: Brake shoe linings or pads worn so far that metal is grinding against drum or disc. Inside of drum is full of lining dust. Remove and replace, or clean out the drum(s). Do not inhale brake dust.

Note: Any operation on the steering and brake systems must be carried out with the necessary care and attention. Always think of your safety and the safety of other road users. Make sure to use the correct fluid for the power-assisted steering and the correct brake fluid.

Faults in an ABS system should be investigated by a dealer.

ELECTRICAL FAULTS

Starter motor failure:	2 to 5, 8, 9
No starter motor drive:	1 to 3, 5 to 7
Slow cranking speed:	1 to 3
Charge warning light remains on:	3, 10, 12
Charge warning light does not come on:	2, 3, 9. 11, 13
Headlamp failure:	2, 3, 11, 13, 14
Battery needs frequent topping-up:	11
Direction indicators not working properly:	2, 3, 9, 13, 14
Battery frequently discharged:	3, 10, 11, 12

Fault Finding Section

Causes and Remedies

1.   Tight engine. Check and rectify.
2.   Battery discharged or defective. Re-charge battery or replace if older than approx. 2 years.
3.   Interrupted connection in circuit. Trace and rectify.
4.   Starter motor pinion jammed in flywheel. Release.
5.   Also 6, 7 and 8. Starter motor defective, no engagement in flywheel, pinion or flywheel worn or solenoid switch defective. Correct as necessary.
9.   Ignition/starter switch inoperative. Replace.
10. Drive belt loose or broken. Adjust or replace.
11. Regulator defective. Adjust or replace.
12. Generator inoperative. Overhaul or replace.
13. Bulb burnt out. Replace bulb.
14. Flasher unit defective. Replace unit.

WIRING DIAGRAMS
Wiring Diagram Index

Cable Colour Code

bl	=	blue	nf	=	natural colour
br	=	brown	rs	=	pink
ge	=	yellow	rt	=	red
gn	=	green	sw	=	black
gr	=	grey	vi	=	violet
el	=	ivory	ws	=	white

Cable identification: a = size, square mm, b = basic colour, c = second colour

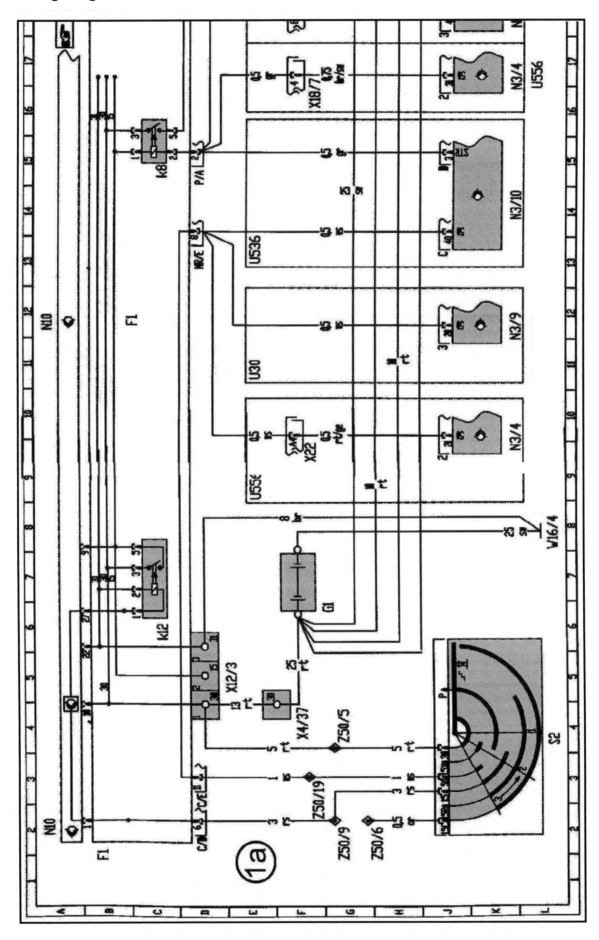

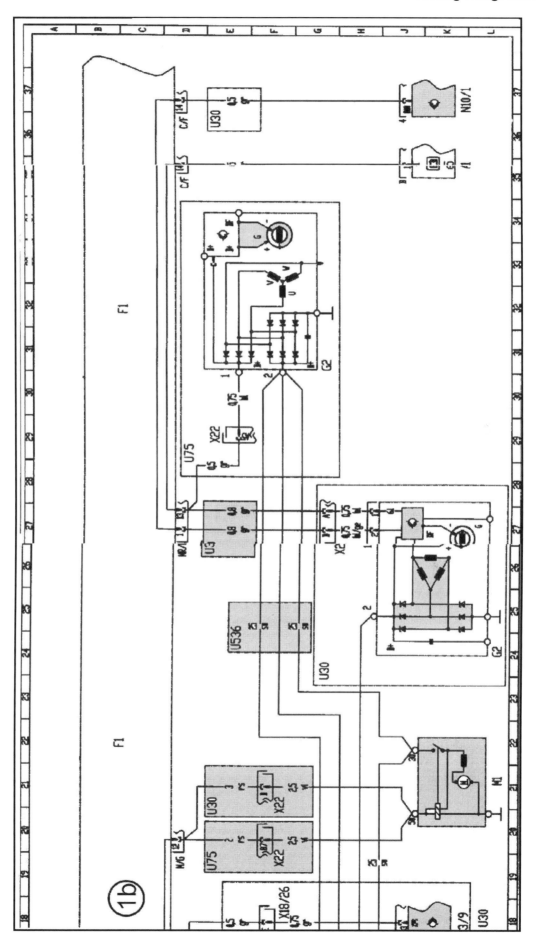

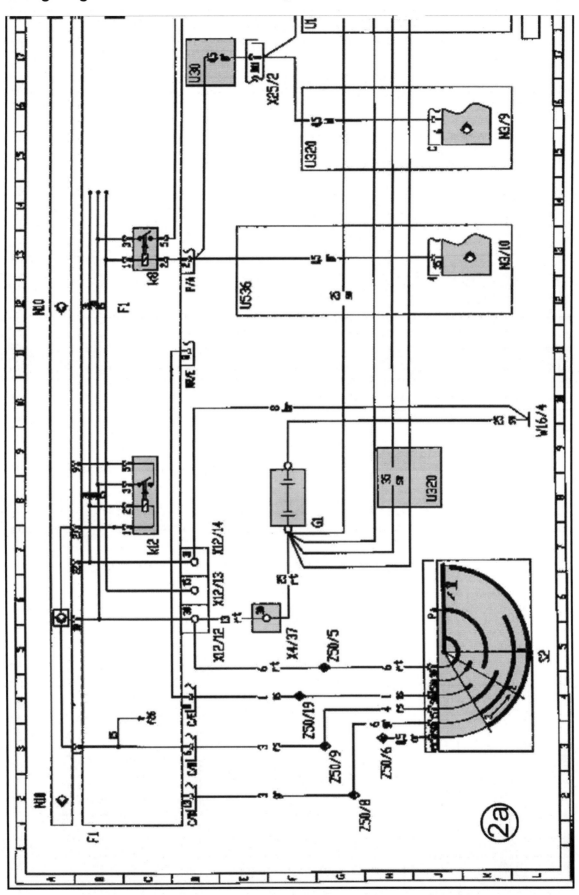

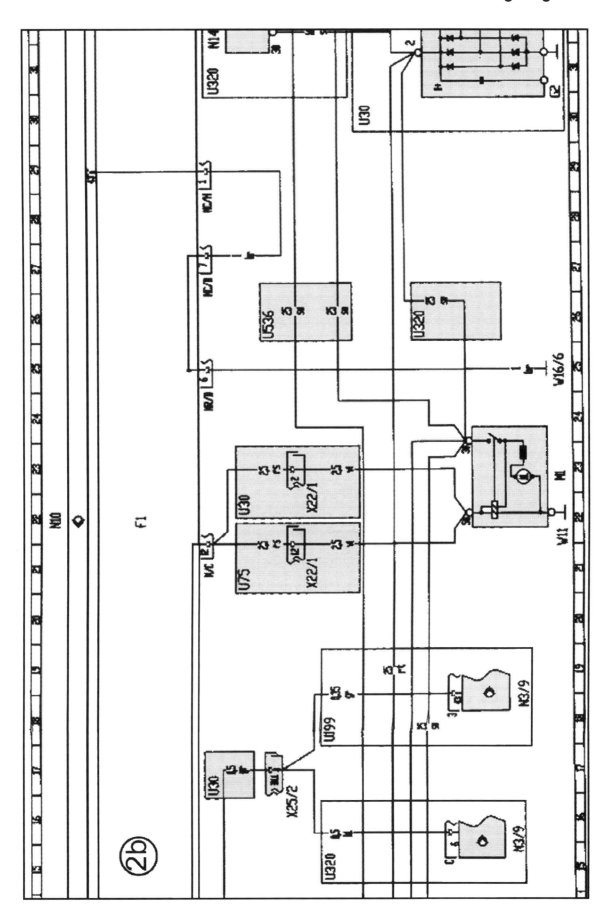

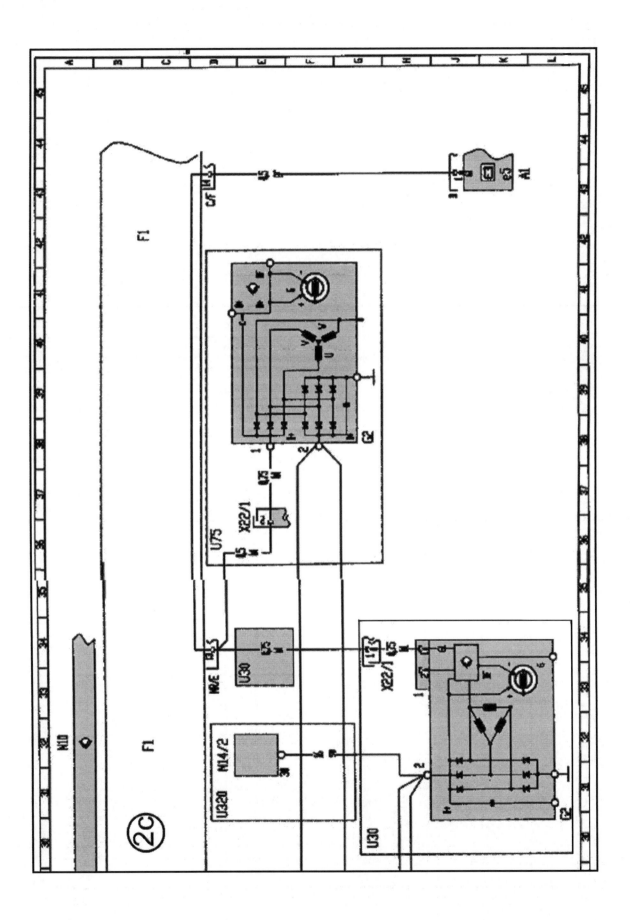

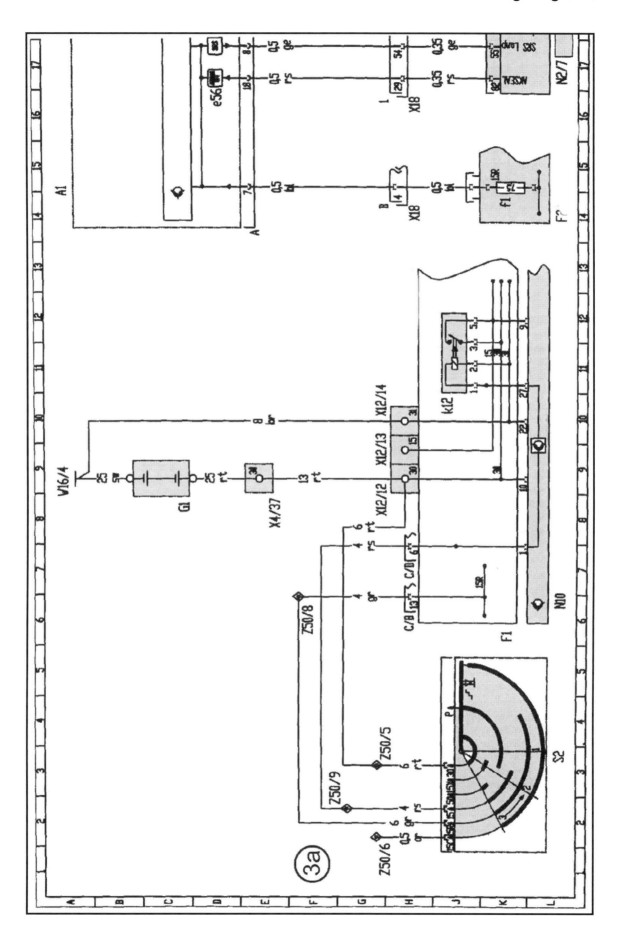

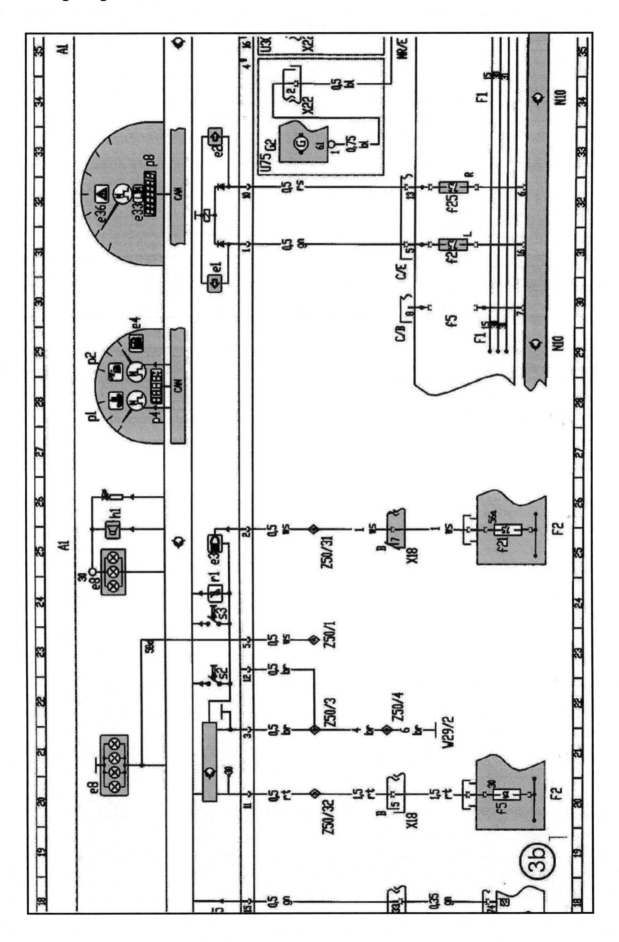

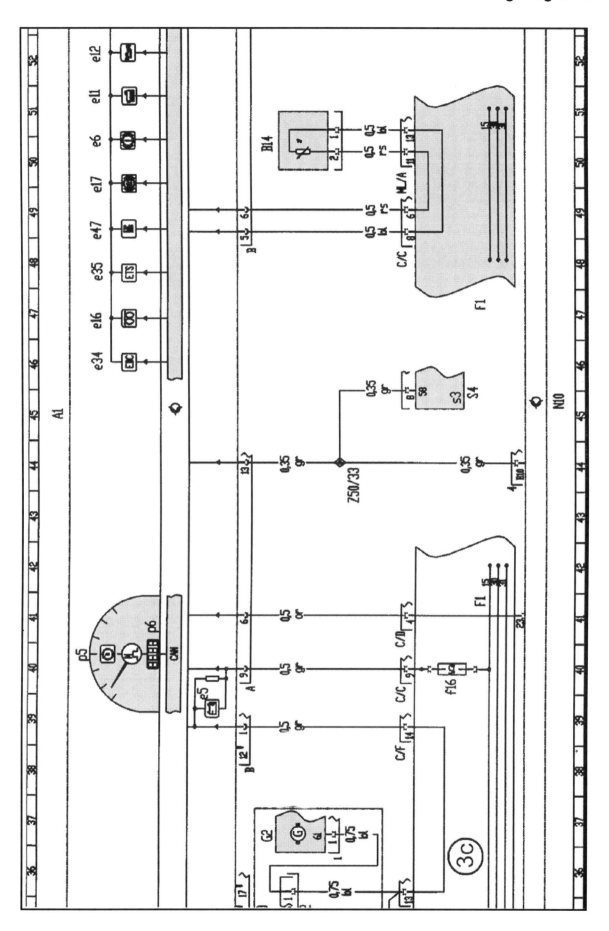

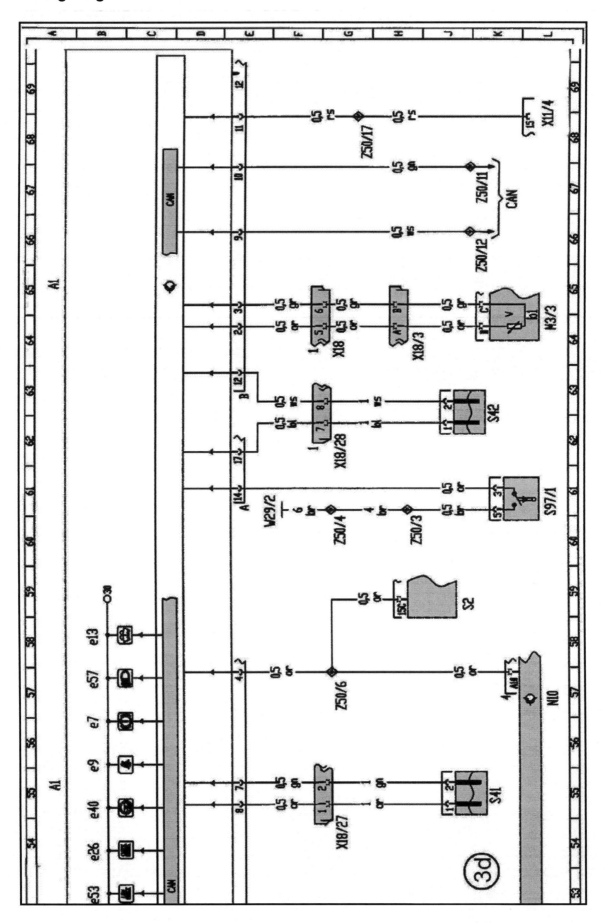

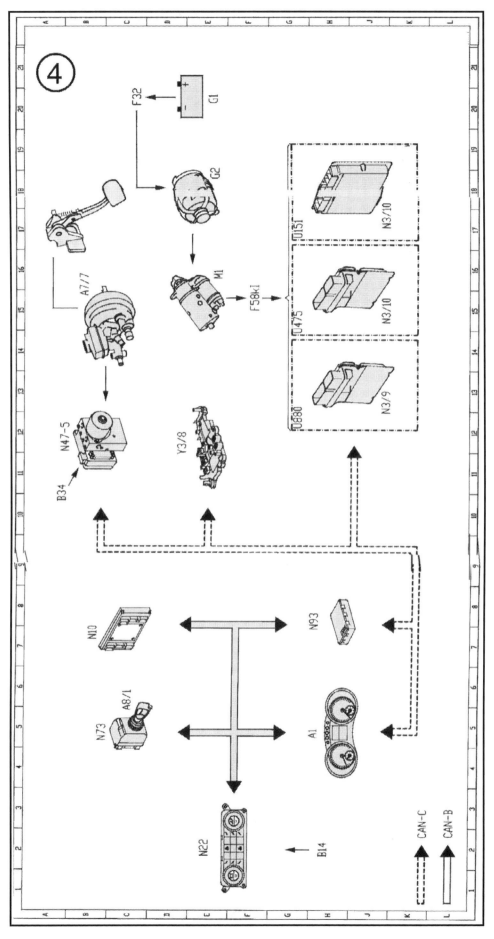

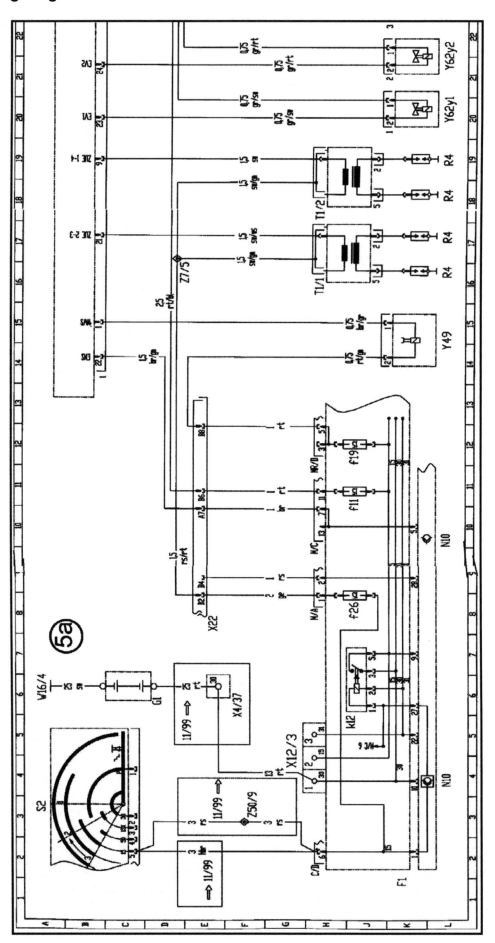

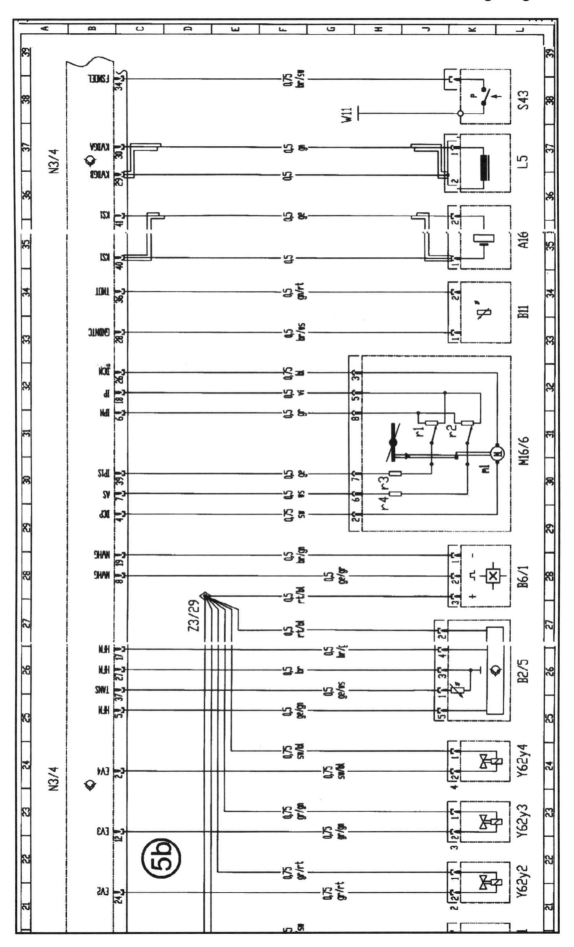

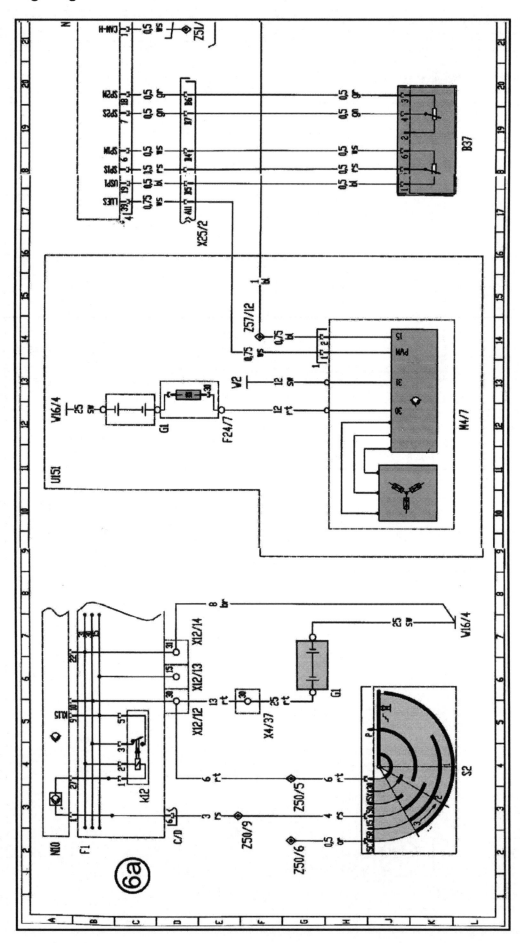

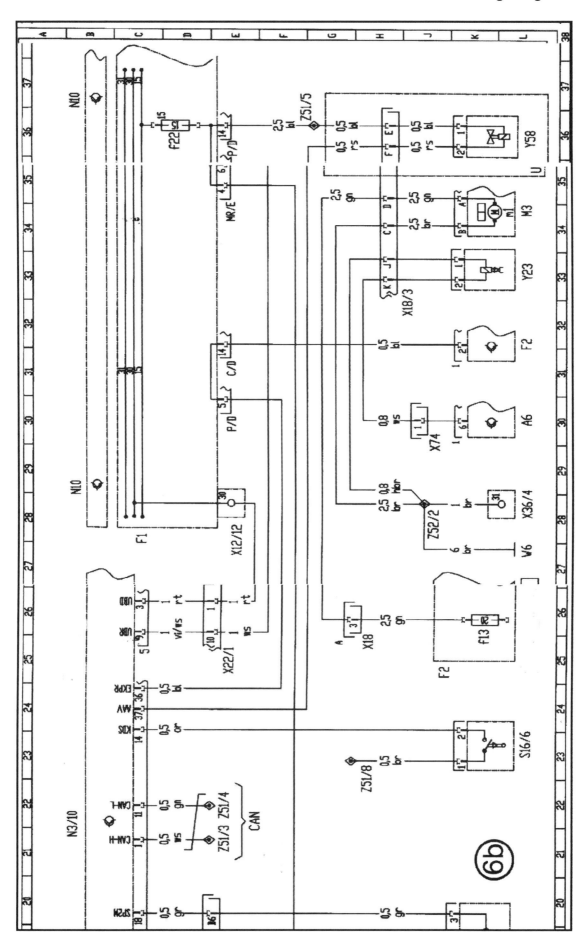

Wiring Diagrams

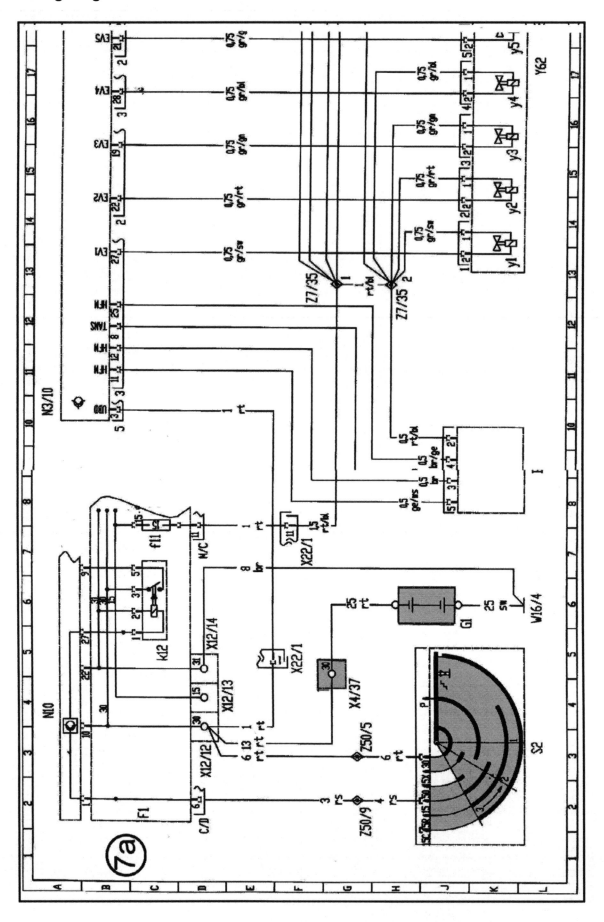

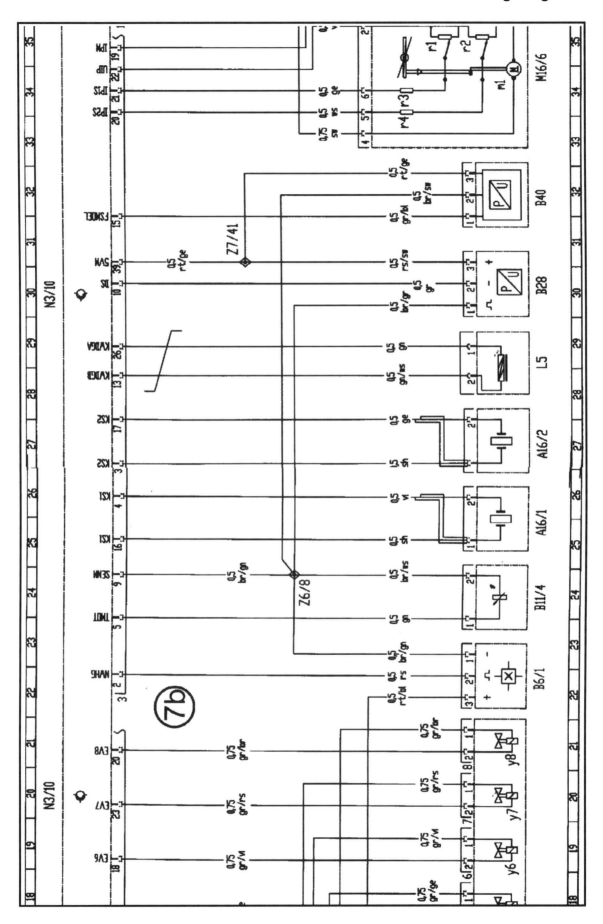

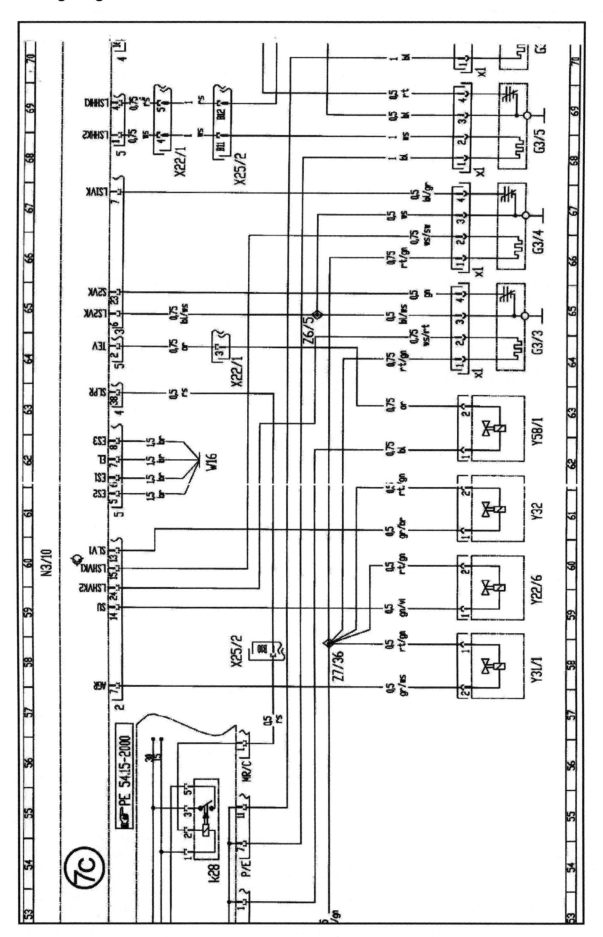

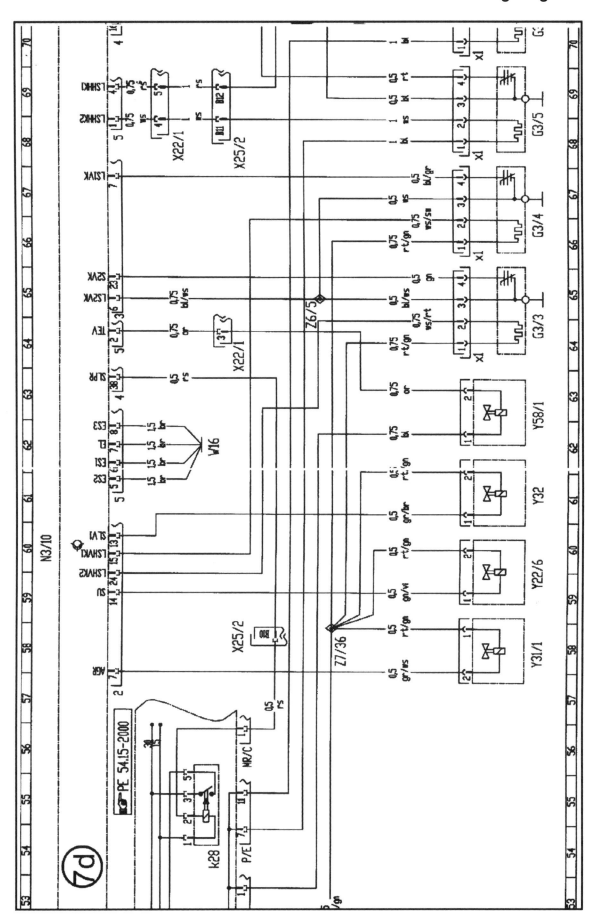

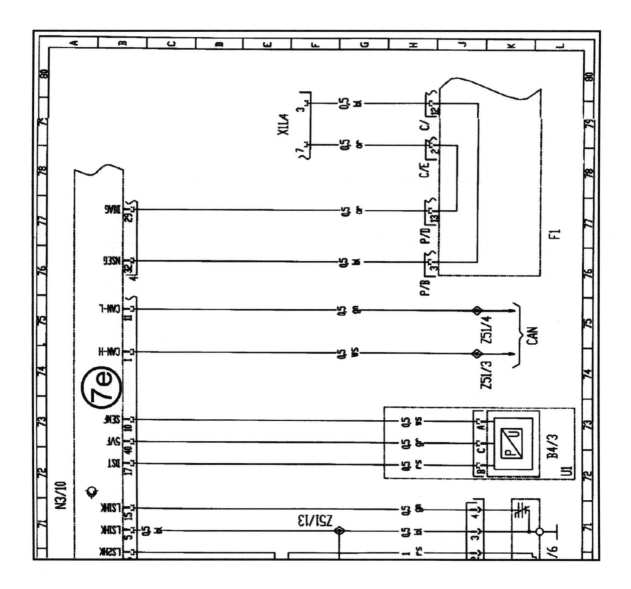

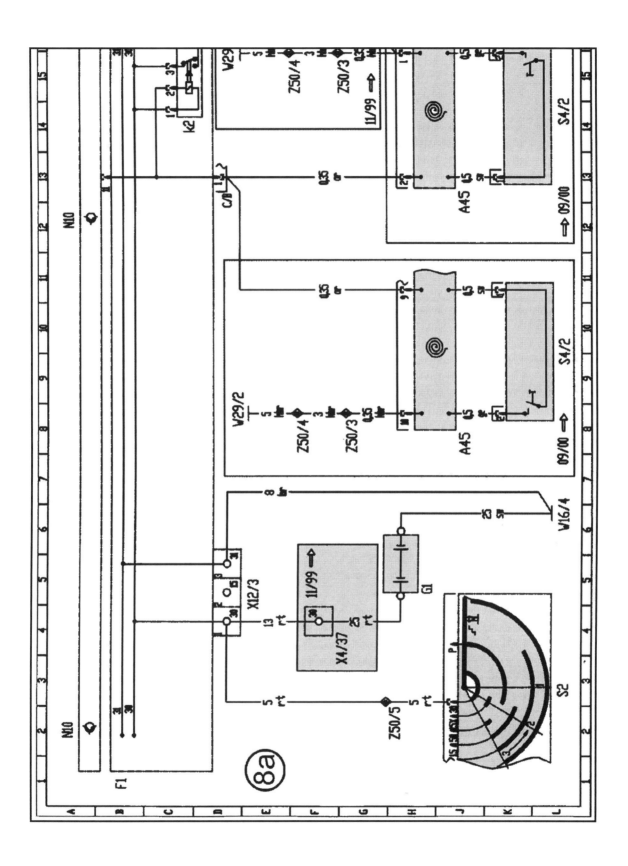

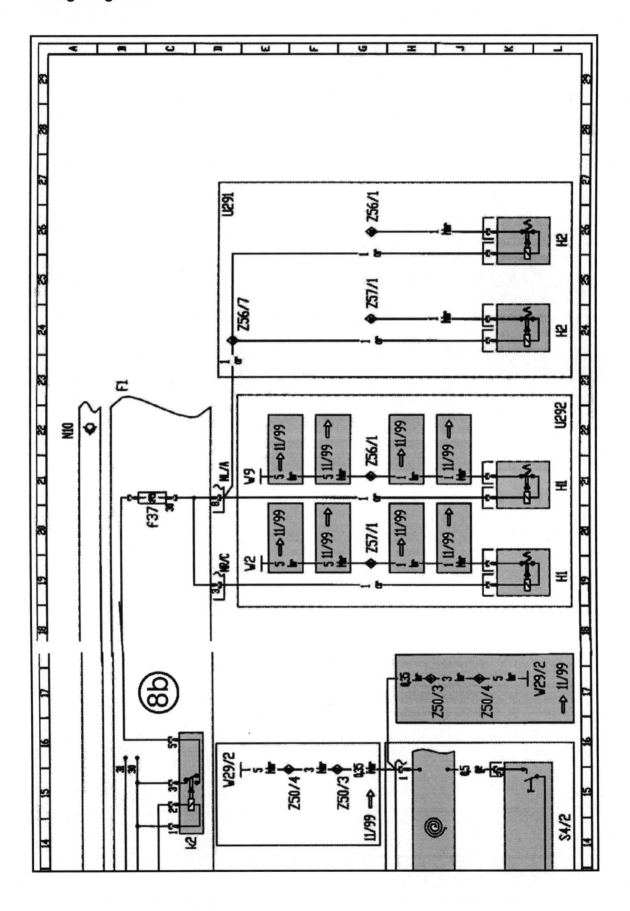

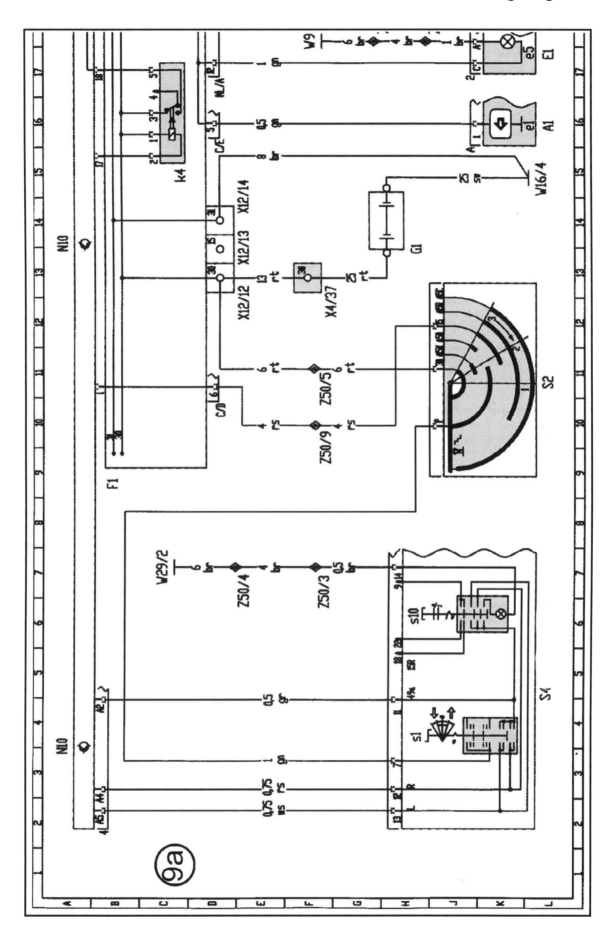

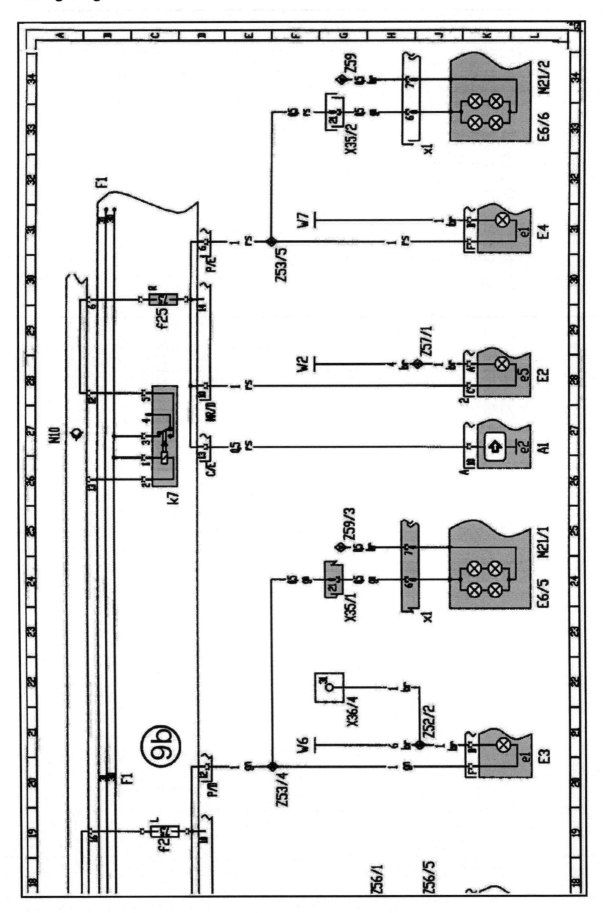

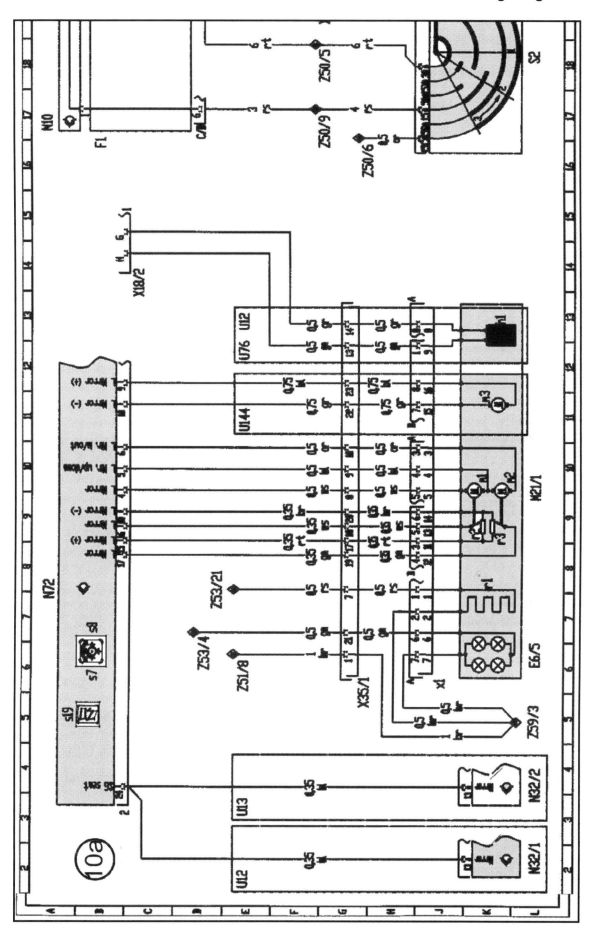

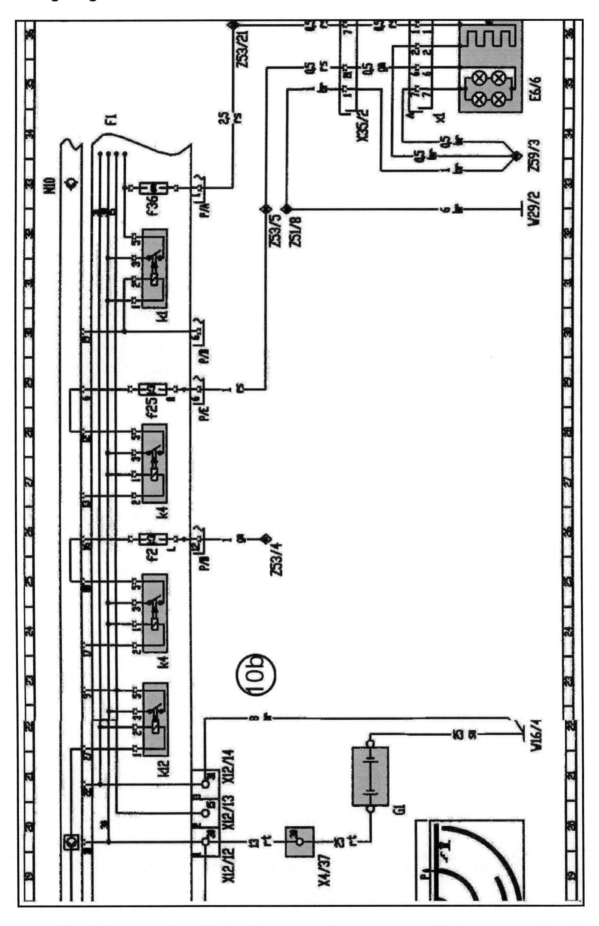

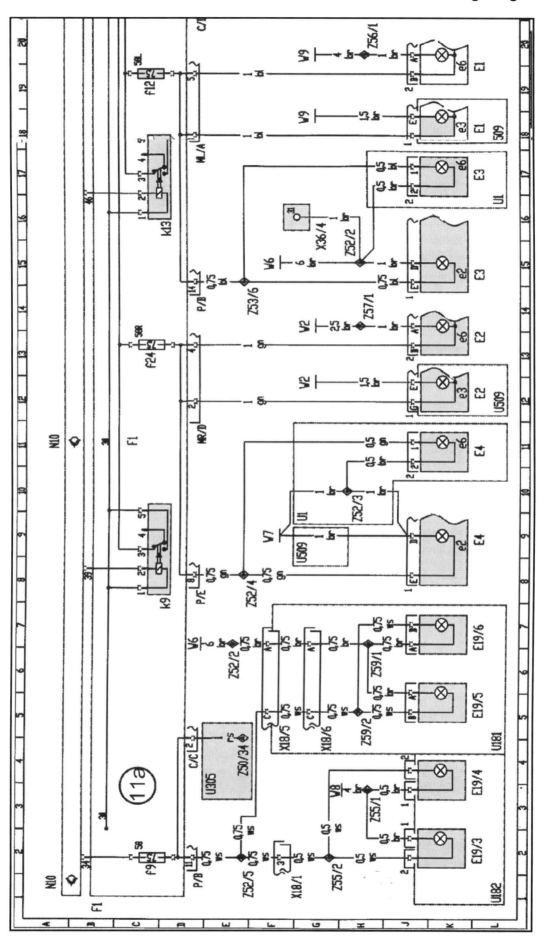

Wiring Diagrams

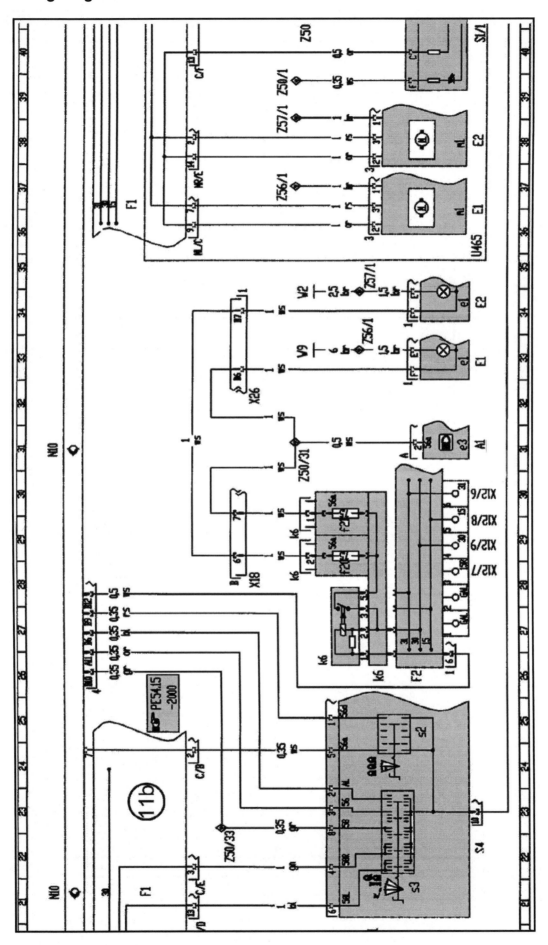

200

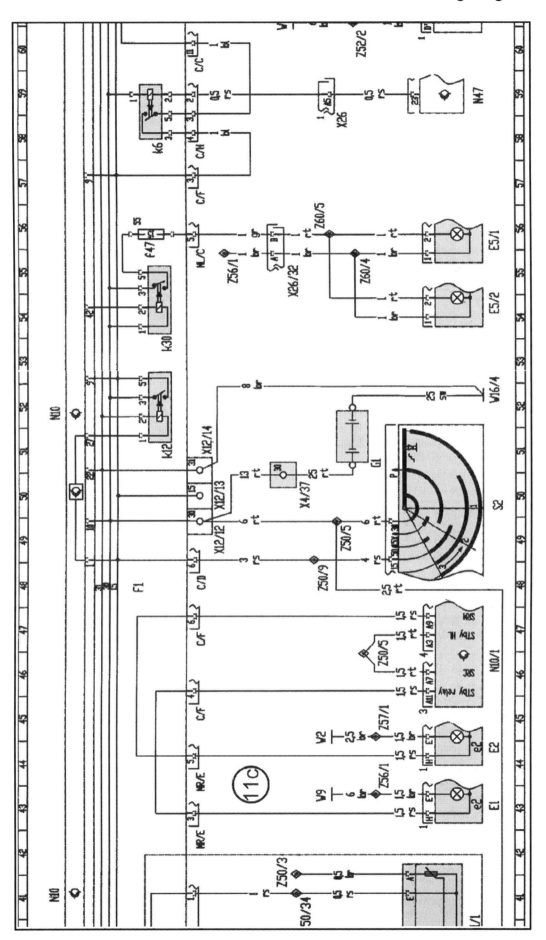

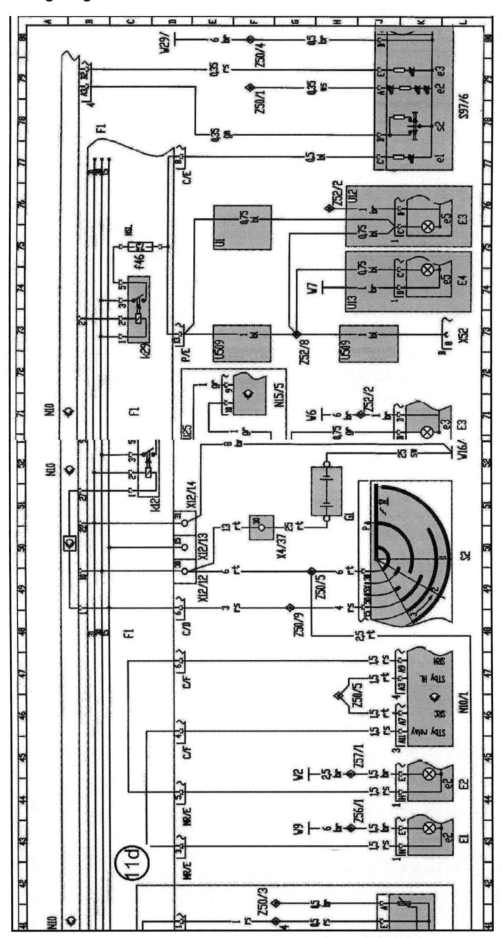

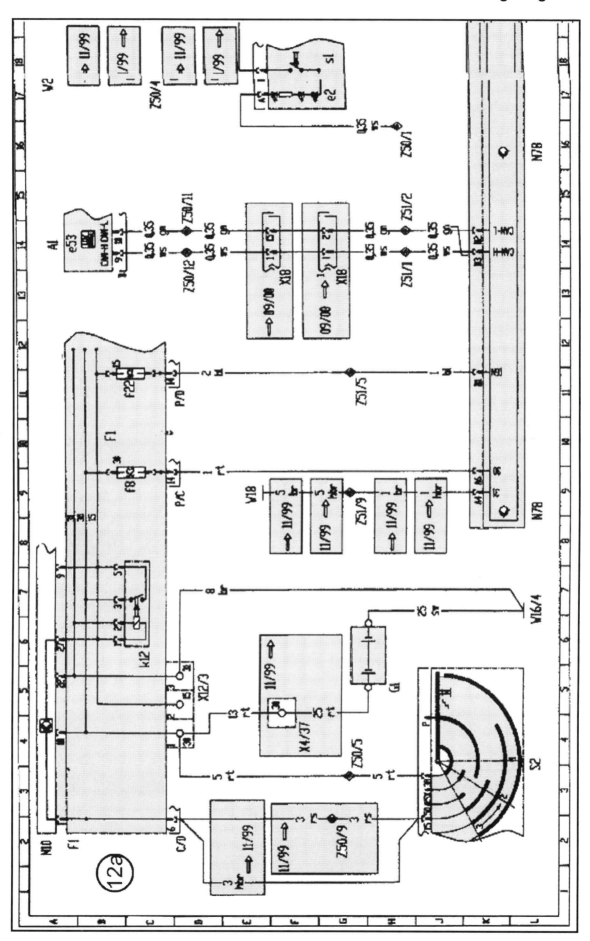

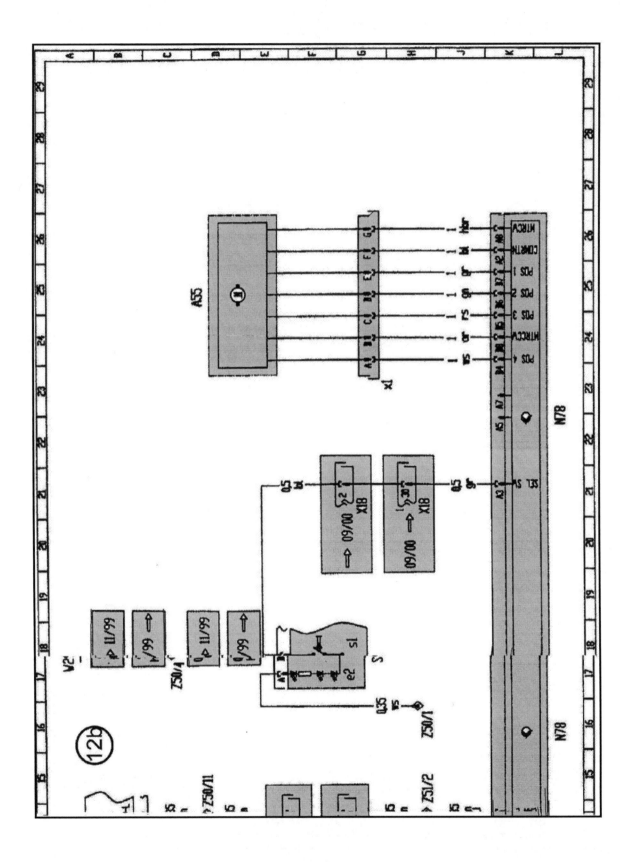

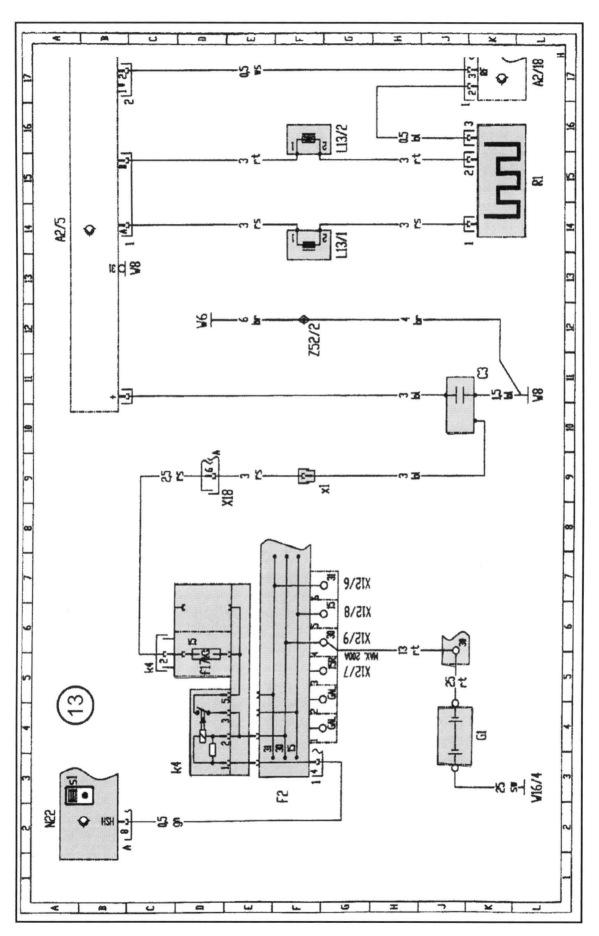

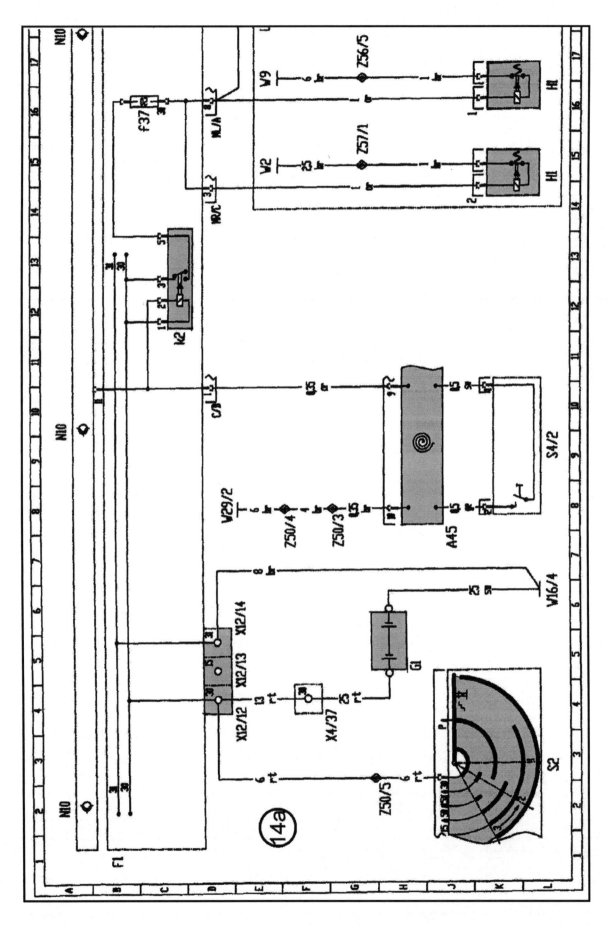

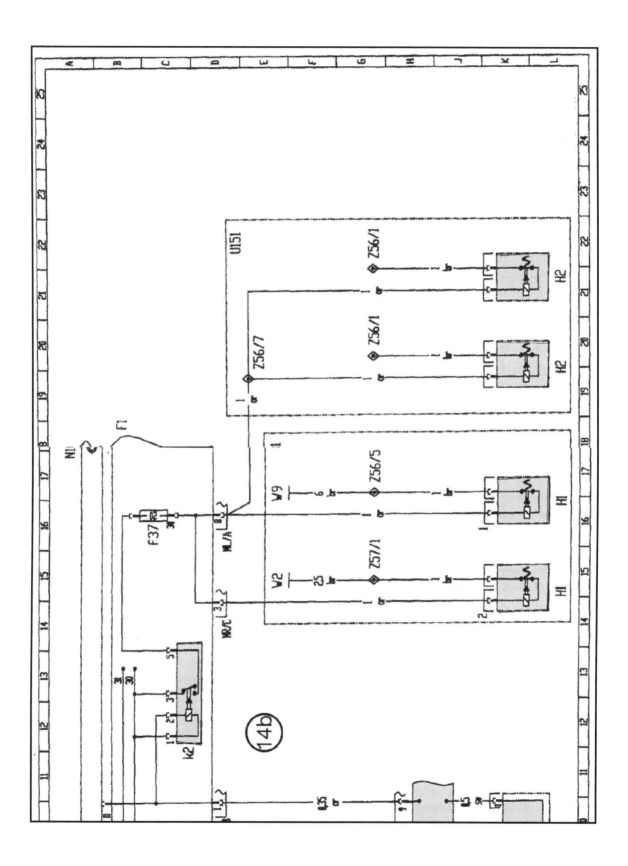

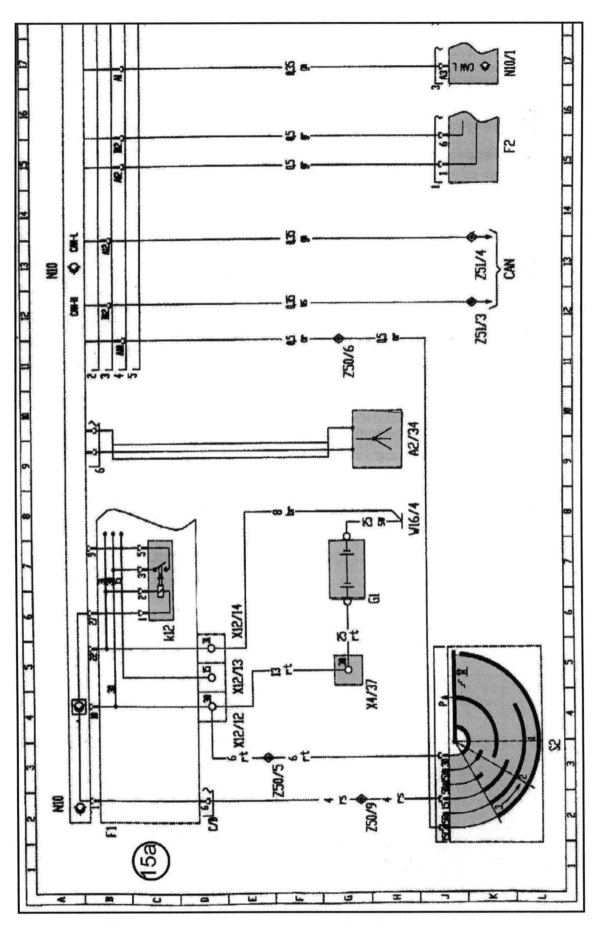

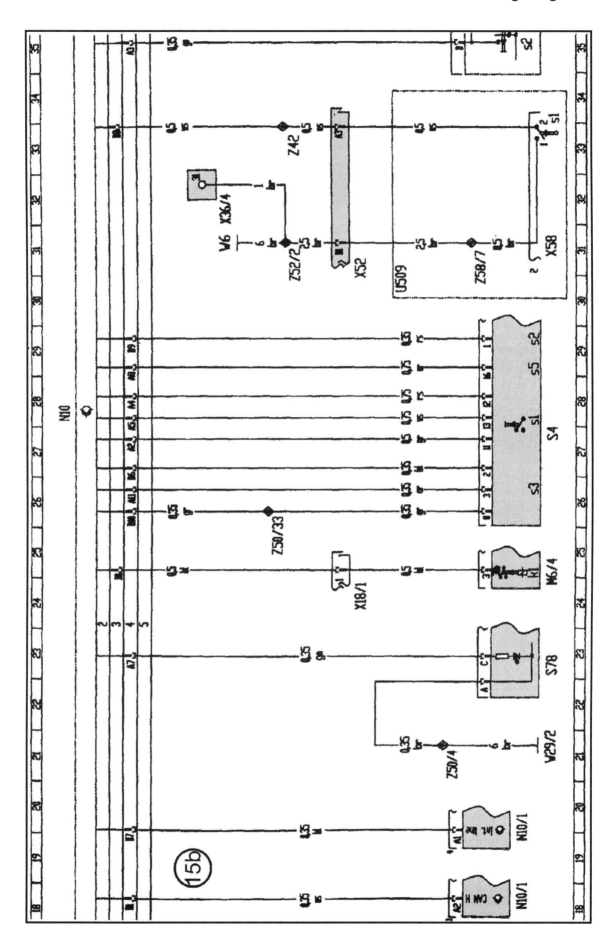

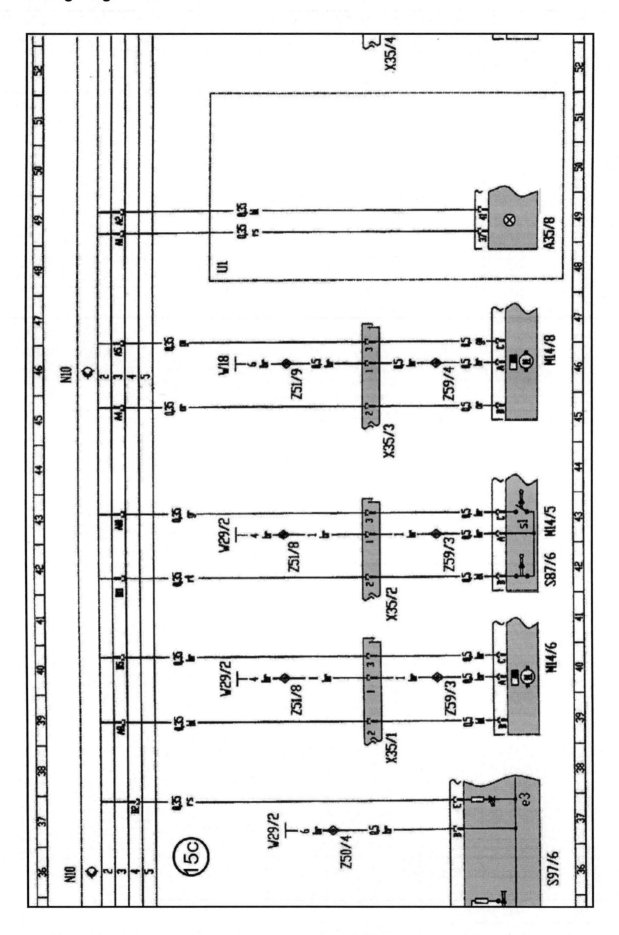

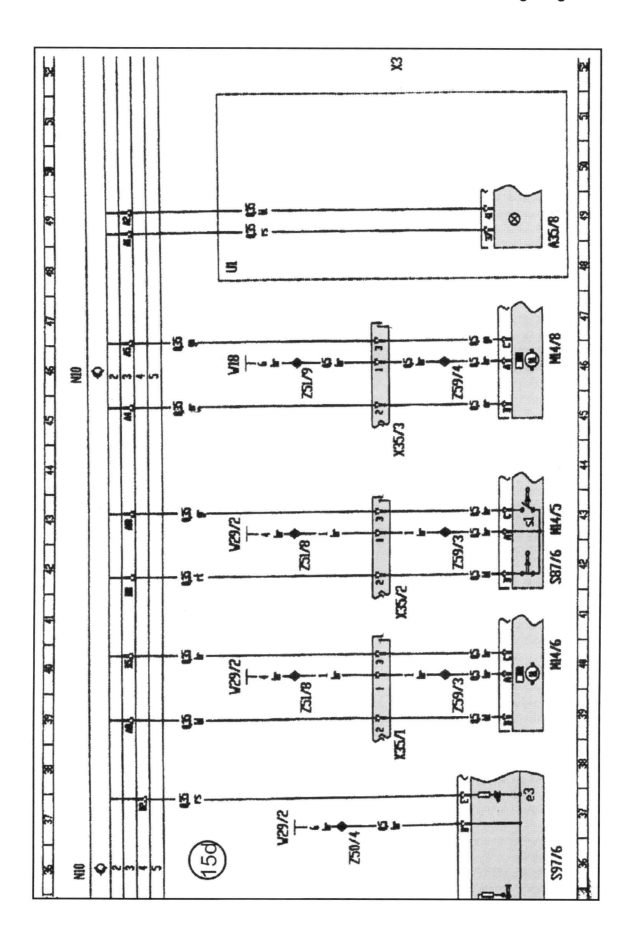

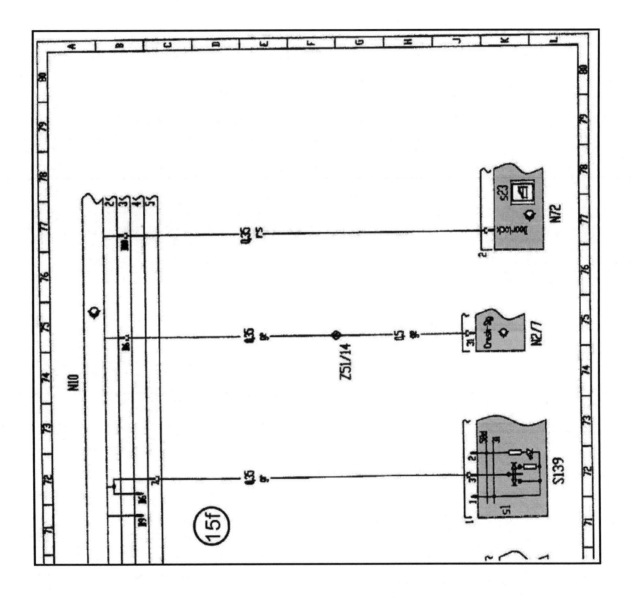

Mercedes-Benz ML Petrol Models to 2006

Legend for Wiring Diagrams, for Alternator and Starter motor, engines M111, M112 and M113 to Aug. 2000

ID.	Consumer	Location
A1	Instrument cluster	35K
A1e5	Generator charging light	35K
F1	Fuse and relay module	1B, 12C, 22C, 32C
F1k12	Circuit 15 relay	6C
F1k8	Starter motor relay	15C
G1	Battery	6G
G2	Alternator	24L, 31G
M1	Starter motor	21L
N3/4	Engine control module	9L, 16L
N3/9	Only applicable to diesel engine	12L, 18L
N3/19	Motor electronics control module	14L
N10	All-activity module	2A, 12A
N10/1	Extended activity module	37K
S2	Starter motor switch	4L
U30	Valid for diesel engines	11E, 18L, 20E, 23G 26E, 36E
U75	Valid for petrol (gasoline) engine	19E. 29D
U536	Valid for 112/113 engine	13E, 24E
W16/4	Earth (output earth, component compartment right-hand side	8L
X4/37	Circuit 30 terminal block	4F
X12/3	Circuit 30, 15, 31 terminal block, 3-pin	5E
X18/7	Interior/engine connector	16F
X18/26	Right interior/engine compartment connector	18FE
X22	Engine compartment and engine connector	9F, 19F,20F, 26H, 29E
Z50/5	Cockpit circuit 30 connector sleeve	4G
Z50/6	Cockpit connector sleeve (circuit 15C)	1H
Z50/9	Cockpit connector sleeve (circuit 15 II)	1G
Z50/19	Cockpit connector sleeve (circuit 50)	2F

Wiring Diagram Legend for Wiring Diagrams 2 – Starter motor, alternator – Engines M112/M112 from Sept. 2002 2002

A1	Instrument cluster	43K
A1e5	Charge warning light	43K
F1	Fuse and relay module	1B, 12C, 22C, 32C, 42C
F1k12	Relay, circuit	15C
K1k8	Starter motor relay	12C
G1	Battery	7G
G2	Alternator	30L, 38G
M1	Starter motor	23L
N10	All-Activity module	2A, 12A. 22A, 32A
N14/2	Pre-glow output stage (diesel only)	31D
N3/10	Injection control unit	13L
N3/9	CDI control unit (diesel only)	15L, 18L
U199	Only valid for 612 diesel engine	18F
U30	Valid for all diesel engines	17D, 22E, 30G, 33E
U320	Only valid for 400 CDI	6J, 15F, 26H, 31D
U536	Only valid for M112/M113 engines	12E, 26E
U75	Only valid for petrol engines	21E, 36ED
W11	Earth (engine-connection point for earth wires)	22L
W16/4	Earth (output earth, component compartment right-hand side	25L
W16/6	Earth, engine compartment, right	25L
X12/12	Circuit 30 terminal block at relay module 1	5E
X12/13	Circuit 15 terminal block at relay module 1	6E
X12/14	Circuit 31 terminal block at relay module 1	7E
X22/1	Engine compartment and engine connector	21F, 22F,33H, 38E
X25/2	Engine compartment/interior compartment connector	18F
X4/37	Terminal block (circuit 30)	5F
Z50/19	Cockpit circuit 50 connector sleeve	3F
Z50/5	Cockpit circuit 30 connector sleeve	5G
Z50/6	Cockpit connector sleeve (circuit 15C)	2H
Z50/8	Cockpit connector sleeve (circuit 15R)	1H
Z50/9	Cockpit connector sleeve (circuit 15 II)	2G

Wiring Diagram Legend for Wiring Diagrams 3 – Instrument cluster/display instruments/warning systems – 163 models from Jan. 2001

A1	Instrument cluster	14A, 25A, 35A, 45A, 55A, 65A
A1e1	L.H. turn signal indicator warning lamp	31D
A1e11	Coolant level waning lamp	51B
A1e12	Low engine oil level warning light	52B
A1e13	Windscreen washer fluid level warning lamp	58B
A1e15	Airbag indicator and warning lamp	18D
A1e15	Pre-glow indicator lamp	47B
A1e17	ABS malfunction indicator lamp	50B
A1e2	R.H. turn indicator lamp	33D
A1e26	CHECK ENGINE indicator lamp	54B
A1e3	High beam indicator lamp	25D
A1e33	Variable speed limit function indicator lamp	32B
A1e34	Electronic diesel control indicator lamp	46B
A1e35	ETS indicator lamp	48B
A1e36	ETS indicator lamp	32B
A1e4	Fuel reserve warning lamp	30B
A1e40	Steering lock warning lamp	55B
A1e47	BAS/ESP malfunction indicator lamp	49B
A1e5	Generator charge warning lamp	40D
A1e55	Low range indicator lamp	53B
A1e56	Airbag OFF indicator lamp	16D
A1e57	Front fog lamp indicator lamp	57B
A1e6	Brake pad wear indicator lamp	50B
A1e7	Brake fluid, handbrake and brake force distribution warning lamp	56B
A1e8	Instrument illumination	20A, 24B
A1e9	Seat belt warning lamp	56B
A1h1	Warning buzzer	26B
A1p1	Engine coolant temperature gauge	28A
A1p2	Fuel level gauge	29A
A1p4	Outside temperature indicator	28C
A1p5	Tachometer	40A
A1p6	Electronic clock	41C
A1p8	Electronic speedometer	33G
A1r11	Instrument illumination variable resistor	25D
A1e2	Clock setting switch	23D
A1e3	Trip odometer reset button	24D
B14	Outside temperature indicator sensor	50E
F1	Fuse and relay module	6K, 29K, 34K, 41K, 47K
F1f16	Fuse 16	40J
F1ff2	Fuse 2	31J
F1f25	Fuse 25	32J
F1f15	Fuse 5	30J
F1k12	Terminal 15 relay	10J
F2	Fuse and relay module in front R:H. footwell	14L, 20L, 25L
F2f1	Fuse 1	14K
F2f5	Fuse 5	20K
G1	Battery	8C
G2	Alternator	33E, 37E
M3/3	Fuel tank sensor	64L
N10	All-activity module (AAM)	6L, 29L, 34L, 45L
N2/7	Restraint system control module	17L
S2	Starter motor switch	59J
S4	Combination switch	46J
S41	Coolant level indicator switch	55K
S42	Windscreen washer fluid level switch	63K
S4s3	Light switch	45J
S97/1	Steering lock switch	61L
U30	Valid for diesel engines	35E
U75	Valid for petrol engines	33E
W16/4	Earth (output earth, component compartment right-hand side	9A
W29/2	Earth (R.H. A-door pillar)	21J
X11/4	Data link connector	68L
X12/12	Circuit 30 terminal block at relay module 1	8G
X12/13	Circuit 15 terminal block at relay module 1	9G
X12/14	Circuit 31 terminal block at relay module 1	10G
W18	Interior and tail lamp wiring harness connector, cockpit	14H, 16H, 20H, 25H, 64G
X18/27	Cockpit and R.H. engine compartment connector	54G
X18/28	Cockpit and L.H. engine compartment connector	62G
X18/3	Interior/fuel tank connector	64H
X22	Engine compartment and engine connector	34F, 35F
X4/37	Terminal 30 terminal block	8E
Z50/1	Cockpit connector sleeve, terminal 58d	23F
Z50/11	Cockpit connector sleeve, CAN-L	67K
Z50/12	Cockpit connector sleeve, CAN-H	66K
Z50/17	Cockpit connector sleeve, instruments	68G
Z50/3	Cockpit connector sleeve, terminal 31, left	22F, 60H
Z50/31	Cockpit connector sleeve, terminal 56A	52F
Z50/32	Connector sleeve, terminal 30, fused	19F
Z50/33	Connector sleeve, terminal 58, unfused	43G
Z50/4	Connector sleeve, terminal 31 II, right	22H
Z50/5	Cockpit circuit 30 connector sleeve	3H
Z50/6	Cockpit connector sleeve (circuit 15C)	1H
Z50/8	Cockpit connector sleeve (circuit 15R)	6F
Z50/9	Cockpit connector sleeve (circuit 15 II)	2F

Electrical function diagram 4 for starter, alternator, battery – Engines M113 and M272 – Series 164

A1	Instrument cluster	5H
A7/7	BAS brake booster	15B
A8/1	Transmitter key	5C
B14	Outside temperature display temperature sensor	2H
B34	ESP brake pressure sensor	10B
F32	Front pre-fuse	20C
F58K1	Starter relay	15F
G1	Battery	20E
G2	Alternator	18E
M1	Starter motor	16E
N3/9	CDI control unit (diesel only)	12K
N10	Front SAM control unit	7B
N22	A/C control and operating unit	2E
N47/5	ESP control unit	12B
N73	EIS control unit	5B
N83	Central gateway control unit	12B
U151	Valid for M113 engine	17G
U475	Valid for M272 engine	14G
Y3/8	Electronic control unit	11D

Wiring diagram Legend for Wiring Diagrams 5 – Fuel injection and ignition system – Engine M111

A61	Knock sensor	35L
B2/5	Hot film MAF sensor	26L
B6/1	Camshaft Hall sensor	28L
B11	Coolant temperature sensor	34L
F1	Fuse and relay module	1K
F1/f11	Fuse 11	10J
F1/f19	Fuse 19	12J
F1/f26	Fuse 26	8J
F1/k12	Circuit 15 relay	5J
G1	Battery	6D
L5	Crankshaft position sensor	37L
M16/6	Throttle valve actuator	30L
M16/6m1	Actuator motor	30K
M16/6r1	Throttle valve actual valve potentiometer	31J
M16/6r2	Drive actual value potentiometer	31K
M16/6r3	Actual value potentiometer (sliding contact 1)	30H
M16/r4	Actual value potentiometer (sliding contact 2)	29H
N3/4	HFM-SF1 control unit	24A , 37A
N10	All-activity module	4L, 10L
R4	Spark plugs	16L, 17L, 18L, 19L
S2	Starter motor switch	3A
S43	Oil level switch	38L
T1/1	Ignition coil cylinder 1	16H
T1/2	Ignition coil cylinder 2	18H
W11	Earth (engine connection point for earth cables)	38G
W16/4	Earth (output earth – engine compartment right-hand side	6A
X4/37	Terminal 30 terminal block	5F
X12/3	Circuit 30, 15, 31 terminal block. 3-pin	4G
X22	Engine compartment and engine connector	7E
Y48	Camshaft timing solenoid	14L
Y62y1	Fuel injector, cylinder 1	20L
Y62y2	Fuel injector, cylinder 2	21L
Y62y3	Fuel injector, cylinder 3	23L
Y62y4	Fuel injector, cylinder 4	24L
Z3/29	Circuit 15, connector sleeve, fused	27D
Z7/5	Circuit 87 connector sleeve	16E
Z50/9	Cockpit connector sleeve, circuit 15 II	3F

Wiring diagram Legend for Wiring Diagrams 6 – Fuel injection and ignition system – Engine M112, M113 in model 163 from Sept. 2002

A6	STH heater unit	30L
B37	Accelerator pedal sensor	9L
F1	Fuse and relay module	2B, 28C
F1/22	Fuse 22	36C
F2	Fuse and relay module in R.H. front foot well	25J, 32L
F24/7	Circuit 30 auxiliary fuse, suction fan	12E
F2f13	Fuse 13	25K
G1	Battery	6H, 12D
M3	Fuel pump	34L
M3m1	Fuel pump 1	34L
M4/7	Electric suction fan	12L
N10	All-activity module	2A, 29A, 31A
N3/10	ME control module (injection)	21A
S16/6	Kick-down switch	23L
S2	Starter switch	4L
U1	Valid for USA	35L
U151	Valid for M113 engine	11A
W16/4	Earth (output earth-component compartment R.H. side	7L, 12A
W2	Earth (at R.H. headlamp unit)	13E
W6	Earth (L.H. wheel housing in boot)	27L
X12/12	Circuit 30 terminal block at relay module 1	5E
X12/13	Circuit 15 terminal block at relay module 1	6E
X12/14	Circuit 31 terminal block at relay module 1	7E
X18	Interior and tail lamp harness connector	25H
X18/3	Interior/fuel tank connector	32H
X22/1	Engine compartment and engine connector	25E
X25/2	Engine compartment/interior compartment connector	18E
X36/4	Fuel tank filler neck/earth screw connection	28L
X4/37	Circuit 30 terminal block	5F
X74	Fuel metering pump connector, 1 pin	30J
Y23	Fuel metering pump	33L
Y58	Activated charcoal filter shut-off valve	36L
Z50/5	Cockpit circuit 30 connector sleeve	3G
Z50/6	Cockpit connector sleeve (circuit 15C)	2G
Z50/9	Cockpit connector sleeve (circuit 15 II)	2F
Z51/3	CAN high 2 interior connector sleeve	21E
Z51/4	CAN low 2 interior connector sleeve	22E
Z51/5	Circuit 15 interior connector sleeve	36F
Z51/8	Interior connector sleeve II (circuit 31)	22H
Z52/2	Interior connector sleeve V (circuit 31)	28J
Z57/12	R.H. engine compartment, circuit 15 sleeve	14F

Wiring diagram Legend for Wiring Diagrams 7 – Fuel injection and ignition system – Engine M113 in model 163 from Sept. 2002

A16/1	Knock sensor 1, right	25L
A16/2	Knock sensor 2, left	27L
B11/4	Coolant temperature sensor	24L
B2/5	Hot film mass air flow meter	9L
B28	Pressure sensor	30L
B4/3	Fuel tank pressure sensor	73L
B49	Oil sensor (oil level, temperature)	32L
B6/1	Camshaft Hall sensor	22L
C4	Radio interference suppression capacitor	37K. 50K
F1	Fuse and relay module	2C, 52B, 77L
F1f11	Fuse 11	7 C
F1f19	Fuse 19	52D
F1f126	Fuse 26	50D
F1f145	Fuse 45	51D
F1k12	Circuit 15 relay	5C
F1k28	Secondary air pump relay	54D
G1	Battery	6J
G3/3	Left O2 sensor upstream of CAT	64L
G3/3x1	Connector for G3/3	64K
G3/4	Right O2 sensor upstream of CAT	66L
G3/4x1	Connector for G3/4	66K
G3/5	Left O2 sensor downstream of CAT	68L
G3/5x1	Connector for G3/5	68K
G3/6	Right O2 sensor downstream of CAT	70L
G3/6x1	Connector for G3/6	70K
L5	Crankshaft position sensor	29L
M16/6	Throttle valve actuator	34L
M16/6m1	Actuator motor	34K
M16/6r1	Throttle valve actual valve potentiometer	35J
M16/6r2	Drive actual valve potentiometer	35J
M16/6r3	Actual valve potentiometer (sliding contact 1)	34H
M16/6r4	Actual valve potentiometer (sliding contact 2)	33H
M33	Electric air pump	51L
N10	All-activity module	4A
N3/10	ME (injection) control module	10A. 20A, 30A 40A, 50A, 60A, 72A
S2	Starter switch	3L
T1/1	Cylinder 1 ignition coil	38L
T1/2	Cylinder 2 ignition coil	40L
T1/3	Cylinder 3 ignition coil	41L
T1/4	Cylinder 4 ignition coil	43L
T1/5	Cylinder 5 ignition coil	44L
T1/6	Cylinder 6 ignition coil	46L
T1/7	Cylinder 7 ignition coil	57L
T1/8	Cylinder 8 ignition coil	48L
U1	Valid for USA	72L
W11/3	Earth (engine, L.H. side)	37G, 50G, 52G
W16	Earth (component compartment)	62D
W16/4	Earth (output earth- component compartment, right	6L
X11/4	Data link connector	79E
X12/12	Circuit 30 terminal block at relay module 1	3D
X12/13	Circuit 15 terminal block at relay module 1	4E
X12/14	Circuit 31 terminal block at relay module 1	5D
X22/1	Engine compartment and engine connector	5F, 7F, 49F, 64E, 68D
X25/2	Engine compartment/interior compartment connector	58E, 68E
X4/37	Circuit 30 terminal block	4G
Y22/6	Variable intake manifold switch-over valve	59L
Y31/1	EGR vacuum transducer	58L
Y32	Air pump switch-over valve	61L
Y58/1	Purge control valve	63L
Y62	Injection valves	17L
Y62/1	Injection valve, cylinder 1	13K
Y62/2	Injection valve, cylinder 2	14K
Y62/3	Injection valve, cylinder 3	15K
Y62/4	Injection valve, cylinder 4	16K
Y62/5	Injection valve, cylinder 5	17K
Y62/6	Injection valve, cylinder 6	19K
Y62/7	Injection valve, cylinder 7	20K
Y62/8	Injection valve, cylinder 8	21K
Z3/29	Circuit 15 connector sleeve (fused)	38F, 48F
Z50/5	Cockpit circuit 30 connector sleeve	3G
Z50/9	Cockpit connector sleeve (circuit 15 II)	1G
Z51/13	Oxygen sensor signal interior compartment connector sleeve, circuit 31	71F
Z51/3	CAN high 2 interior connector sleeve	74K
Z51/4	CAN low 2 interior connector sleeve	75K
Z6/5	Earth connector sleeve (O2 sensor)	65F
Z6/8	Sensor earth connector sleeve	24F
Z7/35	Circuit 87M connector sleeve	12F, 12H
Z7/36	Circuit 87M2e connector sleeve	58G
Z7/41	Sensor supply connector sleeve	31E

Wiring Diagram Legend for Wiring Diagrams 8 – Signal system – 163 models

A45	Fanfare horns and airbag spring contact	8J, 12J
F1	Fuse and relay module	1B, 23B
F1f37	Fuse 37	20C
F1k2	Two-tone horn relay	14C
G1	Battery	5H
H1	Two-tone horn	19L, 21L
H2	Fanfare horns	24L, 26L
N10	All-activity module	2A, 12A, 22A
S2	Starter motor switch	3L
S4/2	FAN switch	9L, 14L
U291	Valid for ML 55 AMG only	26D
U292	Valid for all except ML 55 AMG	22L
W2	Earth (R.H. front headlamp unit)	19E
W9	Earth (L.H. front headlamp unit)	21E
W16/4	Earth (output earth, component compartment right-hand side	6L
W29/2	Earth (R.H. A door pillar)	8D, 15D. 17
X4/37	Circuit 30 terminal block	3G
X12/3	Circuit 30, 15, 31 terminal block, 3 pins	4E
Z50/3	Cockpit connector sleeve, terminal 31, left	8G, 15G, 17J
Z50/4	Connector sleeve, terminal 31 II, right	8F
Z50/5	Cockpit circuit 30 connector sleeve	2H
Z56/1	Connector sleeve in left of engine Compartment, circuit 31 (1)	21G, 26G
Z56/7	Fanfare horns connector sleeve	24E
Z57/1	Connector sleeve R.H. side of engine compartment, circuit 31 (1)	20G, 25G

Wiring Diagram Legend for Wiring Diagrams 9 – Turn signal and hazard warning lights

A1	Instrument cluster	16L, 27L
A1e1	L.H. turn signal indicator lamp	16L
A1e2	R.H. turn signal indicator lamp	27L
E1	L.H. headlamp	17L
E1e5	Turn signal lamp	17L
E2	R.H. headlamp	17L
E2e5	Turn signal lamp	28L
E3	L.H. tail lamp	20L
E3e1	Turn signal lamp	20L
E4	R.H. tail lamp	31L
E4e1	Turn signal lamp	31L
E6/5	L.H. exterior mirror turn signal lamp	24L
E6/6	R.H. exterior mirror turn signal lamp	33L
F1	Fuse and relay module	9B, 20B, 32B
F1f2	Fuse 2	19C
F1f25	Fuse 25	29C
F1k4	L.H. turn signal relay	15C
F1k7	R.H. turn signal relay	26C
G1	Battery	3H
M21/1	L.H. adjustable and heated outside mirror	25L
M21/1x1	Connector for M21/1	23J
M21/21	R.H. adjustable and heated outside mirror	34L
M21/2x1	Connector for M21/21	33J
N10	All-activity module	3A, 13A, 27A
S2	Starter motor switch	11L
S4	Combination switch	5L
S4e1	Left and right turn signal switch	4H
S4s10	Hazard warning light switch	6H
W16/4	Earth, engine compartment, right	15L
W2	Earth (R.H. headlamp)	28F
E29/2	Earth (R.H. A door pillar)	7C
W6	Earth, L.H. wheel house in boot)	21F
W7	Earth, R.H. wheel house in boot)	31F
W9	Earth, L.H. headlamp unit	17F
X12/12	Circuit 30 terminal block at relay module 1	12E
X12/13	Circuit 15 terminal block at relay module 1	13E
X12/14	Circuit 31 terminal block at relay module 1	14E
X35/1	L.H. front door separation point	23G
X35/2	R.H. front door separation point	33G
X36/4	Fuel tank connection earth	21G
X4/37	Circuit 30 terminal block	12F
Z50/3	Cockpit connector sleeve, terminal 31, left	6F
Z50/4	Connector sleeve, terminal 31 II, right	6E
Z50/5	Cockpit circuit 30 connector sleeve	10F
Z52/2	Circuit 31 interior connector sleeve	21J
Z53/4	Interior connector sleeve (circuit L)	20F
Z53/5	Interior connector sleeve (circuit R)	30F
Z56/1	Connector sleeve in left of engine compartment, circuit 31 (1)	18H
Z56/5	Connector sleeve in left of engine compartment, circuit 31 (2)	18J
Z57/1	Connector sleeve in right of engine compartment, circuit 31 (1)	29J
Z59/3	Connector sleeve, front doors, circuit 3125G, 34G	

Wiring Diagram Legend for Wiring Diagrams 10 – Exterior mirrors – from Sept. 2001

A67	Interior mirror unit	51L
A67/e1	L.H. reading light	50J
A67/e2	R.H. reading light	50K
A67/e3	Surround lamp	50K
A67/x1	Interior rear view mirror connector	49H
E6/5	L.H. exterior mirror turn signal lamp	6L
E6/6	R.H. exterior mirror turn signal lamp	35L
F1	Fuse and relay module	16B, 34B, 48C
F1f2	Fuse 2	25C
F1f25	Fuse 25	28C
F1f31	Fuse 31	49C
F1f36	Fuse 36	32C
F1k1	Heated outside mirror relay	30C
F1k12	Circuit 15 relay	21C
F1k4	Left turn signal relay	23C, 26C
G1	Battery	20H
M21/1	L.H. adjustable and heated outside mirror	9L
M21/1h1	Mirror dimming	13K
C	Mirror up/down adjustment motor	38K
C	Mirror in/out adjustment motor	38K
M21/2m3	Mirror folding-in motor	40K
C	Mirror heater	36K
M21/2r2	Mirror up/down adjustment potentiometer	37K
M21/2r3	Mirror in/out adjustment potentiometer	37K
M21/2x1	Connector, R.H. mirror	34J
N10	All-activity module	17A, 33A
N10/1	Extended activity module (EAM) 54A	
N32/1	Left front seat adjustment control module with memory	2L
N32/2	Front seat adjustment control module with memory, right	3L
N72	Lower control panel control module	7A, 40A
N72s19	Outside mirror fold-in/out switch	5A
N72/s7	Outside mirror adjustment switch	6B
N72s8	Left or right mirror adjustment selection switch	7B
S2	Starter motor switch	18L
U12	Valid for L.H. drive models	2E, 13E
U13	Valid for R.H. drive models	3E, 41E
U144	Valid for mirror folding-in feature	11E, 39E
U76	Valid for automatic mirror dimming	12E, 41E, 49H
W16/4	Earth (output earth, component compartment right-hand side	22L
W18	Earth, L.H. front seat crossmember)	42E
W29/2	Earth, R.H. door A-pillar)	32L
W7	Earth (R.H. wheel house in boot)	48G
X12/12	Circuit 30 terminal block at relay module 1	19E
X12/13	Circuit 15 terminal block at relay module 1	20E
X12/14	Circuit 31 terminal block at relay module 1	21E
X18	Interior and tail lamp wiring harness connector, cockpit	44C
X18/2	Interior/roof connector	13C, 50F
X35/1	L.H. door separation point	5G
X35/2	R.H. door separation point	34G
X4/37	Circuit 30 terminal block	19G
Z50/5	Cockpit connector sleeve, circuit 30	18G
Z50/6	Cockpit connector sleeve, circuit 15C	16G
Z50/9	Cockpit connector sleeve, circuit 15 II	16G
Z51/7	Circuit 31 interior connector sleeve	42D
Z51/8	Circuit 31 interior connector sleeve	6E, 32F
Z52/7	Comfort interior connector sleeve	40D, 51C
Z52/9	Interior connector sleeve (reverse lamp)	54E
Z53/1	Interior mirror connector sleeve	7D, 35E
Z53/4	Interior connector sleeve (circuit L)	6D, 25F
Z53/5	Interior connector sleeve (circuit R)	32F
Z54/1	Roof connector sleeve, circuit 15R	51F
Z54/3	Roof connector sleeve, circuit 31	49G
Z54/9	Roof connector sleeve, circuit 31	47F
Z59/3	Front door connector sleeve, circuit 31	8L, 33L

Wiring Diagram Legend for Wiring Diagrams 11 – Exterior lights from Sept. 2002

A1	Instrument cluster	
A1e3	High beam indicator lamp	31K
E1	L.H. headlamp unit	18L, 19L, 33L, 37L, 43L
E19/3	L.H. rear tailgate door licence plate lamp	2L
E19/4	R.H. rear tailgate door licence plate lamp	3L
E19/5	L.H. spare wheel carrier licence plate lamp	5L
E19/6	R.H. spare wheel carrier licence plate lamp	7L
E1e1	L.H. high beam	33K
E1e2	L.H. low beam	43L
E1e3	L.H. standing and parking lamp	18K
E1e6	L.H. side marker lamp	19K
E1m1	L.H. range adjustment motor	37K
E2	R.H. headlamp unit	12L, 13L, 34L, 38L, 44L
E21	Centre high mounted brake light	64L
E2e1	R.H. high beam	34K
E2e2	R.H. low beam	44L
E2e3	R.H. standing and parking lamp	12K
E2e6	R.H. side marker lamp	13K
E2m1	R.H. range adjustment motor	38K
E3	L.H. tail lamp	15L, 17L, 61L, 71L, 76L
E35	High brake light on spare wheel carrier	67L
E3e2	L.H. tail lamp and parking lamp	15K
E3e3	L.H. reversing light	71L
E3e4	L.H. brake light	61L
E3e5	L.H. rear fog light	78L
E3e6	L.H. side marker lamp	17K
E4	R.H. tail lamp	9L. 11L. 62L, 69L, 74L
E4e2	R.H. tail lamp and parking lamp	9K
E4e3	R.H. reversing light	69L
E4e4	R.H. brake light	62L
E4e5	R.H. rear fog light	74L
E4e6	R.H. side marker lamp	11K
E5/1	L.H. fog lamp	56L
E5/2	R.H. fog lamp	54L
F1	Fuse and relay module	1B, 11C, 21C, 37C, 48C, 61C, 71C, 78B
F1f12	Fuse 12	19C
F1f15	Fuse 15	62C

F1f16	Fuse 16	70C
F1f24	Fuse 24	13C
F1f46	Fuse 46	75C
F1f47	Fuse 47	58C
F1f19	Fuse 9	1C
F1k12	Circuit 15 relay	51D
F1k13	Circuit 58L relay	16D
F1k29	Rear fog lamp relay	73C
F1k30	Front fog lamp relay	53D
F1k6	ESP brake light suppression relay	7D
F1k9	Circuit 58R relay	7D
F2	Fuse and relay module in R.H. foot well	26J
F2f20	Fuse 20	28H
F2f21	Fuse 21	29H
F2k6	Relay 6	26H
G1	Battery	51H
N10	All activity module	1A, 11A, 31A, 41A, 52A, 61A
N10/1	Extended activity module	46L
N15/5	Electronic selector lever control module	71G
N47	Traction system control module	59L
S1/1	Electric headlamp range control	40L
S16/2	Reversing light switch	69G
S2	Starter switch	69G
S4	Combination switch	22L
S4e2	Headlamp flasher/main beam switch	25J
S16/2	Reverse lamps switch	69G
S4e3	Light switch	21J
S97/6	Double switch combination	78L
S97/6e1	Rear fog lamp indicator lamp	77K
S97/6e2	Pushbutton unit illumination	79K
S97/6e3	ATA status indicator	79K
S97/6s2	Fog lights, rear fog light switch	78K
U1	Valid for USA only	9G, 16L, 75E
U12	Valid for L.H. drive models	76H
U13	Valid for R.H. drive models	74H
U181	Valid for spare tyre carrier	4L, 66G
U182	Valid without spare tyre carrier	1L
U24	Valid for manual transmission	68E
U25	Valid for automatic transmission	71D
U305	Not valid with Xenon headlamps	3E
U465	Valid for normal headlamp adjustment	38L
U509	Valid for all except USA	8G, 12L, 18L, 73E, 73H
W16/4	Earth (output earth, component compartment, right	52L
W2	Earth, R.H. headlamp unit	12G, 14G, 34G, 45G
W29/2	Earth, R.H. door A-pillar	80D
W6	Earth, L.H. wheel housing in boot	7D, 15F, 61F 68L, 71G
W7	Earth, R.H. wheel housing in boot	9F, 62F, 68G
W8	Earth, tailgate	3G, 64G
W9	Earth, L.H. headlamp unit	18G, 20G, 33G, 43G
X12/12	Circuit 30 terminal block at relay module 1	49E
X12/13	Circuit 15 terminal block at relay module 1	50E
X12/14	Circuit 31 terminal block at relay module 1	51E
X12/6	Circuit 31 terminal block at relay module 2	30L
X12/7	Circuit 15R terminal block at relay module 2	29L
X12/8	Circuit 15 terminal block at relay module 2	30L
X12/9	Circuit 30 terminal block at relay module 2	29L
X18	Interior and tail lamp wiring harness connector, cockpit	28F
X18/1	Interior/tail gate connector	1G, 64F
X18/5	Wheel carrier connector	4F, 66F
X26	Engine compartment/cockpit connector	32F, 58H
X26/32	Front engine compartment/bumper connector	58F
X36/4	Fuel tank filler neck earth connector	15G
X4/37	Circuit 30 terminal block	50G
X52	Trailer coupling connector	73L
Z50/1	Cockpit connector sleeve (circuit 58D)	39F, 78F
Z50/3	Cockpit connector sleeve (circuit 31)	39F, 78F
Z50/31	Cockpit connector sleeve (circuit 56A)	30G
Z50/33	Cockpit connector sleeve (circuit 58)	22E
Z50/34	Cockpit connector sleeve (circuit 58)	4E, 40G
Z50/4	Cockpit connector sleeve (circuit 31)	80F
Z50/5	Cockpit connector sleeve (circuit 30)	46J
Z50/9	Cockpit connector sleeve (circuit 15)	48G
Z52/2	Interior connector sleeve, circuit 31, left rear	6E, 15H, 60H, 65H, 71J, 78H
Z52/3	Interior connector sleeve, circuit 31	9H
Z52/4	Interior connector sleeve, circuit 58R	7F
Z52/5	Interior connector sleeve, circuit 58	1F
Z52/6	Interior connector sleeve, circuit 54	62E
Z52/8	Rear fog lamp connector sleeve	72E
Z52/9	Reversing fog lamps connector sleeve	70G
Z53/6	Interior connector sleeve, circuit 58L	14F
Z55/1	Circuit 31 tailgate connector sleeve	3H, 63H
Z55/2	Tailgate connector sleeve, circuit 31	1G
Z56/1	Left engine compartment connector sleeve, circuit 31 (1)	20H, 33H, 37F, 44J, 55E
Z57/1	Left engine compartment connector sleeve, circuit 31 (1)	14H, 35H, 38F, 45J
Z59/1	Wheel carrier connector sleeve, circuit 31	6H
Z59/2	Wheel carrier connector sleeve, circuit 58	4H
Z60/4	Fog lamp wiring harness connector sleeve	55H
Z60/5	Fog lamp wiring harness connector sleeve	58G

Wiring diagram 12 - Transfer case– 163 models

A1	Instrument cluster	14A
A1e53	LOWER RANGE indicator lamp	14B
A55	Transfer case range selector motor	25D
A55x1	Transfer case range selection motor connector	23H
F1	Fuse and relay module	2A, 10B
F1f8	Fuse 8	9C
F1f22	Fuse 22 11C	
Fk12	Circuit 15 relay	9C
G1	Battery	5H
N10	All-activity module	2A
N78	Transfer case control module	8L, 16L, 22L
S2	Starter motor switch	3L
S97/6	2/fold switch combination	17G
S97/6e2	Switch lighting	17G
S97/6s1	LOW RANGE switch	18G
W16/4	Earth (output earth, component compartment right-hand side	6L
W18	Earth, L.H. front seat crossmember)	9E
W29/2	Earth, R.H. door A-pillar)	17A
X4/37	Terminal block (circuit 30)	4F
X12/3	Circuit 30, 15, 31 terminal block, 3 pins	5D
X18	Interior and tail lamp wiring harness connector, cockpit	13F, 13G, 21G, 21H
Z50/1	Cockpit connector sleeve (circuit 58D)	16H
Z50/4	Cockpit connector sleeve (circuit 31)	17C
Z50/5	Cockpit connector sleeve (circuit 30)	4G
Z50/9	Cockpit connector sleeve (circuit 15)	2G
Z50/11	CAN-low cockpit connector sleeve	14D
Z50/12	CAN-high cockpit connector sleeve	13D
Z51/1	CAN-high interior connector	13H
Z51/2	CAN-low interior connector	15H
Z51/5	Circuit 15 interior connector sleeve	11G
Z51/9	Circuit 31 interior connector sleeve	8G

Wiring Diagram Legend for Wiring Diagram 13 – Rear window defroster– 163 models

A2/18	FM/AM amplifier	17L
A2/18	Antenna splitter, radio	14A
C3	Electrolytic capacitor (rear window)	11K
C3x1	Rear window noise suppression capacitor	9G
F2	Fuse and relay module, front R.H. footwell	3F
F2f17	Fuse 17	5D
F2k4	Relay 4	3D
G1	Battery	4K
L13/1	R.H. antenna coil	13G
L13/2	L.H. antenna coil	18G
L22	AAC push button control module	2A
N22s1	Rear window defroster switch	3A
R1	Rear window defroster	15L
W16/4	Earth (output earth, component compartment right-hand side	3L
W6	Earth, L.H. wheel housing in boot	12D
W8	Earth, tailgate	1L, 13C
X12/6	Terminal block, circuit 13, at relay module 2	7G
X12/7	Circuit 15R terminal block at relay module 2	5G
X12/8	Circuit 15 terminal block at relay module 2	6G
X12/9	Circuit 30 terminal block at relay module 2	6G
X18	Interior and tail lamp wiring harness connector, cockpit	8E
Z52/2	Passenger compartment connector sleeve	11F

Wiring Diagram Legend for Wiring Diagrams 14 – Horn system– 163 models

A45	Fanfare horns and airbag clock spring contact	7J
F1	Fuse and relay module	1B, 18B
F1f37	Fuse 37	16C
F1k2	Two-tone horn system relay	11C
G1	Battery	5H
H1	Two-tone horn system	15L, 16L
H2	Fanfare horns	19L, 21L
N10	All-activity module (AAM)	2A, 9A, 17A
S2	Starter motor switch	3L
U151	Valid for engine M113 (petrol)	22D
U151	Valid for all engines except M113 (petrol)	18E
W16/4	Earth (output earth, component compartment right-hand side	6L
W2	Earth, R.H. headlamp unit	15E
W29/2	Earth, R.H. door A-pillar	8D
W9	Earth, L.H. headlamp unit	16E
X12/12	Circuit 30 terminal block at relay module 1	3E
X12/13	Circuit 15 terminal block at relay module 1	4E
X12/14	Circuit 31 terminal block at relay module 1	6E
X4/37	Circuit 30 terminal block	3G
Z50/3	Cockpit connector sleeve (circuit 31)	7G
Z50/4	Cockpit connector sleeve (circuit 31)	7F
Z50/5	Cockpit circuit 30 connector sleeve	2H
Z56/1	Left engine compartment connector sleeve, circuit 31 (1)	20G, 22G
Z56/5	Left engine compartment connector sleeve, circuit 31 (2)	17G
Z56/7	Left engine compartment connector sleeve, fanfare horns	20E
Z57/1	Right engine comp. connector sleeve	15G

Legend for Wiring diagrams 15 – All-activity module from Sept. 2002

A2&34	Central locking antenna	9H
A35/8	E-call control module	48L
E15/2	Dome lamp with time delay/reading lamp	67L
E15/8	Left rear dome lamp	68L
E15/9	Right rear dome lamp	70L
F1	Fuse and relay module	2B, 55B
F1k12	Terminal 15 relay	6C
F1k15	Central locking relay, unlock tailgate	56C
F2	Fuse and relay module in foot well (RH)	15K
G1	Battery	6H
H3/1	Alarm signal siren with auxiliary battery	62L
M14/5	R.H. front door CL motor	43L
M14/5s1	R.H. front door CL micro switch	43K
M14/6	L.H. front door CL motor	40L
M14/7	Tailgate CL motor	56L
M14/8	Left rear door CL motor	46L
M14/9	Right rear door CL motor	54L
M14/9s1	Right rear door CL micro switch	54K
M6/4	Tailgate wiper motor	24L
M64k1	Tailgate wiper motor relay	25L
N10	All-activity module	2A, 13A, 28A, 36A, 46A, 74A
N10/1	Extended activity module	17K, 18K, 19K
N2/7	Restraint system control module	75L
M41	Trip computer control module	65L
N41b1	Inclination sensor	65L
N41b2	Glass breakage sensor	65L
N72	Lower control panel control module	77L
N72s73	Central locking switch	77K
S139	Overhead control panel switch module	72L
S139s1	Interior lights switch	71K
S2	Starter switch	3L
S4	Combination switch	28L
S4s1	L.H. and R.H. turn signal switch	28L
S4s2	Headlamp flasher and high beam switch	29L
S4s3	Light switch	26L
S4s5	Wiper switch	29L
S78	Rear widow wipe/washer switch	23L
S87/3	R.H. rear door rotary tumbler switch	53L
S87/6	R.H. front door rotary tumbler switch	42L
S88/1	Tailgate rotary tumbler switch	59L
S97/6	Twin switch combination	36L
S97/6e3	ATA status indicator	37K
S97/6s2	Fog lamp and rear fog lamp switch	35L
U1	Valid or USA	48D
U180	Valid for ATA with siren	61G
U509	Valid for all except USA	30H
W16/4	Earth connection	8H
W18	Earth (crossmember, L.H. front seat)	48D
W19	Earth (crossmember, R.H. front seat)	54D
W29/2	Earth (R.H. A-pillar)	21L, 37E, 40D, 42D
W6	Earth (L.H. wheel house in boot)	31D
W8	Earth (tailgate)	59G
X12/12	Circuit 30 terminal block at relay module 1	3E
X12/13	Circuit 15 terminal block at relay module 1	4E
X12/14	Circuit 31 terminal block at relay module 1	6E
X18/1	Interior/tailgate connector	24G, 58G
X35/1	Left front door separation point	38H
X35/2	Right front door separation point	41H
X35/3	Left rear door separation point	44H
X35/4	Right rear door separation point	52H
X36/4	Fuel filler neck earth screw connection	32D
X4/37	Terminal 30 terminal block	4H
X52	Trailer coupling connector	31G
X58	Trailer hitch socket, 13 pin	31L
X58s1	Trailer recognition connector sleeve	33L
Z42	Parktronic system connector sleeve	33F
Z50/33	Cockpit connector sleeve, terminal 58	25E
Z50/4	Cockpit connector sleeve, terminal 31	21J
Z50/5	Cockpit connector sleeve, terminal 30	2F
Z50/9	Cockpit connector sleeve, terminal 15 II	2H
Z51/14	Interior connector sleeve, crash signal	74G
Z51/8	Interior terminal 31 connector sleeve	39F, 42F
Z51/9	Interior terminal 31 connector sleeve	45F
Z52/1	Interior terminal 31 connector sleeve	30F
Z53/1	Interior central locking motor 1 sleeve	57E
Z55/1	Tailgate terminal 31 connector sleeve	58J
Z57/3	Right engine compartment connector sleeve, terminal 31 (2)	62F
Z58/7	Trailer socket connector sleeve, term. 31	30K
Z59/3	Front door connector sleeve, term. 31	39J, 42J
Z59/4	Rear door connector sleeve, term. 31	45J, 52J

Cable Colour Code

bl	blue	nf	natural colour
br	brown	rs	pink (rosa)
el	ivory	rt	red
ge	yellow	sw	black
gn	green	vi	violet
gr	grey	ws	white

Further reading on
MERCEDES-BENZ

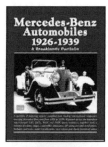

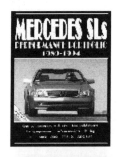

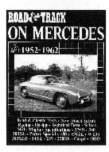

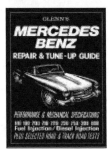

Mercedes-Benz 190 & 200 1959-1968 Owners Workshop Manual	Mercedes-Benz 230 1963-1968 Owners Workshop Manual	Mercedes-Benz W123 1976-1986 Owners Workshop Manual	Mercedes-Benz W124 1985-1995 Owners Workshop Manual	Mercedes-Benz Sprinter CDI Diesel Models 2000-2006 Owners Workshop Manual
Mercedes-Benz ML Petrol 1997-2006 Owners Workshop Manual	Mercedes-Benz ML Diesel 1998-2006 Owners Workshop Manual	Mercedes-Benz Vito & V-Class Petrol & Diesel up to 2000 Owners Workshop Manual	Mercedes-Benz Vito & V-Class Petrol & Diesel 2000-2003 Owners Workshop Manual	Mercedes-Benz Vito & Vanio Petrol & Diesel 2004 on Owners Workshop Manual

From specialist booksellers or, in case of difficulty direct from the distributor:

Brooklands Books Ltd., P.O. Box 146, Cobham, Surrey, KT11 1LG, England, UK
Phone: +44 (0) 1932 865051   info@brooklands-books.com   www.brooklands-books.com

www.brooklands-books.com

5/15/21 - 85,554 MI

- OIL CHANGE - FILTER (MANN HU7R/5x); 7.5L
- AIR FILTERS - MANN C 3698/3-2(2)
         - MANN CUK 2646-2 (CABIN/CARBON)

7/2/23 - 95,150 MI; OIL/FILTER CHANGE

Made in the USA
Coppell, TX
08 May 2021